THE EMERGENCE
OF JUDAISM

THE EMERGENCE OF JUDAISM

Christine Elizabeth Hayes

Greenwood Guides to Historic Events of the Ancient World
Bella Vivante, Series Editor

GREENWOOD PRESS
Westport, Connecticut • London

Library of Congress Cataloging-in-Publication Data

Hayes, Christine Elizabeth.
    The emergence of Judaism / Christine Elizabeth Hayes.
       p. cm.—(Greenwood guides to historic events of the ancient world)
    Includes bibliographical references and index.
    ISBN 0-313-33206-1 (alk. paper)
    1. Judaism—History—To 70 A.D.   2. Judaism—History—Talmudic period,
    10–425.   3. Bible. O.T.—History of Biblical events.   4. Judaism—History.
    I. Title.
  BM165.H39   2007
  296.09′014–dc22   2006028863

British Library Cataloguing in Publication Data is available.

Library of Congress Catalog Card Number: 2006028863
ISBN: 0–313–33206–1

First published in 2007

Greenwood Press, 88 Post Road West, Westport, CT 06881
An imprint of Greenwood Publishing Group, Inc.
www.greenwood.com

Printed in the United States of America

The paper used in this book complies with the
Permanent Paper Standard issued by the National
Information Standards Organization (Z39.48–1984).

10 9 8 7 6 5 4 3 2 1

CONTENTS

Photo essay follows Chapter 7

SERIES FOREWORD

As a professor and scholar of the ancient Greek world, I am often asked by students and scholars of other disciplines, why study antiquity? What possible relevance could human events from two, three, or more thousand years ago have to our lives today? This questioning of the continued validity of our historical past may be the offshoot of the forces shaping the history of the American people. Proud of forging a new nation out of immigrants wrenched willingly or not from their home soils, Americans have experienced a liberating headiness of separation from traditional historical demands on their social and cultural identity. The result has been a skepticism about the very validity of that historical past. Some of that skepticism is healthy and serves constructive purposes of scholarly inquiry. Questions of how, by whom, and in whose interest "history" is written are valid questions pursued by contemporary historians striving to uncover the multiple forces shaping any historical event and the multilayered social consequences that result. But the current academic focus on "presentism"—the concern with only recent events and a deliberate ignoring of premodern eras—betrays an extreme distortion of legitimate intellectual inquiry. This stress on the present seems to have deepened in the early years of the twenty-first century. The cybertechnological explosions of the preceding decades seem to have propelled us into a new cultural age requiring new rules that make the past appear all the more obsolete.

So again I ask, why study ancient cultures? In the past year, after it ousted that nation's heinous regime, the United States' occupation of Iraq has kept that nation in the forefront of the news. The land base of Iraq is ancient Mesopotamia, "the land between the rivers" of the Tigris and

Euphrates, two of the four rivers in the biblical Garden of Eden (Gen. 2). Called the cradle of civilization, this area witnessed the early development of a centrally organized, hierarchical social system that utilized the new technology of writing to administer an increasingly complex state.

Is there a connection between the ancient events, literature, and art coming out of this land and contemporary events? Michael Wood, in his educational video *Iraq: The Cradle of Civilization*, produced shortly after the 1991 Gulf War, thinks so and makes this connection explicit—between the people, their way of interacting with their environment, and even the cosmological stories they create to explain and define their world.

Study of the ancient world, like study of contemporary cultures other than one's own, has more than academic or exotic value. First, study of the past seeks meaning beyond solely acquiring factual knowledge. It strives to understand the human and social dynamics that underlie any historical event and what these underlying dynamics teach us about ourselves as human beings in interaction with one another. Study of the past also encourages deeper inquiry than what appears to some as the "quaint" observation that this region of current and recent conflict could have served as a biblical ideal or as a critical marker in the development of world civilizations. In fact, these apparently quaint dimensions can serve as the hook that piques our interest into examining the past and discovering what it may have to say to us today. Not an end in itself, the knowledge forms the bedrock for exploring deeper meanings.

Consider, for example, the following questions. What does it mean that three major world religions—Judaism, Christianity, and Islam—developed out of the ancient Mesopotamian worldview? In this view, the world, and hence its gods, were seen as being in perpetual conflict with one another and with the environment, and death was perceived as a matter of despair and desolation. What does it mean that Western forms of thinking derive from the particular intellectual revolution of archaic Greece that developed into what is called rational discourse, ultimately systematized by Aristotle in the fourth century B.C.E.? How does this thinking, now fundamental to Western discourse, shape how we see the world and ourselves, and how we interact with one another? And how does it affect our ability, or lack thereof, to communicate intelligibly with people with differently framed cultural perceptions? What, ultimately, do we gain from being aware of the origin and development of these fundamental features of our thinking and beliefs?

In short, knowing the past is essential for knowing ourselves in the present. Without an understanding of where we came from, and the journey we took to get where we are today, we cannot understand why we think or act the way we do. Nor, without an understanding of historical development, are we in a position to make the kinds of constructive changes necessary to advance as a society. Awareness of the past gives us the resources necessary to make comparisons between our contemporary world and past times. It is from those comparisons that we can assess both the advances we have made as human societies and those aspects that can still benefit from change. Hence, knowledge of the past is crucial for shaping our individual and social identities, providing us with the resources to make intelligent, aware, and informed decisions for the future.

All ancient societies, whether significant for the evolution of Western ideas and values, or whether they developed largely separate from the cultures that more directly influenced Western civilization, such as China, have important lessons to teach us. For fundamentally they all address questions that have faced every human individual and every human society that has existed. Because ancient civilizations erected great monuments of themselves in stone, writings, and the visual arts—all enduring material evidence—we can view how these ancient cultures dealt with many of the same questions we face today. And we learn the consequences of the actions taken by people in other societies and times that, ideally, should help us as we seek solutions to contemporary issues. Thus it was that President John F. Kennedy wrote of his reliance upon Thucydides' treatment of the devastating war between the ancient Greek city-states of Athens and Sparta (see the volume on the Peloponnesian War) in his study of exemplary figures, *Profiles in Courage*.

This series seeks to fulfill this goal both collectively and in the individual volumes. The individual volumes examine key events, trends, and developments in the world history in ancient times that are central to the secondary school and lower-level undergraduate history curriculum and that form standard topics for student research. From a vast field of potential subjects, these selected topics emerged after consultations with scholars, educators, and librarians. Each book in the series can be described as a "library in a book." Each one presents a chronological timeline and an initial factual overview of its subject, three to five topical essays that examine the subject from diverse perspectives and for its various consequences, a concluding essay providing current perspectives on the event, biographies of key players, a selection of primary documents, illustrations, a glossary, and an index. The concept of the series is to provide ready-reference materials that include a quick, in-depth examination of the topic and insightful guidelines for interpretive analysis, suitable for student research and designed to stimulate critical thinking. The authors are all scholars of the topic in their fields, selected both on the basis of their expertise and for their ability to bring their scholarly knowledge to a wider audience in an engaging and clear way. In these regards, this series follows the concept and format of the Greenwood Guides to Historic Events of the Twentieth Century, the Fifteenth to Nineteenth Centuries, and the Medieval World.

All the works in this series deal with historical developments in early ancient civilizations, almost invariably postdating the emergence of writing and of hierarchical dynastic social structures. Perhaps only incidentally do they deal with what historians call the Paleolithic ("Old Stone Age") periods, from about 25,000 B.C.E. onward, eras characterized by nomadic, hunting-gathering societies, or the Neolithic ("New Stone Age"), the period of the earliest development of agriculture and hence settled societies, one of the earliest dating to about 7000 B.C.E. at Çatal Höyük in south-central Turkey.

The earliest dates covered by the books in this series are the fourth to second millennia B.C.E. for the building of the Pyramids in Egypt, and the examination of the Trojan War and the Bronze Age civilizations of the eastern Mediterranean. Most volumes deal with events in the first millennium B.C.E. to the early centuries of the first millennium C.E. Some treat the development of civilizations, such as the rise of the Han Empire in China, or the separate volumes on the rise and on the decline and fall of the Roman Empire. Some highlight major personalities and their empires, such as the volumes on Cleopatra VII of Ptolemaic Egypt or Justinian and the beginnings of the Byzantine Empire in eastern Greece and Constantinople (Istanbul). Three volumes examine the emergence in antiquity of religious movements that form major contemporary world systems of belief—Judaism, Buddhism, and Christianity. (Islam is being treated in the parallel Medieval World series.) And two volumes examine technological developments, one on the building of the Pyramids and one on other ancient technologies.

Each book examines the complexities of the forces shaping the development of its subject and the historical consequences. Thus, for example, the volume on the fifth-century B.C.E. Greek Peloponnesian War explores the historical causes of the war, the nature of the combatants' actions, and how these reflect the thinking of the period. A particular issue, which may seem strange to some or timely to others, is how a city like Athens, with its proto-democratic political organization and its outstanding achievements in architecture, sculpture, painting, drama, and philosophy, could engage in openly imperialist policies of land conquest and of vicious revenge against any who countered them. Rather than trying to gloss over the contradictions that emerge, these books conscientiously explore whatever tensions arise in the ancient material, both to portray more completely the ancient event and to highlight the fact that no historical occurrence is simply determined. Sometimes societies that we admire in some ways— such as the artistic achievements and democratic political experiments of ancient Athens—may prove deeply troublesome in other ways—such as what we see as their reprehensible conduct in war and brutal subjection of other Greek communities. Consequently, the reader is empowered to make informed, well-rounded judgments on the events and actions of the major players.

We offer this series as an invitation to explore the past in various ways. We anticipate that from its volumes the reader will gain a better appreciation of the historical events and forces that shaped the lives of our ancient forebears and that continue to shape our thinking, values, and actions to-day. However remote in time and culture these ancient civilizations may at times appear, ultimately they show us that the questions confronting human beings of any age are timeless and that the examples of the past can provide valuable insights into our understanding of the present and future.

Bella Vivante
University of Arizona

PREFACE

The term Judaism refers to an evolving *religious* tradition most, but not all, of the adherents of which are *ethnically* Jewish. While religious elements dominate Jewish history and civilization, they are not identical with it. This book does not pretend to be a comprehensive study of the history and civilization of the entire Jewish people (the Jewish *ethnos*). Rather, its focus is on *Judaism*—the religious traditions, texts, practices, and ideas developed among and nurtured by Jews through late antiquity—with attention to the historical, cultural, and ideological circumstances contributing to their emergence.

The period that saw the consolidation of the ethnic-religious tradition Judaism in its classical form runs from approximately 200 C.E. to the seventh century C.E.[i] However, the roots of classical Judaism stretch back for more than a millennium before this period. The historical experiences and traditional literature of the ancient Israelites (ancestors of the Jews dating from approximately 1300 B.C.E.) are the well-spring from which classical Judaism emerged. Any study of classical Judaism must begin therefore with a survey of the religious ideas, traditions, and practices of the ancient Israelites and their relation to Ancient Near Eastern civilization generally. These ideas, traditions, and practices are available to us primarily through an anthology of writings known as the Hebrew Bible (roughly corresponding to the Protestant Old Testament).

---

i. Throughout this book, the abbreviations C.E. (Common Era) and B.C.E. (Before the Common Era) will be employed instead of the corresponding abbreviations A.D. (Anno Domini) and B.C. (Before Christ). So for example the year 586 B.C.E. = 586 B.C. and the year 220 C.E. = 220 A.D.

After surveying the biblical sources and related extra-biblical evidence (Chapters 2 and 3), we will examine the development and transformation of the ancient Israelite heritage by a variety of Jewish groups in the centuries before the first century C.E. (Chapter 4). This in turn will set the stage for an account of the gradual rise of classical rabbinic Judaism, which was to become increasingly influential from the fourth century C.E. on (Chapter 5). By the end of our period (late seventh century C.E.), classical rabbinic Judaism—particularly as developed in Babylonia—had established itself as the normative tradition of the Jewish people (Chapter 6). A final chapter surveys Judaism's manifestations and transformations to the modern period.

This volume is a textbook designed to lay out the major contours of its subject matter, rather than a monograph presenting original research. The work draws upon and synthesizes a vast body of scholarship on biblical Israel and rabbinic Judaism. In particular, the presentation of biblical Israel is indebted to the writings of Michael Coogan, Moshe Greenberg, Yehezkel Kaufman, Jonathan Klawans, Jacob Milgrom, Nahum Sarna, and the excellent scholarly essays in *The Jewish Study Bible* edited by Adele Berlin and Marc Brettler. The presentation of the Second Temple period and rabbinic Judaism is indebted to the writings of Shaye J.D. Cohen, Daniel Boyarin, Seth Schwartz, Jeffrey Rubenstein, and Richard Kalmin as well as the present author. Full bibliographic details of the major works of these scholars can be found in the Annotated Bibliography. Generalized references to "scholarly opinion" in the body of the text summarize the insights and research of these and other scholars.

Following the main body of the book, the reader will find descriptions of a number of important literary and historical figures in Jewish tradition as well as a sampling of primary sources from biblical and rabbinic literature, with commentary. A brief glossary of selected terms is followed by an extensive annotated bibliography. An index for easy reference to specific topics in the text concludes the book.

Throughout this book, the terms "Hebrew," "Israelite," and "Jew" will be used with terminological precision. The term "Hebrew" is the name employed in early biblical sources to designate the most ancient ancestors of the Jews. It is a primarily an ethnic and linguistic term denoting persons who spoke Hebrew, a Canaanite dialect. The Hebrews are thought to have established themselves in the land of Canaan (roughly modern-day Israel) by about 1200 B.C.E. The term "Israelites" (literally, "the children of

Israel") is generally used to refer to the twelve Hebrew tribes who inhabited Canaan, eventually forming themselves into a united kingdom around 1000 B.C.E. The kingdom of Israel later split into a northern and southern kingdom, destroyed in 722 and 586 B.C.E. respectively. Falling under Persian rule at the end of the sixth century, the area around Jerusalem was named Yehud and the name given to its restored inhabitants was "Yehudites" or Jews (singular Yehudi = Jew). Centuries would pass before the term Jew was understood to designate an adherent of the tradition of Judaism, rather than an inhabitant of the province of Yehud. A complex relationship between the ethnic and the religio-cultural components of Jewish identity continues to the present day.

In this work, references to the Israelite and Jewish deity will be capitalized as "God," not in order to enshrine the theological belief in a single divinity, but to make it clear that the object of our discussion is the deity of Jewish tradition rather than a generic deity (god).

Citations of biblical texts (primary documents 1-7) are taken from *Tanakh, The Holy Scriptures: The New JPS Translation According to the Traditional Hebrew Text* (Philadelphia: The Jewish Publication Society, 1988). This translation now appears in *The Jewish Study Bible*, ed. Adele Berlin and Marc Zvi Brettler (Oxford: Oxford University Press, 1999). Citations of Babylonian Talmud (primary documents 8c, 10b, 10c, 10d, 11, 12, 13c) are based on the translations that appear in *The Babylonian Talmud*, ed. Isadore Epstein (London: Soncino Press, 1935–1952), though modified upon consultation with the original sources. Citations of other rabbinic sources are based on the translations that appear in the following works, though modified upon consultation with the original sources: *Rabbinic Stories*, Jeffrey L. Rubenstein (New York: Paulist Press, 2002), primary sources 8a and 8b; *Mekhilta de-Rabbi Ishmael*, Jacob Z. Lauterbach (Philadelphia: Jewish Publication Society, 2004), primary source 13a; *Pesikta de-Rab Kahana*, William G. Braude and Israel J. Kapstein (Philadelphia: Jewish Publication Society, 2002). Other translations are those of the author.

I owe a special debt of gratitude to Professor Bella Vivante, a kind and patient editor whose excellent suggestions have greatly improved this volume. Finally, I would like to thank Greenwood Press for the opportunity to participate in this series.

CHRONOLOGY OF EVENTS

The earliest dates are approximate and some of the earliest events of Israelite history—including the patriarchal narratives, the Exodus and entry into Canaan—are unverifiable. The increasing historical verification for many events and personages provided by extra-biblical sources after the turn of the first millennium B.C.E. affords a greater though not absolute confidence in the later dates and events.

B.C.E.

2000–1900	3rd dynasty of Ur in Mesopotamia; XII Dynasty in Egypt
1900–1800	1st Babylonian Dynasty
1728–1686	Period of Hammurabi, the historical setting for the patriarchal narratives, spanning four generations from Abraham to the sons of Jacob
1700–1600	Hyksos invade Egypt; Babylonia declines. Possible Hebrew migration into Egypt
1290–1211	XIX Dynasty in Egypt, Pharaohs Ramses II, and Merneptah: the historical setting for the story of the Jews' enslavement in Egypt, the rise of Moses, and the Exodus
End of 13th c.	An entity known as Israel is attested in Canaan
1200–1000	Philistines settle along the coast of Canaan; the historical setting for the events recounted in the book of Judges—Israelite tribes inhabit tribal areas throughout Canaan, at

	times forming alliances against common enemies under the leadership of "judges"
1100–1000	Philistine ascendancy in Canaan; the prophet Samuel anoints Saul first king in Israel
1000–961	King David consolidates the Israelite tribes in a united kingdom and establishes Jerusalem as the national capital
961–922	King Solomon builds the Temple in Jerusalem
922	Upon Solomon's death, the ten northern tribes rebel creating Israel in the north, ruled by Jeroboam I and Judah in the south, ruled by Rehoboam
876–842	In Israel: The Omri Dynasty; the prophet Elijah (c. 850) rails against Baal worship under Ahab and his queen, Jezebel
	In Judah: Jehoshaphat rules, followed by Jehoram
842	In Israel: Jehu establishes a dynasty and pays tribute to Assyria.
	In Judah: Athaliah rules
786–746	In Israel: Jeroboam II reigns; the prophets Amos and Hosea deliver their oracles
750–730	Aggressive Assyrian expansion; the prophet Isaiah begins his prophetic career in Judah (c. 742–700)
732	Syria falls to the Assyrians; soon after, the prophet Micah delivers oracles in Judah
722	Assyrians under Shalmaneser V conquer Samaria, the capital of Israel; Sargon II makes Samaria an Assyrian province, marking the end of the northern kingdom; mass Israelite deportation
715	Hezekiah reigns in Judah and initiates religious reforms in line with Deuteronomistic ideology.
701	Sennecharib of Assyria lays siege to Jerusalem; Judah becomes a tributary vassal of Assyria

687–642	Manasseh reigns in Judah and reintroduces foreign cultic practices
640–609	Josiah reigns in Judah; initiates religious reforms, centralizing the worship of Yahweh in the Jerusalem temple; Short period of Judean independence
628–622	Zephaniah prophesizes
626–587	Jeremiah prophesizes
612	Babylonians and Medes raze Ninevah, the capital of Assyria; Babylonians soon establish dominance over the Ancient Near East
609	Judean King Josiah killed in the Battle of Megiddo
605	Habakkuk prophesizes
597	Nebuchadnezzar of Babylonia attacks Judah; first deportation to Babylonia includes Judah's king Jehoiachin
587/6	Jerusalem falls to the Babylonians; second deportation includes Judah's King Zedekiah; the prophet Jeremiah flees to Egypt
539	Babylon falls to Cyrus II of Persia; period of the prophecies of Second Isaiah
538	Cyrus' edict permits Jews to return to Judah and rebuild the temple; first exiles return under Sheshbazzar
520–515	Jerusalem temple is rebuilt; the prophets Haggai and Zechariah are active; Judah (Yehud) is a semi-autonomous province of the Persian Empire
5th c.	Malachi prophesizes; a second return under Ezra occurs—date uncertain
445	Nehemiah arrives in Judah; rebuilds the walls of Jerusalem
336–323	Alexander conquers the Ancient Near East; Hellenistic period begins

300–200	Palestine falls under the control of the Ptolemies of Egypt; rise of the Jewish community of Alexandria in Egypt
200	Palestine falls under the control of the Seleucids of Syria
175–163	Seleucid King Antiochus IV Epiphanes inflames factional violence in Jerusalem; Judah Maccabee and his sons lead a revolt in 167
164	Maccabeean victory; the desecrated Temple is rededicated to Yahweh. Judea becomes an independent kingdom under the Hasmoneans
163–140	Emergence of Jewish sects—Sadducees, Pharisees, Essenes
140	Simon, son of Judah Maccabee becomes high priest and *ethnarch* of Judaea
134–104	John Hyrcanus (Simon's son) reigns as king
103–76	Alexander Janneus, second son of John Hyrcanus, extends Judean control over Palestine and Transjordan
63	Pompey of Rome captures Jerusalem; John Hyrcanus II becomes high priest; Antipater becomes administrator in Judaea
40	Parthian invasion of Judea; Herod, son of Antipater, flees to Rome
37	Herod, Roman appointed king of Judaea, captures Jerusalem; reigns 33 years
4	Herod dies; the kingdom is divided between sons Archelaus (ethnarch in Judaea and Samaria), Herod Antipas (tetrarch in Galilee and Peraea) and Philip (tetrarch in Southern Syria)

C.E.

6	Archelaus is deposed; Judaea becomes a Roman province administered by prefects (later procurators); Torah scholars Hillel and Shammai are active

26–36	Pontius Pilate is Roman governor of Judaea; increasing hostilities between Jews and Roman overlords
40	Philo heads delegation from Jewish community of Alexandria to the emperor in Rome, after violent clashes with Alexandrian Greeks
66–70	Jewish revolt against Rome; Titus, son of emperor Vespasian, takes Jerusalem; the temple is destroyed; thousands are enslaved
74	Masada, the last remaining fortress of the rebels, falls to the Romans
1st–2nd c.	Tannaitic period; rabbinic sages form informal disciple circles, study Torah and transmit oral teachings
114–117	Jewish revolt in Egypt, Cyrene, and Cyprus
132–135	Unsuccessful Jewish revolt in Judaea led by Simeon bar Kosiba (Kochba) believed by some to be a messianic figure
170–217	Judah I is *nasi*; appoints judges for Jewish courts, sends envoys to diaspora communities, collects monies; credited with the redaction of the Mishnah c. 220 C.E.
3rd c.	Amoraic period; rabbinic movement in Palestine centers in Tiberius; rise of the Babylonian rabbinic movement; exilarch in Babylonia
306–337	Roman Emperor Constantine extends official toleration to Christians and reverses hostile position of predecessors
4th c.	First legal restrictions on Jews; period of synagogue construction in Palestine; major scholars in Babylonia include Rava and Abbaye
400	Redaction of the Palestinian Talmud
425	Abolition of the office of Patriarch
455–475	Period of persecution of Jews in Babylonia.
476	Fall of the western empire

527–565   Justinian conquers the western Mediterranean; Justinian Code

6th–7th c. Formation/redaction of the Babylonian Talmud; major academies (yeshivot) are centers of Torah study

CHAPTER 1

The Emergence of Judaism to 650 c.e.: A Narrative Overview

EARLIEST BEGINNINGS

The ancient ancestors of the Jews were the Israelites—relatively insignificant players in the several millennia of history in the Ancient Near East, who enjoyed an independent existence as a united and then a divided kingdom in the tiny land of Canaan or Palestine from about 1000 to 586 B.C.E. In 586 B.C.E., the last of the Israelites were conquered by the Babylonians and sent into exile. In the ancient world, such an event would usually spell the end of a particular ethnic-national group. Yet, despite the demise of their national-political base in 586 B.C.E., some Israelites survived and emerged into the modern period with a continuous identity and historical consciousness. Known as Jews in the centuries following the exile, they carried with them the sacred literature (the Hebrew Bible), ideas, and traditions that laid the foundation for the three major religions of the Western world: Judaism, Christianity, and Islam.

The ancient Israelites were profoundly influenced by the great civilizations of the lands of the Ancient Near East: southern Mesopotamia, Ancient Egypt, and the central areas of the Fertile Crescent including the Levant region (Canaan and Syria), home to the kingdoms of the ancient Israelites. The first eleven chapters of the biblical book of Genesis, the so-called "primeval history," owe a great deal to Ancient Near Eastern mythology. The creation story in Genesis 1:1–2:3 shows great similarities with the Babylonian creation epic *Enuma Elish*, while the story of the first human pair in the Garden of Eden (Genesis 2:25–3:24) has clear affinities with the *Epic of Gilgamesh*, a Babylonian and Assyrian epic in which the hero embarks on a search for immortality. The story of Noah and the flood (Genesis 6:5–9:17) is an Israelite version of an older flood story found in the Mesopotamian *Epic of Atrahasis* and also incorporated in a modified form in the *Epic of Gilgamesh*.

The ancient Israelites and later Jews understood their relationship with God to be played out on the stage of history, and thus much of Israel's sacred literature—the Hebrew Bible—takes the form of a national history. The myths in Genesis 1–11 span twenty-five hundred years and serve as a cosmic and universal prologue for the national history that begins in Chapter 12. The rest of Genesis (Chapters 12–50) covers just four generations of one family represented in the Bible as the earliest ancestors, or patriarchs and matriarchs, of the Israelites: Abram and Sarai (later Abraham and Sarah), their son Isaac and his wife Rebekah, their son Jacob and his wives Rachel and Leah, and Jacob's twelve sons and one daughter.

Set in the second millennium Levant, the dramatic stories of Genesis 12–50 recount the migration of Abraham and Sarah from Ur in Mesopotamia to the land of Canaan, a journey depicted as commanded by God; Abraham's efforts to produce an heir; the marriage of Abraham's son Isaac to Rebekah, an active and purposeful matriarch who secures the birthright for her younger son Jacob; the rivalry between Jacob, a classic trickster type, and his older brother Esau; Jacob's marriage to Leah and Rachel; and the birth of Jacob's one daughter and twelve sons, from whom the twelve tribes of Israel will descend. The final section of the book of Genesis (37:1–50:26) contains the story of Joseph, the youngest of Jacob's twelve sons, born of his favorite wife Rachel. Joseph is betrayed by his jealous brothers, who sell him to slave traders on their way to Egypt. Joseph's descent into Egypt and stunning rise to political power set the stage for the reformation of his brothers' characters and eventually the descent of all the Israelites into Egypt in search of food during a time of famine. They are said to live peacefully and prosperously in Egypt for some generations until a Pharaoh rises who does not know Joseph and all he had done for Egypt. This pharaoh enslaves the Israelites and embitters their lives.

In contrast to the mythic material in Genesis 1–11, Genesis 12–50 is often referred to as "historical narrative." This is not to say that the patriarchal stories are a historically accurate representation of the events they describe. The stories have a striking folktale quality. The biblical authors develop psychologically complex characters, weave dramatic plot lines, and employ many of the tools of the *literary* trade, such as dialogue, wordplay, parallelism, and allusion. The result is a work of great literary artistry and imagination that does not pretend to be and should not be read as "objective history."

Nevertheless, it would be a mistake to view the Bible as *only* a fanciful work of the imagination. At some level, the biblical narrative extending from Genesis 12 through the end of 2 Kings tells the foundational story of a real people, and thus serves as an important record of that people's *reactions to* and *interpretations of* its national experience. The Bible's goal, ultimately, is didactic. The biblical narrators were concerned to show what they believed to be the finger of God in the events and experiences of the Israelite people. The patriarchal narratives express the fundamental conviction that God had acted in history, setting in motion a chain of events that would bind a nation to him forever. Thus, although the historicity of the events described in the Bible are far from certain, the role that these stories and their continued interpretation played in shaping the national religious culture of the ancient Israelites and later Jews is quite certain.

THE EMERGENCE OF ISRAEL—THE BIBLE AND ARCHAEOLOGY

Exodus 1:1–15:21 contains the story of Israel's enslavement in Egypt, Moses' birth and exposure to the Nile River, his rescue by Pharaoh's daughter and upbringing in Pharaoh's own palace, God's call to Moses to lead his people out of Egypt, Pharaoh's stubborn resistance to Moses' demand through ten devastating plagues, and the Israelites' escape through the parted waters of the Red Sea. In Exodus 15:22–17:16, Moses leads the Israelites to Sinai, a mountain in the wilderness, where they will enter into a covenant relationship with the God who liberated them. The Israelites agree to abide by the rules and moral instruction ("Torah") conveyed to them by Moses and in so doing they will become God's people—"a kingdom of priests and a holy nation" set apart from the other nations in its singular devotion to the teachings of God (Exodus 18:1–24:18). Chapters 25–40 detail the construction of a sanctuary, a portable tent-like structure that houses the Ark of the Covenant (a box containing two tablets inscribed with the Ten Commandments) and in which sacrificial worship and divine communication take place. After a forty-year journey through the wilderness, a new generation of Israelites are said to arrive at the Jordan River—the eastern border of the land of Canaan—where they prepare to cross over and occupy the land promised to them by God. Moses dies without entering the Promised Land, and leadership of the people passes to Joshua. The biblical books of Joshua and Judges relate the story of the conquest of the land of Canaan by the Israelites, the division of the land among the tribes, and the early years of the settlement.

The historical value of the story of the exodus from Egypt—whether and when such an event occurred—and the conquest of Canaan by the Israelites has exercised scholars for generations. Second millennium Egyptian records mention foreigners entering the eastern Nile delta for food and water in times of famine and working on royal building projects, as the Israelites are said to have done in the Bible. A later Egyptian inscription (the stele of Merneptah) mentions a nonsedentary people named Israel in the land of Canaan by 1220 B.C.E. It is *possible* that some type of exodus of foreign slaves from Egypt—much smaller in scale than indicated in the biblical materials—took place in the thirteenth century B.C.E. and that some of these slaves may have ended up in Canaan. Nevertheless, the biblical account of the exodus shows evidence of a long process of transmission, revision, and literary editing and cannot be taken at face value. Its purpose is didactic and ideological rather than strictly historical. More important than historical verifiability is the conviction of the ancient Israelites who received and transmitted these traditions that God had rescued them from bondage and concluded a covenant that articulated the nation's aspirations. Exodus does not pretend to be objective history. It is a celebratory myth of origins explaining Israel's special relationship with God, a theological interpretation of the great events that were believed to bind Israel and her God Yahweh (which is the presumed pronunciation of YHWH) together forever.

Did a group of escaped slaves invade and conquer Canaan in the mid-thirteenth century B.C.E., establishing the nation of Israel? The biblical account is self-contradictory on this point, and archaeological research does not support the picture of a rapid and wholesale conquest. Archaeologists have found hundreds of small sites that were newly established in the thirteenth to eleventh centuries B.C.E., in places that the Bible identifies as strongholds of Israel. However, because these settlements are in their material culture (pots, jars, houses, etc.) entirely Canaanite, many scholars believe that they were established by disaffected Canaanites who for some reason chose to withdraw, establish their own settlements, and worship a liberator God. They may have been joined by immigrants—as this was a period of great migrations throughout the Ancient Near East—and by escaped slaves. Scholars have suggested that these slaves may have brought with them the story of a marvelous escape from Egypt understood at some point to have been the doing of Yahweh, and the mixed group that would emerge in the late thirteenth century as the nation of Israel adopted the national story of the Exodus as its own.

The Hebrew tribes themselves were likely still in the process of formation, but the tribal structure of Israelite society that would develop would be strengthened by the natural division of the land into geographically distinct districts. The religious center and symbol of this tribal confederation was the peripatetic shrine housing the Ark of the Covenant. There was no supertribal government—the twelve tribes were bound together by their mutual covenant with the deity. In times of national crisis the tribes would act together. The book of Judges describes several inspired leaders (judges) said to be sent by God when Israel's enemies threatened. Particularly troubling were the Philistines who arrived in Canaan from the Aegean islands at the beginning of the Iron Age (1200 B.C.E.). With their superior technology, the Philistines expanded north and east and by the mid-eleventh century constituted a serious threat to Israelite control of the land.

Partly in response to the Philistine threat, Israel changed its form of government from tribal confederacy to monarchy. Saul was anointed king by the prophet Samuel around 1025 B.C.E. But it was Israel's second monarch, King David, who consolidated his rule over all Israel and brought relative peace to the region. The Bible touts the reigns of David and his son Solomon as a golden age. Solomon's construction of a great Temple to Yahweh in Jerusalem (ca. 950 B.C.E.) inaugurates the so-called First Temple Period, which lasts until the destruction of 586 B.C.E. However, as life in the royal court became increasingly lavish under Solomon and the power of the state increased, so did the burdens on the lower classes in the form of heavy taxation and the much-hated corvée (forced labor on state projects). Many viewed the increasing social and economic schisms as a violation of the older traditions of Hebrew tribal society united by covenant with Yahweh and guided by prophets and priests rather than kings. Over the next centuries, prophetic figures such as Amos, Hosea, Isaiah, and Micah excoriated the wealthy for their insatiable greed, exploitation of the poor, and social injustice.

When King David's son and successor King Solomon died in 922 the structure erected by David fell into two rival states of lesser importance— Israel (comprising ten tribes in the north) and Judah (including the tribes of Judah and Benjamin in the south), each with its own king. The names of many kings of Israel and Judah are verified in Assyrian sources. Sometimes the two kingdoms were at war; sometimes they formed an alliance against outside enemies. But two centuries later the northern kingdom of Israel fell to the Assyrians (722) and much of the population was exiled to Assyria only to disappear from the pages of history. The southern kingdom of Judah, though still viable, was reduced by the Assyrians to tributary status. Judah was finally destroyed in 586 by the Babylonians who had defeated the Assyrians and assumed control over the Ancient Near East. The Temple was destroyed and the population decimated by death and exile.

The exiles were for the most part members of the Judean ruling class and skilled artisans. Those left behind in Judah eked out a subsistence living. While some exiles surely assimilated into mainstream Babylonian culture, others viewed recent events as confirmation rather than disproof of the sovereignty of Israel's God who had chosen to punish Israel for her many sins in violation of the covenant. As we shall see, the community of the exile played a key role in the eventual transformation of the nation of ancient Israel into the religion of Judaism.

THE SECOND TEMPLE PERIOD (539 B.C.E.–70 C.E.)

The Persian Period (539–332 B.C.E.)

In 539 B.C.E. the Babylonians were defeated by Cyrus of Persia, whose empire stretched from Egypt, through Asia Minor to eastern Iran. The Persians held to a policy of religious autonomy for their conquered subjects and in 538 B.C.E. Cyrus authorized the rebuilding of the Temple of Jerusalem and the return of the Temple vessels, a decree verified by archaeological findings. In addition, the exiles would be allowed to return to Yehud—the name of the Persian province of Judah—and establish a kind of Commonwealth under Persian hegemony in what scholars refer to as the period of the Restoration. The Second Temple was completed between 521 and 515 B.C.E., inaugurating the Second Temple period that extends until the Temple's destruction by the Romans in 70 C.E. During this period hegemony over the land of Israel passed from the Persians, to the Greeks

(332 B.C.E.), and after a period of Jewish independence (142–63 B.C.E.), finally to the Romans.

Leadership in the Persian period is associated with Nehemiah and Ezra, two prominent diaspora Jews authorized by the Persian king. The small community of Yehud was beset with problems. Frequent conflicts with the neighboring territories of Samaria, Geshur, and Ammon, as well as internal conflicts threatened the community's very survival. Ezra and Nehemiah instituted reforms and zealously promoted a renewed commitment to the Mosaic covenant. Increasingly, community life was organized around the Torah book.

The Hellenistic Period (332–167 B.C.E.)

Alexander of Macedon's conquest of the Ancient Near East was concluded in the 320s B.C.E. In Alexander's time tens of thousands of Greeks and Macedonians migrated to all parts of his vast empire. Greek culture flourished from Italy to Central Asia until the rise of Islam in the seventh century. In political terms, the Hellenistic period in Palestine extends from 332 to 167 B.C.E., when the Jews asserted their political independence from the Greeks. In cultural terms, however, the Hellenistic period in Palestine extends until the rise of Islam, for even under native Jewish rule, Roman rule and later Byzantine rule, Jews in Palestine were thoroughly immersed in Hellenistic *culture*.

Rulers of the Hellenistic period encouraged the construction of new cities and the conversion of old cities into towns with Greek institutions such as: the assembly of citizens, the election of magistrates, educational athletic centers (the gymnasium), civic cults honoring the Olympian gods as well as local deities. In addition, there was a wide adoption of the Greek language, of Greek dress, material culture, art, and modes of thought particularly among the upper middle classes of the Ancient Near East. That Jews participated in and were deeply influenced by Hellenistic culture is attested in an array of writings expressing new ideas, and in the formation of sectarian movements with diverse understandings of God's will for Israel: Sadducees, Pharisees, Essenes, and messianic and apocalyptic movements.

After Alexander's death in 324, his generals fought for control of the empire. By 301 Egypt was held by Ptolemy, while Mesopotamia and the Levant (Palestine) were held by Seleucus. However, the Ptolemies occupied most of the Levant and for a century the two great powers struggled for control of the region, the Seleucids finally prevailing by 198 B.C.E.

The struggle had a significant impact on the internal politics of Jerusalem and Judah, with pro-Ptolemaic and pro-Seleucid factions in conflict. After gaining control of Judea in 198, the Seleucids rewarded the pro-Seleucid faction, by providing support for the Temple, granting tax concessions, and confirming local autonomy. But the early second century B.C.E., saw a struggle over the office of high priest in which various contenders for the position paid the Seleucid king, Antiochus Epiphanes, for his support. Problems arose when a man named Menelaus attempted to raise money to buy the king's support by taking treasures from the Temple. Fighting broke out between the supporters of Menelaus and a certain Jason, who favored establishing Jerusalem as a polis. Antiochus suspected a revolt, recaptured the city, and plundered the Temple in 169–168 B.C.E. He garrisoned troops in Jerusalem and reorganized the Temple under pagan rites to accommodate his soldiers. The Temple was rededicated to Zeus Olympius (the Syrian god Baal Shamem) and Menelaus presided as high priest over the proceedings. Many Jews were outraged however, and the suppression of traditional Jewish observances such as circumcision and Sabbath observance, prompted a full-scale revolt known as the Maccabean revolt.

The Maccabean Revolt and the Hasmonean Period (167–63 B.C.E.)

The revolt was led by Judas Maccabeus of the Hasmonean family, and his sons. Among the rebels were Hasidim or "pious ones," whose goal was to purge the Temple of its "pagan pollution" and restore it to Yahweh. This was achieved in December, 164 B.C.E.—an event commemorated by Jews to this day in the Festival of Hanukkah. During the revolt many zealots were tortured and killed, generating the first written accounts of Jewish martyrs, that is, persons who willingly accept death rather than violate the injunctions of their religion against, for example, eating pork or offering sacrifice to the king's god.

The Hasidim, concerned only about the pure worship of Yahweh and not about national independence, broke with the Hasmoneans once it was clear that the latter were bent on the further goal of national independence. Though they lost the support of the Hasidim, the Hasmoneans met with military success, assisted in their efforts by a mutual defense treaty with Rome. In 142 B.C.E., independence from the Seleucids and expulsion of their army was achieved. The Hasmonean family ruled the small kingdom of Judea for several generations, assuming the offices of both king and high priest even though the high priesthood was a hereditary office to which they had no legitimate claim. The Hasmoneans ruled until Pompey's armies captured Jerusalem in 63 B.C.E. and established Roman hegemony.

The Roman Period (from 63 B.C.E.)

Under Roman rule Jews had some semblance of autonomy and religious independence. However, the Judean kings, princes, and high priests were all appointed by Rome and were expected to bear allegiance to Rome. Major segments of the Jewish population were unwilling to relinquish the political independence they had experienced under the Hasmoneans, and opposition to the Romans was manifest from the outset. Many Jews never ceased to view Roman rule as illegitimate, and the hope for a *messiah* (anointed leader), who would defeat the enemy and restore the nation, burned bright in some quarters. From 63 to 40 B.C.E., Judea was a vassal state of Rome, but great civil and political unrest led the Romans to appoint a local loyalist king—King Herod. Herod ruled from 37 to 4 B.C.E and undertook extensive and ambitious building projects including a magnificent renovation of the Temple in Jerusalem. However, he was hated by many Palestinian Jews not only for his unswerving loyalty to Rome but also because he was viewed as an illegitimate king. He was not from the house of David, which had been promised perpetual sovereignty by Yahweh; indeed, his Jewish lineage was suspect since he was descended from a family of forced converts. In 6 C.E., Rome opted for a plan of direct rule for Judea as a Roman province headed by Roman governors. But relations between the Jews and the Roman authorities deteriorated, and the Emperor Caligula's demand that his statue be set up in the Jerusalem Temple almost provoked a rebellion.

Finally, in 66 C.E., a full-scale war did break out resulting in massive slaughter, the destruction of the Temple in 70 C.E., and a permanent transformation of Jewish life. Although the Temple was not the exclusive center of Jewish religious life, it nevertheless served critically important symbolic and ritual functions. It was the only site of the collective worship of the entire nation and the focus of great religious events, particularly the three pilgrimage festivals (Passover, Shavuot, and Sukkot) and the Day of Atonement (Yom Kippur). In addition, the Temple was a forum for lectures and the dissemination of ideas and the seat of the Sanhedrin (high court). The Sanhedrin was a legislative and judicial body of seventy or seventy-two members that convened in a special area of the Temple and held authority in matters of law and religion in Jewish life. The destruction of this central institution was an event of major significance.

Messianic agitation continued in the ensuing decades climaxing in the Bar Kokhba Revolt. When Hadrian decided in 132 to turn the Holy City of Jerusalem into a Roman colony renamed Aelia Capitolina, zealots and messianists rebelled ready to fight a new war. Simon bar Kosiba (also Kokhba), believed by some to be the messiah, commanded the army and was head of an interim rebel administration. But after a dreadful and bloody war the rebellion was crushed. The Roman government decided that a radical solution was necessary. They expelled Jews from in and around Jerusalem. They suppressed two central religious practices—circumcision and the teaching or study of Torah—and engaged in persecution for two or three years after the war. When Hadrian died in 137 he was succeeded by Antoninus Pius who opted for a more lenient, tolerant policy. He repealed most of the oppressive edicts.

But the Jewish population had been hard hit, decimated by two wars and rising emigration. The collapse of the community's central institutions in combination with severe economic problems eroded adherence to a Jewish way of life. The Romans imposed direct rule after the Bar Kokhba revolt, replacing local rulers with Roman officials. All legal authority and political power was in the hands of the Roman state and its representatives, and even in the Jewish cities of Palestine, public life was predominantly pagan in character.

Yet during this period a small and peripheral group with some connection to pre-70 scribes and Pharisees, preserved and developed a Torah-centered Judaism. It would be at least two centuries before these sages, or rabbis, would begin to win broader influence and even judicial authority over the general Jewish populace as a result of Patriarchal patronage. The Patriarch was the chief representative of the Jews to the Romans, whose power and prestige grew considerably through the third and fourth centuries. The patriarchs appointed rabbis as judges and religious functionaries, and in the fourth through sixth centuries the rabbis reached out to the broader Jewish community, preaching in synagogues and serving as teachers. The major works of the Palestinian rabbinic movement include a collection of legal teachings and disputes known as the Mishnah (ca. 220 C.E.), a further commentary and elaboration of the Mishnah known as the Palestinian Talmud (ca. 380 C.E.) and sundry works of biblical exegesis (or Midrash), liturgical compositions, and mystical speculation.

CHRISTIANITY AND THE JEWS

Christianity began as a movement within the Jewish community. A small number of Palestinian Jews and Greek-speaking Diaspora Jews centered in Jerusalem believed that a Jewish man named Jesus put to death by the Romans in the early first century C.E., was God's anointed (messiah); as such he would reappear for the ultimate redemption of the Jewish people. These early Jesus-peoples identified themselves as Jews, conducted themselves as Jews, and worshipped the God of Israel in the Temple. Gentiles who wished to join this Jesus movement adopted Jewish religious identity and practice (observing the many laws of the Torah, including circumcision, and dietary and purity regulations). Members of this early community headed by James, the brother of Jesus in Jerusalem, did not view belief in Jesus' messiahship as the negation of Judaism and the laws and commandments of the Hebrew Bible, but as a natural part of it. It was Paul, a Jew active in the second half of the first century, who did the most to bring the new movement to non-Jews. Paulines believed that Christianity's vocation was its mission to the Gentiles and that this mission would be eased without the requirement to observe the laws of the covenant. Paul forbade Gentiles to become circumcised, to adopt the Jewish dietary system, or obey the commandments of the Hebrew Bible. Consequently, there soon existed a variety of Christian sects with greater and lesser degrees of antagonism toward the covenantal religion of the Hebrew Bible.

As the Pauline version of Christianity gained in strength, and increasing numbers of non-Jews joined the church, hostility and antagonism toward Jews increased. These negative attitudes, as dangerous as they were, were a limited threat in the pluralistic society of the early second and third centuries. But with the creation of a Christian state and society in the fourth century, long-standing theological and cultural hostilities were translated into proscriptions that had the force of law. With the rise of monastic movements and waves of religious emotionalism, attacks on non-Christians became more energetic. Monks were particularly zealous in the war against both paganism and Judaism. Successive Christian emperors lobbied by a powerful church passed increasingly severe legislation against the Jewish community.

With Christianity as the official faith of the Roman Empire, Judaism gradually assumed a position of legal inferiority. In general the anti-Jewish legislation followed a certain consistent line: Jews should be allowed to survive but dispersed, few in number, abased and poor because then they served as a testimony to the truth of Christianity. Hence Christian doctrine supported legal harassment and subjugation of the Jews. The Code of Justinian in 527 C.E. contained discriminatory legislation that was to influence European legal systems for centuries. The term "heretic" was redefined to include Jews, and Jews were entitled to no real legal protections. The Justinian code also declared that the canons of the church had the force of law. Synagogues were taken over as churches and there were instances of forced baptism. Jews in Caesarea rioted, but were severely suppressed. Yet, despite the marginalization and hardship (or perhaps because of it), many Jews chose to constitute themselves as religious communities formed around synagogues, and in the fourth to sixth centuries numerous synagogues were built in Palestine. The synagogue and local community became the chief organizing institutions of Jewish life in late antiquity and remained so until the modern period.

Byzantine Christian rule of the Holy Land ended in 637 with the Moslem conquest which brought generally better conditions for the Jews. Nevertheless, the Jewish community in Palestine was by this time dwarfed—numerically, intellectually, and spiritually—by the Jewish community of Babylonia.

THE BABYLONIAN JEWISH COMMUNITY

In the ancient period, Jewish communities flourished outside the land of Israel, particularly in Alexandria, Egypt and in Babylonia to the east. The community in Babylonia was outside the sphere of Greek, Roman, and ultimately Christian dominion. Although the Babylonian Jewish community confronted problems and persecutions of its own, its relative freedom from subjugation to a Christian state and from the economic, political, and religious hardships that prevailed in Palestine was largely responsible for its development into a vibrant center of Jewish intellectual and cultural life, until it finally surpassed the Palestinian community in its leadership of world Jewry.

Israelites first arrived in Babylonia during the time of the exile in 586 B.C.E. In later periods there was some immigration from Palestine, but it was not until the Hadrianic persecutions after the Bar Kochba revolt in the 130s C.E. that large numbers of scholars made their way to Babylonia and established a home there. Over the next several centuries as the status of Babylonian scholarship grew in prestige, immigration increased.

From 140 to 226 C.E., the Parthian-Arsacide dynasty ruled Babylonia. The Parthians permitted the establishment of a civil authority among the Jews of Babylonia so that by the end of the second century there was an exilarch in Babylon just as there was a patriarch in Palestine. The exilarch was a high government official in the Parthian administration and had military resources and direct access to the throne. In 226 the Parthian empire fell to the Sassanians, an Iranian peoples. The Sassanians established a state church (Zoroastrianism or Mazdeanism) and attempted to centralize the faith of the nation. Other religions were persecuted: Brahmans, Shamans, Buddhists, Christians, and Jews. This initial period of persecution was relieved by emperor Shapur I, who favored a policy of toleration, and Jews worked out a *modus vivendi* with the Persian regime, articulated in the famous principle "the law of the land is law." Scholars generally understand this principle to mean that the Jews agreed to observe the rules of the state in all civil affairs in exchange for the freedom to run their internal community affairs according to Jewish law. Despite some periods of persecution initiated by religious zealots (the Zoroastrian priest Kartir at the end of third century, the emperor Yazdegird II in the fifth century), Jews in Babylonia generally fared better than the Jews of Palestine.

In the early Sassanian period, the exilarch, an aristocratic grandee, played a major role in Jewish communal life and exercised considerable judicial authority. The rabbis were exilarchic bureaucrats, local judges, and administrators. However, as the rabbinic movement expanded and developed through the fourth to sixth centuries, it became increasingly independent. Rabbis saw their authority as deriving from their knowledge of Torah rather than the exilarch's support. By the end of the Talmudic period (seventh century C.E.), the exilarch had faded from view and large-scale rabbinic academies called yeshivot (sing. *yeshivah*) provided the Babylonian Jewish community with its distinctive character and culture.

The curriculum of the rabbinic academy centered on the Mishnah, a collection of primarily legal traditions and disputes on all aspects of civil, criminal, personal status, and religious law produced in Palestine and carried to Babylonia in the early third century. Generations of Babylonian sages discussed the Mishnah and related teachings, ultimately producing a compendious supercommentary known as the Babylonian Talmud. Rabbinic or classical Judaism is the Torah-centered way of life that finds expression in the vast sea of materials produced by Palestinian and Babylonian rabbis of the classical age (70–630 C.E.), most prominently the Talmud of Babylonia. This classical rabbinic Judaism achieved a remarkable degree of cultural hegemony in Jewish communities worldwide, a hegemony that, despite local variations, withstood serious challenge well into the early modern period.

BIBLICAL ISRAEL: MANY VOICES

WHAT IS THE HEBREW BIBLE?

A study of the contents and major ideas of the Hebrew Bible begins with an exploration of the work's general nature and composition. The Bible is not a book in the sense of a work penned at one time by a single author. Rather, it is a library or anthology of short books by various writers from approximately 1000 B.C.E. to 200 B.C.E., each responding to particular issues and historical circumstances. As such, it does not have a uniform style and message and, as we shall see, some passages express points of view that diverge from or plainly contradict the points of view of other passages. There are many types, or genres, of material in the Bible—narratives; legal collections; cultic/ritual texts; records of the messages of prophets; psalms of petition, praise, and thanksgiving; laments; love poetry; proverbs; and more. The Bible is written largely in Hebrew, with a few passages in Aramaic.

The product of ancient Israelite culture, these writings have had a profound and lasting impact on three world religions: Judaism, Christianity, and Islam. For Jews, the Hebrew Bible is, first and foremost, a record of God's eternal covenant with the Jewish people. Jews refer to the Bible as the TaNaKh, an acronym comprised of the initial letters of its three chief sections (Torah, Nevi'im, and Khetuvim). The first section, containing the first five books of the Bible (Genesis, Exodus, Leviticus, Numbers, and Deuteronomy) is known as the Torah, which means "instruction, teaching." The second section, Nevi'im or "Prophets," is further subdivided into the Former Prophets and the Latter Prophets. Included in the Former Prophets are books of historical narrative (the books of Joshua,

Judges, 1 and 2 Samuel, 1 and 2 Kings) in which prophetic figures such as Samuel, Elijah, and Elisha play an important role. Included in the Latter Prophets are books that purport to convey the oracular utterances of prophets who carried the word of God to the ancient Israelites over the course of several centuries. The books associated with the three major prophets—Isaiah, Jeremiah, and Ezekiel—precede smaller books associated with twelve minor prophets. The third section of the Hebrew Bible referred to as Khetuvim ("writings") is a miscellaneous collection of works of various types. Here one finds religious and lyrical poetry (Psalms, the Song of Songs), historical narratives (Ezra and Nehemiah), short stories (Ruth and Esther), wise sayings (Proverbs), and deep reflection on fundamental questions of human existence (Job and Ecclesiastes). The books of the Torah likely reached an authoritative status first, then the books of the Prophets, and finally the books contained in the Writings. The entire canon of the Hebrew Bible appears to have been closed by the end of the first century C.E.

Different Bibles serving different communities developed over the centuries. One of the earliest translations of the Hebrew Bible was the translation into Greek known as the Septuagint, intended to facilitate the reading of the Bible by Greek-speaking Jews in Egypt after the third century B.C.E. There are some significant divergences between the Greek translation and the traditional Hebrew text of the Bible as we now have it, including a different order for the books and the inclusion, in some copies, of books not included in the Hebrew canon but accepted in the early Christian canon. The Septuagint became the Bible of Christianity, or more precisely it became the Old Testament of the Christian Bible.

Not only has there been variation regarding the definition of the biblical canon among various communities, there has also been some fluidity in the actual text itself. We do not of course have the "original" copies of any individual biblical book. The centuries-long process of transmitting the Hebrew Bible began with the handing down of separate traditions and literary units, first in oral form and then in written form, during the course of which it was subject to expansion and revision. Our oldest biblical manuscripts (found among the Dead Sea Scrolls) date to the third and possibly fourth century B.C.E. These fragments are not identical in every respect to the traditional Hebrew text of the Bible, but there is a high enough degree of correspondence that we can speak of a relatively stable textual tradition from ancient to modern times.

MODERN CRITICAL STUDY OF THE BIBLE AND THE DOCUMENTARY HYPOTHESIS

Over time the belief developed that the Pentateuch—or Torah—consisting of the first five books of Genesis to Deuteronomy was written entirely by Moses, although the Bible itself does not make this claim. However, as early as the Middle Ages some biblical scholars noticed anachronisms, contradictions, repetitions, and other features that were evidence of the composite structure and multiple authorship of the Bible. With the rise of rationalism in the modern period, traditional notions of the divine and Mosaic authorship of the Pentateuch were called into question. The modern critical study of the Bible began with Baruch Spinoza (1632–1677) who first suggested that the Bible should be studied and examined like any other book without presuppositions or dogmatic claims as to its divine origin or composition. But it was a Catholic priest, Richard Simon, who first argued that Moses did not write the Torah and that it contained many anachronisms and errors.

Close literary analysis of the Bible in the eighteenth and nineteenth centuries led ultimately to the Documentary Hypothesis, according to which the Pentateuch (Genesis through Deuteronomy) is seen as an amalgam of four main sources or "documents"—referred to as J, E, P, and D—that have been edited or "redacted" together beginning in the Babylonian exile (after 586 B.C.E.). In 1878, the classic statement of biblical source theory was published by Julius Wellhausen. Wellhausen argued that the Bible's source documents date to different periods and tell us not so much about the times or situations they purport to describe but about the beliefs and practices of Israelites in the period in which they were written.

The designations J and E are based on the names for God that these two hypothetical sources use in the book of Genesis. The J source uses the personal name Yahweh (in German, Jahwe, hence "J") while the E source uses the generic term Elohim, which means simply God. Once these two sources were separated by the name of the deity, each could be analyzed so as to identify its characteristic style, terminology, and theological perspective. The J source has a vivid and earthy style, describing God anthropomorphically: God walks in the Garden of Eden, shuts the door of Noah's ark, smells Noah's sacrifice, and so on. Wellhausen dated the J source to tenth-century B.C.E. Judah.

The E source, which seems to occur first in Genesis 15, is the most fragmentary and difficult source to isolate but the style is more abstract and God is described less anthropomorphically. Because E is concerned primarily with the northern tribes, scholars have suggested that it was composed in the northern kingdom of Israel in the ninth century. According to the Documentary Hypothesis, J and E were combined, probably in the late eighth century. The combined JE source forms the backbone of the Pentateuchal narrative and, beginning in Genesis 2, includes the stories of earliest humankind, Israel's early ancestors (known as patriarchs), the story of Moses and the Exodus from Egypt in the book of Exodus, and the wanderings in the wilderness in Numbers. J continues in the books of the Former Prophets.

To this JE substratum are superadded two large units representing two important streams of tradition: the priestly cultic tradition (P) which emphasizes holiness, and the Deuteronomic tradition (D) which emphasizes covenant. The P source, which uses the term Elohim in the early material and the name Yahweh starting with Moses, is found mostly in Leviticus and the nonnarrative portions of Numbers. P is chiefly concerned with religious institutions, the sacrificial system, the Sabbath and holidays, circumcision, the Passover, dietary restrictions (*kashrut*), the system of ritual purity and impurity, and ethical and cultic holiness. P does have some narrative including the creation story of Genesis 1 and some of the flood story. In P, God is transcendent yet reveals himself to his people in his *kavod*, a sort of cloud-encased fire often translated "glory." The dating of P is much contested. Rather than assigning fixed dates for the sources in a sequence, some scholars prefer to speak of the various streams or strands of tradition (J, E, P) as roughly contemporaneous in origin, but crystallizing slowly and at various times over the centuries, with P reaching its final form in the period following the destruction (after 586 B.C.E.).

D refers to the book of Deuteronomy. Because it insists that sacrificial worship of God must take place only in the central sanctuary, Deuteronomy is associated with the program of religious reforms and cultic centralization of King Josiah in 622 B.C.E. However, D reflects older northern traditions as well and so it is thought to have been composed earlier in the north, then brought to Jerusalem after the fall of the northern kingdom. It was rediscovered and championed by King Josiah of Judah, but it probably did not reach its final form until after the destruction.

In the Babylonian exile and after, the written versions of these diverse strands of Israelite tradition took final shape. In the Persian period, the Torah as a whole was transplanted back to Yehud.

While most biblical scholars today accept some version of the source theory, there are serious disagreements over both the identity and dating of the sources. While it is an important and worthwhile project to analyze these component sources and examine their specific concerns and contribution, we must remember that the sources were woven together with great skill and care by a final redactor or redactors.

Multiple Voices in the Bible

The anonymous scribe or editor who combined these various sources did not see a need to remove contradictions or doublets (two accounts of a single event or story). Thus, Genesis 1–3 contains two creation stories side by side. In P's account (Gen 1:1–2:4a), God is transcendent, creating cosmos by his word alone and on the sixth and final day creating the human—male and female simultaneously—in the image of God. J's account (Gen 2:4a–3) is much more anthropomorphic—God walks about, fashions a single human out of clay, and breathes life into him. Moreover, the male human is created before the animals, and last of all, woman is separated from the male's side. Elsewhere in the Bible, doublets do not appear side by side but are interwoven. This occurs in the flood story (Gen 6–9), long recognized as a combination of J and P flood stories. The two interwoven accounts differ in many details, creating a contradictory story (compare Gen 6:14–22 and 7:1–5, or Gen 7:17 and 7:24).

Although biblical writers and editors drew upon older sources and traditional material it is clear that they blended and shaped these materials in a particular way. This brings us to a critical problem facing anyone who seeks to reconstruct ancient Israelite religion and culture on the basis of the biblical text—*the conflicting perspectives of the older source materials and of the final redactors of those materials.* The narrative books that relate the early history of Israel down to the mid-sixth century B.C.E.—the books of the Torah (Genesis–Deuteronomy) and the Former Prophets (Joshua–2 Kings)—reached their final form centuries after the events they purport to relate. Those responsible for the final redaction of these books have a decidedly monotheistic world view and attempt to impose that world view on the earlier source materials. They represent Israel's earliest heroes—the patriarchs and matriarchs—as the world's first monotheists called by the one God to mark a new beginning and a special destiny for the ancient Hebrews.

In the premodern world, the dominant approach to reading the Hebrew Bible focused on the level of final redaction without concern for the diverse perspectives of older sources. As modern students of the Bible, we have the opportunity to deepen our knowledge of the text and its meanings by attending to the diverse voices of the sources prior to their redaction, as well as the voices of the redactors who wove the sources into a larger whole. In short, the Bible can be read both analytically and synthetically, combining an awareness of origins and sources with sensitivity to the final composition.

ISRAELITE RELIGION VERSUS BIBLICAL RELIGION

For more than a century, scholars have acknowledged a distinction between the actual religion of the inhabitants of Israel and Judah (Israelite-Judean religion) and the religion promoted by later writers and redactors of the biblical narrative (biblical religion).[i] Israelite-Judean religion is attested in early sources incorporated into the Bible, as well as the archaeological record. Most scholars conjecture that ancient Israelite-Judean religion was monolatrous (promoting Israel's worship of her god, Yahweh, without denying the existence of other nations' gods) rather than monotheistic (asserting the reality of one god only). Moreover, Yahweh was in many respects similar to the gods of Canaanite religion whose exploits are recorded in recently discovered texts. These gods include the sky god El, the father of various gods and humans; El's wife Asherah, a mother goddess; their daughter Anat, goddess of love and war, and their son Baal, a dying and rising storm god, who is depicted in mythological literature as defeating both the chaotic sea god Yam and the god of death,

---

i. For a full and accessible discussion of Israelite-Judean religion and biblical religion as summarized here, see Stephen Geller, "The Religion of the Bible" in *The Jewish Study Bible*, ed. Adele Berlin and Marc Zvi Brettler (New York: Oxford University Press, 2004), pp. 2021–2040. See also Michael Coogan, *Introduction to the Old Testament: A Historical and Literary Introduction to the Hebrew Scriptures* (New York: Oxford University Press, 2006).

Mot. El dwells in a tent atop a mountain and is the head of the council of gods. He is referred to as "father of all creatures," "bull," and "king." He is also a protector of patriarchal figures—a "god of the father"—guiding them, protecting them, and promising them descendants.

Many biblical passages depict Yahweh as the head of a council of divine beings and he is occasionally described with the epithets associated with El (father of all creatures, bull, king). In the patriarchal narratives (Gen 12–50), Yahweh refers to himself as the "god of the father" guiding, protecting, and making promises to Abraham and his heirs. Other descriptions of Yahweh are reminiscent of the storm god Baal. Like Baal, God is said to ride on the clouds (Ps 68:5) and his revelations are accompanied by thunder, lightning, rain, and earthquakes (Ex 19:16). Poetic fragments allude to Yahweh's victory over a watery foe, a motif associated with Baal (Ps 74:12–15). Finally, the influence of Ancient Near Eastern holy war traditions may be discerned in descriptions of Yahweh as an armed warrior leading his hosts in battle.

Continuities with Canaanite and Ancient Near Eastern religions are also apparent in the worship practices of ancient Israel and Judah. Canaanite religious rituals took place in small temples housing cultic statues, stone pillars (symbols of the gods or memorials to the dead), and altars for animal, cereal, and liquid sacrifices. Similarly, Yahweh was worshipped at various "high places"—shrines with altars, cultic pillars, and wooden poles (called *asherot*; singular: *asherah*). Although small female figurines have been found at excavated Israelite-Judean shrines, no figures of Yahweh have been found, which scholars view as evidence of the strong aniconic tendency of this tradition. Many "high places" seem to have been associated with some kind of contact with ancestors, or cult of the dead.

Like his Ancient Near Eastern counterparts, the god of Israel was worshipped with sacrifices. Pilgrims visited local shrines, particularly on the three major pilgrimage festivals (later Passover, Shavuot, and Sukkot). Child sacrifice was practiced in Canaanite religion. Biblical texts denounce the practice, and the story of Abraham's binding of Isaac for a sacrifice that is not carried out (Gen 22) may be read as a rejection of it. Nevertheless, such denunciations suggest that child sacrifice may have been practiced in some quarters of Israel, necessitating rebukes to desist. A remembrance of the practice may be found in the Israelite idea that the first-born child belongs to Yahweh and must be "redeemed" by a payment of money.

While Israelite-Judean religion, as just described, enjoyed many points of contact with other religions and cults in the Ancient Near East, *biblical religion*—evidenced in certain passages of the Torah and Prophets (seventh to fifth centuries B.C.E.)—breaks with Ancient Near Eastern and much Israelite-Judean religion. Time and again, older sources that reflect traditions of Israelite-Judean religion have been altered or reframed to reflect the viewpoint of later editors. Scholars have identified the typical features of this later biblical religion as opposed to earlier Israelite-Judean religion. The most important of these characteristic features is the strong tendency toward monotheism, as seen in the Deuteronomist's polemic against idolatry (Deut 12:2–5; 13:7–12) and expressions of God's uniqueness (Deut 4:35, Deut 6:4). The move toward a stricter monotheism is also expressed in the demythologization and desexualization of Israel's deity in the priestly source.

BIBLICAL RELIGION—THE DEUTERONOMIC TRADITION

Many scholars conjecture that biblical religion originated in the activity of zealous prophets in the northern kingdom of the ninth century who, according to 1 Kings, violently opposed attempts to establish the worship of Baal. Prophets like Elijah and Elisha were Yahwists who tolerated no other deities. After the fall of the northern kingdom to Assyria, this Yahwism grew in strength in the southern kingdom also, consolidating into the Deuteronomic school by the late seventh century and influencing the reforms of King Josiah in the 620s B.C.E. Citing a recently found "book of instruction" (probably something like Deuteronomy) King Josiah called for a centralization of Yahweh worship in Jerusalem and forbade local high places as "idolatrous," destroying the images, cultic pillars, and altars associated with them (2 Kings 23).

The centralization of the cult in Judah must be understood against the political backdrop of the late seventh century. The Assyrian threat loomed large. The northern kingdom had already been destroyed, the southern kingdom was a tribute-paying vassal to Assyria, and a certain amount of religious syncretism had occurred. Josiah's reforms have been described by scholars as an attempt to assert political, religious, and cultural independence for Judea. Unregulated worship throughout the land was no longer acceptable. Uniting the people around a central standardized religious cult purged of foreign influence was deemed necessary to survive the Assyrian threat.

At the heart of the Deuteronomic strand of biblical religion is the concept of covenant. Deuteronomy expresses Israel's relationship with God as a legal covenant, or treaty, concluded at Mount Horeb—elsewhere, Sinai—after the Israelites' escape from Egypt. In a direct revelation to the people, God announced the Decalogue, or Ten Commandments. Moses then receives and transmits the remaining terms of the covenant—a collection of civil, criminal, agricultural, cultic, and ethical laws detailed in Exodus through Deuteronomy. The covenant, which was sealed by a formal oath, entails mutual obligations: God will protect the Israelites as his people and give them the land of Canaan if they will obey his commandments. Unlike the unconditional covenant with Noah, and the unilateral and promissory covenant with Abraham, the covenant with Israel at Horeb/Sinai is conditional. If Israel does not fulfill her obligation by obeying God's commands and living in accordance with his will, then God will revoke the right of residence in his land and withdraw his protection and blessing. Deuteronomy 28 lists the curses that will attend disobedience.

Many scholars have demonstrated the influence of seventh-century Assyrian vassal treaties on Deuteronomy's formulation of the covenant (particularly the curses). Assyrian vassal treaties were loyalty oaths. This is true of Deuteronomy also, but Deuteronomy urges the Israelites to pledge their loyalty to God rather than a human king. The biblical exhortations to "love the Lord your God," "to go after," "to fear," and "to listen to the voice of" God—are all paralleled in the Assyrian treaties where the vassal must love the ruler, listen to the voice of the ruler, etc. The Deuteronomist has borrowed a political form, and applied it to the nation's relationship to God. One scholar has referred to Deuteronomy as a subversive "counter-treaty" attempting to shift the people's loyalty from the Assyrian overlord to God, their true sovereign (see Document 5).

In the Deuteronomic tradition, the sanctuary is understood to be a house of worship, as much as a cultic center, in which Israelites and foreigners alike may deliver prayers to God who dwells in heaven. God is not said to dwell in the Temple, rather it is the dwelling place of his "name," pointing perhaps to a greater abstraction and transcendence of the deity in the Deuteronomic tradition. Deuteronomy emphasizes social justice, personal ethics, and neighborly responsibilities. God's own righteous activity on behalf of the weak and oppressed, his assistance to the orphan, the widow, and the stranger is the basis of the humanitarianism that runs through the laws of Deut 12–26. Each member of the community stands in equality before the law.

In Deuteronomy we find for the first time an expression of the particularity of Israel and its unique relationship with God expressed by the term "bahar" = to elect, or choose. Yahweh has chosen Israel in an act of freely bestowed love to be his special property just as an Ancient Near Eastern sovereign might single out a vassal for the status of special property. However, Deuteronomy warns repeatedly that it is by no special virtue or merit that Israel was chosen, and Moses admonishes the Israelites not to suppose that their inheritance of the land of Canaan is due to their own powers or on account of their righteousness or virtue. On the contrary, Israel was chosen to be God's treasured people (Deut 7:6) in an act of spontaneous love for the patriarchs and it is no cause for Israel to boast (Deut 7:6–8).

In Deuteronomy, God's election of Israel means that Israel is a holy people—that is, a people consecrated to God. This consecration entails separation *from* alien peoples and practices that are inconsistent with the worship of God. Hence intermarriage with the Canaanites is prohibited—indeed the latter are to be utterly destroyed—and all alien practices are to be removed from the covenant community. However, this separation entails also the positive aspect of separation—separation *to* God's service which is the observance of his laws. Being a people consecrated to God entails obligations and responsibilities. It should be noted that since Canaanites no longer existed as a group at the time of Deuteronomy's composition, the term may well refer to "Canaanizers"—those who adhered to older, less strictly monotheistic Israelite-Judean religion.

BIBLICAL RELIGION—THE PRIESTLY CULTIC TRADITION

The priestly cultic tradition is a second major articulation of biblical religion (as opposed to Israelite-Judean religion), shaping cultic and purity practice in the light of fundamental monotheistic convictions. Like the other peoples of the Ancient Near East, the ancient Israelites engaged in cultic practices and sacrifices presided over by priests. Literature from Ancient Near Eastern cultures suggests that a central function of the rituals performed in sanctuaries was to protect the deity from intrusion by demons or other hostile gods. In this way one secured the perpetual aid of a well-disposed deity.

Ancient Israelites also hoped to secure the perpetual aid, blessing, and protection of their deity and may have seen little difference between their own and their neighbors' cultic activities. However, the writers and editors of the priestly source present a highly monotheized portrait of the Israelite cult. Because the one transcendent and moral God lacks divine antagonists, ritual actions are not designed to protect God from demons or evil gods. They are designed to protect God from impurities that defile the sanctuary and render it uninhabitable by him. By keeping the sanctuary pure, Israel's priests attract and maintain God's presence in the sanctuary.

The terms "pure" and "impure" denote states of qualification for or disqualification from contact with the holy, respectively.[ii] That which is impure is anathema to the holy. There are two main types of impurity in the priestly sources. One type of impurity, often called ritual impurity, arises from substances connected with death (corpses, wasting skin disease) and sexuality (genital fluxes such as semen and menstrual blood). It is surely interesting and significant that Israel's priests did not declare urine, feces, nasal mucus, and the like to be impure as many other societies did and do. Instead they specifically chose substances and physical states associated with death and sexuality in order to construct their symbolic system. The highly monotheistic priestly sources conceive of God as an immortal and asexual being. Death and sexuality are thus antithetical to the divine. They have no place in God's sanctuary, and recent association with death and/or sexuality disqualifies one from entering the holy sanctuary. This is not to say that one must not deal with death or sexuality in the ordinary course of life. On the contrary, God explicitly commands humans to be fruitful and multiply in the priestly creation story and he also commands proper care of the dead. The priestly source even commands priests to defile themselves to bury their kin. It is prohibited only to enter the holy sanctuary when one is symbolically defiled by contact

---

ii. For an accessible discussion of the biblical purity system, see Jonathan Klawans, "Concepts of Purity in the Bible" in *The Jewish Study Bible*, ed. Adele Berlin and Marc Zvi Brettler (New York: Oxford University Press, 2004), pp. 2041–2047.

with death and sexuality or by failing to purify oneself after contact with impurity.

The second type of impurity is moral impurity which—unlike ritual impurity—arises through sin. Moral impurity arising from heinous sins is said to symbolically defile not only the sanctuary but also the holy land, and even God's holy name.

According to P, the blood of expiatory sacrifices was assigned by God to purge the sanctuary of, and effect atonement for, moral and ritual impurity, thereby ensuring God's continued residence among—and blessing of—the Israelites. Recent scholarship on Israel's purity system describes the symbolism of the system as follows: If the sanctuary symbolizes the presence of God and if impurity represents the wrongdoing of persons, then by saying that impurity is anathema to God and defiles his sanctuary, the priestly source graphically conveys the idea that sin forces God out of his sanctuary and out of the community. The moral message at the root of this complex symbolic picture is that human actions determine the degree to which God can dwell on earth among his people. Humans and humans alone are responsible for the reign of wickedness and death or the reign of righteousness and life in their society.

A subsection of the priestly source, referred to as the Holiness Code (Lev 17–26), emphasizes the themes of moral purity and holiness. According to the Holiness Code, all holiness in the world derives from God. God alone is holy, and God imparts holiness to persons, places, and things by bringing them into a specific kind of relationship with him, best described as a relationship of ownership. To be holy, or sacred, is to "belong to" God.

Holiness necessarily entails selection and separation. The Sabbath day is separated from the other days of the week to belong, or be holy, to God. The distinctive status of a holy entity is only preserved by observing rules that mark it as separate. Thus the sanctity of the Sabbath day is preserved by observing the rules that mark it as holy and distinct from the profane (i.e., common or non-holy) days of the week. One does not work on the Sabbath, or light a fire, or travel or engage in business as one might do on an ordinary weekday. These rules or safeguards are addressed to humans who are charged with the task of preserving holiness wherever it resides on earth. Thus, although holiness derives from God, humans have a crucial role in sanctifying (making holy) the world. God may have sanctified the Sabbath at creation, but Israel must affirm and preserve its sanctity by observing those rules and prohibitions that mark it off as holy. If not, the Sabbath is automatically desecrated (Ex 31:14).

Likewise, Israel's status as a holy people is not actualized or preserved unless Israel observes those rules that distinguish it from the other nations and mark it as the special possession of God, as holy. Those rules include circumcision, the dietary system, and the many other laws and regulations of the covenant. Indeed, in the Holiness Code Israel's status as a holy nation, as the Lord's special possession, is always connected with an exhortation to faithfully observe all the details of the Torah or certain key elements thereof such as the Sabbath or dietary laws: "you shall sanctify yourselves and be holy, for I the Lord am your God. You shall faithfully observe my laws: I the Lord make you holy" (Lev 20:7–8); or again: "Thus you shall be reminded to observe all My commandments and to be holy to your God" (Num 15:40, Lev 22:31–32).

From the foregoing it is clear that holiness involves a collaboration of divine effort and human effort. This collaboration reaches its most profound expression in the priestly source in the idea that God and Israel sanctify each other. First, God sanctifies Israel: God redeemed Israel and made her his own special possession from among the nations, sealing the relationship with the giving of a Torah that would serve as the blueprint for Israel's holy vocation. In turn, Israel sanctifies God by living out that vocation, by faithfully observing the commandments and becoming a holy people. Israel's failure would be a profanation of God's name. His reputation would be sullied in the eyes of the world. But if Israel succeeds in her sacred calling, God too will be known as Holy. In the covenant relationship God and Israel meet in a reciprocal sanctification. This is the language, logic, and meaning of Lev 22:31–32.

> You shall faithfully observe my commandments; I am the Lord. You shall not profane my holy name, so that I may be sanctified in the midst of the Israelite people—I the Lord who sanctify you, I who brought you out of the land of Egypt to be your God, I the Lord.

In short, holiness in the priestly source must be understood as a remarkable divine-human collaboration which awards to humans a most awesome responsibility. To depict Israel as God's essential partner in the process of sanctification is to represent humans as full-fledged moral agents, each a powerful force for good (or evil) in the world. This is the moral vision at the heart of the priestly concept of holiness.

CONCLUSION

The Deuteronomic tradition and the priestly cultic tradition were superadded to the older narrative traditions of the nation—traditions that were often less clearly monotheistic. The Hebrew Bible is therefore a compromise document that includes many voices, some of which stand in tension with one another. In the next chapter we will survey the major themes of biblical literature that were foundational to later Judaism.

CHAPTER 3

THEMES OF BIBLICAL LITERATURE

As numerous scholars have demonstrated, biblical authors and editors drew upon a common Near Eastern literary heritage, transforming it so as to express distinctive Israelite conceptions of the divine, the natural world, and humankind. Late biblical writers represent the ancient Israelites as breaking with the polytheism of their neighbors. In these writers' view, the difference between monotheism and polytheism is not so much a difference in the *number* of gods worshipped (one vs. many), as it is a difference in the *nature* of the gods worshipped: the God of the monotheistic strands of the Bible is not identical with, but *transcends*, nature. God is experienced not as a force of nature, but through history, historical events, and a peculiar relationship with humankind.

In polytheistic religions, the gods are born (or created); they live lives very similar to human beings but on a grand scale. They are sexually active and they even die. Theogonies are tales of the births of gods, and mythologies are tales of the lives of the gods. Both are found in polytheism. Because gods and humans are both created, the distinction between them is soft, and the interpenetration of divine and human is believed possible. The merging of the divine and human realms finds expression in the pagan belief in divine descent (a king might be said to be the son of a god and a human female, for example) and *apotheosis*, that is, humans actually becoming gods. Apotheosis, or divinization of humans, may be confined to royalty (e.g., the king becomes divine upon ascending to the throne) or may be more universally conceived in a general notion of an afterlife in which humans take on the divine attribute of immortality after death.

The mythologies of polytheistic religions are populated by divine beings of diverse character. Just as there are good gods well disposed toward humanity, there are also evil gods who seek to destroy both humans and the other gods. Thus, in polytheistic systems, *evil is an independent reality.* The universe is characterized by a constant cosmic struggle between good and evil forces—a struggle in which humans are often unwitting victims. There is no single absolute divine will enforcing a single absolute divine morality.

As noted in Chapter 2, the Hebrew Bible contains numerous source materials that exhibit features of contemporary polytheisms. In Genesis 6, divine beings (Nefilim) descend to earth to mate with female humans (Gen 6:1–4). In many passages, Yahweh is represented as presiding over a council of gods (Gen 3:22, Ps 82, Job 1:6–12). Other passages assume the existence of other gods worshipped by other nations (Num 21:29, Deut 4:19, 29:25; Judg 16:23–24). Nevertheless, the most strongly monotheistic sources of the Bible posit a god that is qualitatively different from the gods that populated the mythology of Israel's neighbors and Israelite-Judean religion. This biblical deity is himself the source of all. Because he does not emerge from a preexisting realm and has no divine siblings, this god's will is absolute and sovereign. Moreover, biblical monotheism assumes that this god is inherently good, just, and compassionate and that human morality is conformity to his will. Because certain texts of the Bible posit an absolutely good God who places absolute moral demands upon humankind, biblical monotheism is often referred to as *ethical monotheism.*

Many scholars have enumerated the differences between the God of the monotheizing sources of the Bible and the gods of surrounding Mesopotamian literature. These differences are apparent from the very first chapter of Genesis, attributed to the priestly source. Unlike the Baby-lonian creation myth *Enuma Elish,* in which deities are created by a pro-cess of sexual generation from primordial waters, Genesis 1 contains no theogony and no mythology. God is not born or generated. He does not grow up and mature, find a consort and bear children, age and die. In Genesis 1, we meet an unlimited God who is timeless, ageless, desexu-alized, incorporeal, and eternal. Moreover, this god transcends nature so that the line of demarcation between God and the natural world is clear. God is not identified with any natural phenomenon or force. Nature is not divinized; it becomes merely the stage for God's activity, the canvas upon which God expresses his will and purpose. Similarly, this wholly transcendent god is not kin to humans in any way. God and humans are utterly distinct and there is no interpenetration of human and divine beings in the most strictly monotheistic representations of biblical thought: no apotheosis—humans becoming gods; incarnation—gods becoming humans; or immortality—life after death.

Since God is the supreme and transcendent source of all, there is no realm of power beyond him that can be harnessed through ritual or magical techniques to coerce or manipulate him. Indeed, strict biblical monotheism condemns magic as sinful rebellion against God insofar as it is based on a material conception of power that rivals God's own.

In biblical monotheism sin and evil are also *demythologized*. There are no divine antagonists of God to battle with him, no demonic powers to incite sin and work evil in the universe. Instead, sin and evil arise from the conflict between God—who is represented as absolutely good—and humans—who alone have the freedom to disobey and oppose God. In strict biblical monotheism, evil is thus a *moral* reality, arising as it does from the choices made by human beings. It has no concrete independent existence. The demythologization of sin and evil makes possible a critically important ethical claim. If evil is a moral, and not a metaphysical, reality then human beings are responsible for, rather than victims of, the state of the world. Through their moral choices—namely, by eschewing sin and choosing actions that promote life and blessing—humans can bring about a better world.

In short, the ethical monotheism of the Hebrew Bible posits an absolute and absolutely good God who creates a cosmos that is inherently good. Evil is not built into the structure of the universe but is the product of human choices. Humans are free moral agents and this freedom is both an opportunity and a power for good and a potential source of evil and disaster. These ideas are contained in the opening chapters of Genesis in which Mesopotamian cosmogonies are rewritten and demythologized to express the ethical monotheism of the biblical authors.

The absence of mythology in the Bible is not to be understood as an absence of myth. A myth is a traditional story, often fanciful and imaginative, relating events usually in order to explain some practice, natural phenomenon, religious rite, or belief. The Bible does not contain full-blown mythologies (stories of the lives of gods) but it does contain myths in its opening chapters. The creation story (Gen 1), the Garden of Eden story (Gen 2–3), the story of Cain and Abel (Gen 4), the story of Noah and the flood (Gen 6–9), and the tower of Babel story (Gen 11) are all biblical myths invented to explain various aspects of the human experience.

It is not clear when monotheism became dominant in ancient Israel. Neither do we know whether monotheism took root in all levels of society or was confined to a more elite group responsible for the final form of the nation's sacred traditions. It is clear, however, that a monotheistic perspective has informed the final editing of the primeval myths (Gen 1–11), the stories of Israel's patriarchs and matriarchs (Gen 12–50), the account of the leadership of Moses, the emergence of the nation Israel (Ex-Deut), and the history of the kingdoms of Israel and Judah down to the fall of Judah in 586 B.C.E. (Josh-2 Kings). What are the major themes of this literature that will serve as a foundation for later Judaism?

THE MYTHS OF BIBLICAL RELIGION IN THEIR ANCIENT NEAR EASTERN CONTEXT

Scholars have noted that the common Mesopotamian account of creation as the sequel to a cosmic battle between powerful deities was certainly known in Israel, and is alluded to in many poetic passages of the Bible (Job 26:12–14, Ps 74:12–17, 89:10–11, 104, Isa 51:9–10). However, the creation story that appears in Genesis 1:1–2:4 presents a demythologized account of creation, rejecting the idea of a divine antagonist with whom God does battle. In Genesis, a single uncontested God by the power of his word or will creates cosmos, imposing order on preexisting but inert elements (see Document 1).

One of the most striking differences between the mythological and the biblical creation accounts lies in their descriptions of humankind. In the Bible, the human is the *telos* or goal of all creation, rather than a menial created to relieve the gods of labor, as in the Babylonian creation myth *Enuma Elish*. Most important is the biblical statement that humans are created "in the image of God" (1:26–28) a phrase that seems to connote the endowment of a range of special faculties required for humankind's special mission as God's steward over creation. Moreover, being created in the image of God implies the sanctity of human life. So in Genesis 9:6, God declares the prohibition of murder in these terms: "whoever sheds the blood of man, in exchange for that man shall his own blood be shed, for in the image of God was man created."

In the Genesis 1 creation account there is no implication that man and woman stand in an unequal relationship before God. Genesis 1:27 states that God created the *adam* (not a proper name, but a word that means "earthling") in his image—"male and female created he them." He creates these earthlings to be the stewards of creation and he blesses them with the commandment to be fruitful, and increase, and fill the earth.

The Bible contains two myths dealing with the creation of humans. In the second creation story of Genesis 2:4–3:24, God fashions an "earthling" (*adam*) from the dust of the earth (or clay) and breathes life into it. The human thus draws its life source directly from God, another indicator of special status. Finding no equal companion or fit partner for this creature among the animals, God forms a female from the earthling's own flesh and bone. While many traditional commentators have read this story as implying a subordinate status for woman, there is little in the text to support such a reading. Genesis 2 suggests a genuine and mutually beneficial partnership of male and female. The woman is greeted by the earthling as, at last, bone of his bones and flesh of his flesh—a companion befitting him. Further, the creation of both male and female in the image of God (Gen 1) and their creation from a common flesh and bone (Gen 2) can be connected with a central and highly positive biblical conception of sexuality and marital union. The author of Genesis idealizes marriage as the (re-)union of male and female to become again one flesh (2:24) as at creation.

The created world is portrayed positively in the biblical creation accounts. After each act of creation God declares that "it is good" (Gen 1:4, 10, 12, 18, 21, 25), and after the creation of living things God finds all that he has made to be *very* good (v. 31). The principle of the essential goodness of the world at creation is a rejection of the concept of an inherent evil built into the structure of the universe. What then, in the biblical view, is the source of evil in the world?

Many scholars surmise that the Garden of Eden myth seeks to express the idea that evil is not a metaphysical reality. Evil is not built into the structure of the universe; rather, it is a moral reality, the result of human choices and actions. The first human couple is placed in a garden planted by God and given unlimited access to the fruit of the trees of the garden—including the tree of life—except for one: the tree of the knowledge of good and evil (Gen 2:15–17). By eating of this forbidden tree, Adam and Eve learn that they have the power to disobey God, that they have moral freedom. God observes that the humans have now become "like gods" knowing good and evil. Were humans to add immortality to their newfound moral freedom, they would be true rivals to God. Thus, God banishes the humans from the garden and posts guards to block the way to the tree of life (Gen 2:22–24). The mortality of humans is henceforth a given, necessary concomitant of moral freedom.

While there has been a long tradition of interpreting the sin of the first humans as sexual—particularly within the Christian tradition—there is little in the Genesis story that would support such a reading. Indeed, fertility, reproduction, and child-bearing appear to exist as part of the original Edenic creation; see Gen 1:28, 2:24–25, 3:16. It can be argued that for the biblical writer, the god-like wisdom gained by the first human pair is moral in nature, not sexual.

Despite their recently acquired mortality, humans have become a force to be reckoned with—unpredictable to the very God who created them. The cosmic struggles between good and evil divinities featured in the mythologies of Israel's neighbors are replaced in biblical myths by the struggle between a good God and the morally free creature that can defy him and corrupt his plans. This then is the one limitation that biblical religion places upon its all-powerful God: the free moral agency of humans.

The self-destructive potential of humankind's moral freedom is apparent in the story of the first murder—the murder of Abel, son of Adam and Eve, by his own brother Cain. Despite God's warning to the jealous Cain that he has the power to choose what is right and to master the urge to sin (Gen 4:6–7), the brooding Cain sets upon his brother and kills him. Cain's very culpability assumes the operation of a basic moral principle: the sanctity of human life. The biblical God demands reverence for life from his creatures.

In the biblical flood story that follows, God sees the continuing wickedness, violence, and lawlessness of humankind and regrets having created humans. In Genesis 6, he announces to Noah, a man righteous in his generation, his decision to put an end to all flesh. He instructs Noah to build an ark and take his family and animals of all species on board. He opens windows in the firmament, and the upper waters of the great deep burst forth and flood the earth. When all life has been destroyed, Noah emerges from the ark, builds an altar to God and offers a sacrifice that is pleasing to God.

We have several Ancient Near Eastern accounts of a divinely sponsored flood similar in many details to the Genesis story of the flood in the time of Noah. The biblical writers assimilated these ancient Mesopotamian narratives but rewrote them so as to establish a clear moral rationale for the flood. The earth's inhabitants are to be destroyed because they have filled the earth with *hamas* (violence, bloodshed, oppression). Noah is saved because of his righteousness. God does not act capriciously but in accordance with his own immutable moral standard—punishing the corruption and wickedness of the human beings he so lovingly created and whose degradation he cannot bear to witness. The deeper message of the flood story seems to be that the moral corruption of human society endangers the very existence of that society—indeed, of creation as a whole.

The Noah story ends with the ushering in of a new era, a second creation. God establishes a covenant with Noah and humankind receives its first laws (Gen 9:1–7). At the heart of this covenant is the blood prohibition. Although God's original plan for creation was one that entailed no killing, he recognizes the human appetite for violence and power, and concedes to humans the right to kill animals for meat. However, this concession does not extend to the killing of humans. Moreover, although animals may be killed and consumed, the blood that flows through the animal's veins, which is the life force of the animal, may not be consumed. It must be poured out on the ground and returned to God, since all life—human and animal—is sacred to God. The blood prohibition of the Noahide covenant—no consumption of animal blood, no spilling of human blood—is an expression of the basic principle of the sanctity of life and a central tenet of the dietary laws of later Judaism. (The Jewish practice of salting meat to absorb every last drop of blood before preparation derives from this verse.) Reciprocally, the Noahide covenant also entails God's promise to restore the rhythm of life and nature and never again to destroy the earth. The rainbow is established as a symbol of this eternal covenant.

Themes of the Patriarchal Stories (Gen 12–50)

The story of Abraham expresses the theme of *divine promise* and *blessing*. God orders Abraham to leave his home and travel to a land God will show him. God promises that he will make Abraham the progenitor of a great nation (see Document 2) and bless him. A few verses later when Abraham reaches Canaan, God adds a promise of land to his earlier promise. This threefold promise of descendants, blessing, and land is a central motif of biblical literature and later Judaism. In Chapter 15, the ownership of the land is sealed in a covenant ritual and, in Chapter 17, circumcision is instituted as a sign of the eternal covenant with Abraham.

This patriarchal covenant is a *unilateral* obligation assumed by God—to provide progeny and land—without any reciprocal responsibility being imposed on Abraham. Nevertheless, Abraham exhibits great faith in obeying God's summons, setting forth from his home in the high civilization of the East to travel to an unknown backwater. The Bible makes much of Abraham's faith—exhibited most dramatically and disturbingly in his willingness to prepare his son Isaac for slaughter at God's command (Gen 22)—and later Jewish tradition comes to regard Abraham as the paradigmatic man of faith, who endured numerous trials in his devotion to God (see Document 3).

Many scholars have pointed to another prominent theme of the patriarchal narratives: the subversion of the Ancient Near Eastern custom of *primogeniture*—inheritance by the first-born. Time and again, the younger brother, the unlikely son, rises to claim the blessing and promise given to Abraham: Isaac over his older half-brother Ishmael, and Jacob over his brother Esau. Indeed, Jacob and Esau are locked in a struggle for the birthright almost from the time of conception it would seem, and the name Jacob means "supplanter, uprooter." The rivalry of the two brothers leads Jacob to flee to his mother's homeland where he dwells for many years, acquiring his two wives Leah and Rachel.

It is during Jacob's return to Canaan that a mysterious and transformative incident occurs. Alone in the night, Jacob struggles with a mysterious man who is in some way representative of God. The two wrestle all night in the darkness, neither prevailing, though Jacob is wounded. Jacob is then given a new name by the angel: Yisrael (Israel) meaning "he who has struggled with God"—for indeed as the stranger says, Jacob has striven and wrestled all his life with men, and now even with God.

The ancient Israelites take their name from this most interesting and complex of patriarchs—they are the children of Israel, the children of the one who struggled with God. This story provides an important metaphor for Israel's relationship with God—one that remains in the consciousness of Jews in subsequent generations—the metaphor of struggle. At times the Israelites and later the Jews will feel themselves to be locked in an eternal struggle with God, neither prevailing yet both forever changed by the encounter.

Themes of the Exodus Story (Ex 1–40)

Genesis depicts God as creator and thus sovereign over nature. Exodus focuses on God as the redeemer of his people and thus sovereign over the course of history. Aware of the plight of the Israelites enslaved in Egypt, and remembering his covenant with the patriarchs, God summons Moses to free the Israelites from Egypt. In his dialogue with Moses, God identifies himself as the God of Abraham, Isaac, and Jacob, preparing us for the transfer of the patriarchal promises to the entire nation of Israel that will be formed by Moses after the Exodus from Egypt.

God also reveals his name to Moses: Yahweh (the probable pronunciation of YHWH). Related to the Hebrew verb "to be," this four-letter name (or Tetragrammaton) is understood by some scholars as expressing the quality of being or causation. This God is one who brings new things into being, whether a cosmos out of inert matter, or a new nation out of a group of runaway slaves.

In the story of liberation that follows we see a battle of wills between God and the proud and mighty Pharaoh. In defeating Pharaoh, God shows himself to be on the side of the powerless and weak—a lesson repeated again and again in Israel's story. The exodus event becomes the paradigm of God's salvation of his people, God's mighty deeds on behalf of Israel.

God's redemption and election of Israel set the stage for Israel's response. At a mountain in the wilderness (Sinai or Horeb) a covenant is formed between God and the new nation. Israel agrees to hear and obey all of the words that the Lord has spoken, and by virtue of which she will become God's treasured possession, "a kingdom of priests and a holy nation" (Ex 19:6). This bilateral covenant covers every aspect of the people's lives: it contains civil law, criminal law, cultic law, moral injunctions, a festival calendar, and more. The bond it establishes cannot be unilaterally rescinded by Israel. The covenant concept is central to all of subsequent Judaism and to a Jewish understanding of the relation between God and Israel. The entire history of Israel as portrayed by various biblical writers is governed by this one outstanding reality of a covenant. Israel's fortunes are seen to ride on its degree of faithfulness to the covenant.

The Ten Commandments that introduce the covenant establish yet another innovation: the observance of the sabbath as a day of rest consecrated to God. In imitation of God, who created the world in six days and rested and was refreshed on the seventh, Israelites are commanded to observe every seventh day as a day of rest and re-creation (see Document 4).

Themes of the Deuteronomistic History

The narrative books of the Deuteronomistic History (Joshua, Judges, 1 and 2 Samuel, 1 and 2 Kings) describe Israel's transition from a loose tribal confederacy led in times of crisis by God-inspired charismatic judges to a monarchy. These biblical books include various views of monarchy in ancient Israel. Some sources signal a deep-seated distrust of monarchy as a usurpation of the kingship of God, and God himself is said to be angered by Israel's request for a king. Israel's kings are represented as fully human and far from perfect. They are not above God's laws and are criticized by God's prophets for their failings. Elsewhere, however, God himself commissions his prophet Samuel to anoint a king and in 2 Sam 7:8–17 God pledges through his prophet Nathan that the house of David will rule in Israel in perpetuity.

The Hebrew word "messiah" means "anointed" and is applied to kings and high priests of Israel since both are initiated into office by means of anointment with sacred oil. Every king in Israel was therefore a messiah (anointed one) of God. Later, when living in exile, Jews would pray for another messiah, another king of the house of David appointed by God and anointed by a prophet to rescue them from their enemies and reestablish them as a nation at peace. The Israelite hope for a messiah was thus political and national, involving the restoration of the nation in its land. The idea that God would one day send another Davidic messiah-king to save his people from hardship and trial was so strong that the Christian messiah, Jesus, is represented not only as son of God but also as son of David (see the genealogy provided in Matthew 1:1–17).

David is credited by the biblical writer with establishing a royal capital in Jerusalem. The ark containing the tablets of the Sinaitic covenant was brought to Jerusalem. The city became thereby not only the city of David and his dynasty but a permanent symbol and center of the religion of Israel. David planned a magnificent temple that would become the cultic center of the Israelites, though its construction was left to his son Solomon.

The Deuteronomistic books report the history of the nation, through its division into two kingdoms, the defeat and exile of the northern tribes of Israel in 722 B.C.E., the defeat and exile of the southern tribes of Judah in 586 B.C.E. and the destruction of God's sanctuary in Jerusalem. These events raised a critical theological dilemma: Why had God allowed his people to be defeated? Perhaps he was not the sole and omnipotent sovereign of all the earth, or perhaps he had faithlessly abandoned his promises to the patriarchs and to the house of David.

The response of the Deuteronomistic school to this theological dilemma was this: God is both omnipotent *and* faithful, but God's eternal promises to Israel and David did not preclude the possibility of punishment for sin. Despite the continued warnings of God's messenger prophets, and recurring bouts of repentance and forgiveness, Israel's kings repeatedly led the people to the worship of other gods. In 2 Kings 17, the Deuteronomistic writer attributes the destruction of the northern kingdom in 722 B.C.E. to the idolatrous sins of King Jeroboam who led his people astray by establishing an alternative cultic center adorned with golden calves. The destruction of Judah in 586 and the subsequent exile is blamed on King Manasseh (reigned ca. 698–642 B.C.E.) who sponsored an influx of pagan cults in his time.

The Deuteronomistic School wrote its history so as to influence its generation to learn from the past and to reject idolatry. The result of this interpretation was remarkable. In many societies the defeat of one nation by another would be seen as the defeat of that nation's God by the other nation's God and the conquered nation would turn to the worship of the new ascendant God. Undoubtedly, many sixth-century Israelites despaired and abandoned Yahwism. We know of one group of Judeans exiled in Egypt who attributed their tragic situation to a failure to attend to the cult of Ishtar (Jer 44:15–19). But many others accepted the Deuteronomistic interpretation of the national tragedy as an *affirmation* of both God's power and the necessity of total obedience to his covenant.

Themes of the Prophetic Tradition

Prophets were widespread in the Ancient Near East. We know of ecstatic prophets in second-millennium Mesopotamia and seventh-century Assyria who delivered oracles, and sometimes rebukes, to kings. Ecstatic prophets employed music and dance to induce a frenzy of raving while other prophets might employ mechanical means of divination (throwing lots, consulting spirits). Many of these features are found also in the biblical prophetic tradition.

Not all biblical prophecies had an ecstatic character. Especially in later biblical religion we encounter apostolic (apostle = *messenger*) prophecy in which God initiates communication rather than responding to a prophet's petition. Apostolic prophets are seen as the instrument of God's desire to reveal himself to his people. Like Moses, most prophets are said to experience a sudden, unexpected encounter with, or call from, God. The prophet is often reluctant but eventually surrenders to God's summons (Amos 7:14–15, 3:8; Isa 6:5; Jer 1:6, 20:7 and 9).

Starting in the eighth century, the words of some apostolic prophets were preserved. These oracles were subject to revision, interpolation, and alteration, appearing eventually in the biblical books that bear the names of the prophets. This phenomenon of literary, or classical, prophecy spanned more than three hundred years from 750 to 430 B.C.E. and clustered around four critical periods. During the Assyrian crisis Amos and Hosea warned of the coming destruction in the north, while Micah and Isaiah prophesied in the south. In the Babylonian crisis Habakkuk and Jeremiah advised the Judean leadership to submit to Babylon. In the exilic period Ezekiel both castigated and consoled his countrymen in exile. Finally, in the postexilic/Restoration period Haggai and Zechariah promised a better future while Joel and Malachi added eschatological hope into the mix.

The prophetic writings are replete with powerful rhetoric because the prophets spoke with exaggeration and drama. Their behavior was often bizarre; they were sometimes ridiculed and even persecuted, but in time, their words were preserved and incorporated into the nation's sacred heritage.

What are the major themes of prophetic literature? The oracles of the classical prophets are characterized by an aggressive denunciation of the social injustice and immorality of contemporary Israelite society. They rail against even commonplace venial crimes and insensitivities (bribe-taking, short-changing customers, indifference toward the poor) in terms more commonly applied to heinous crimes of violence and murder (Amos 2:6–8, 4:1–3; Micah 6:9–15; Isa 5:1–24). In prophetic thinking, morality is central to Israel's relationship with God and cultic service performed without moral purity is offensive to God (Amos 5:21–24; Isa 1:10–17). Some view morality as far superior to cultic service. For the prophets of Israel, morality is an absolute religious value. Because they see morality as essentially divine, they proclaim the imitation of the moral attributes of God as the highest goal of humankind (see Document 6).

Like the Deuteronomistic historian, the prophets interpreted the destructions of 722 and 586 as divine punishment for sin that only confirmed rather than negated God's power. However, in the prophetic view, it is not merely idolatry that decides the nation's fate. Rather, all sin, no matter how venial can be punished by national destruction. A further difference between the Deuteronomistic school and the classical prophets is that many of the latter provided a message of hope and consolation, transforming earlier Israelite eschatologies. An eschatology (literally means an "account of the end") is a tradition that describes the end of troubled times and the coming of an era of perfect peace, believed to be brought about by a messianic (divinely appointed and prophetically anointed) ruler. For Israel's prophets, God's punishment was designed to chasten and purge the nation in readiness for lasting peace and prosperity (Amos 9:13–15; Zeph 3:11–13). A repentant and righteous remnant would survive the nation's affliction, and enjoy a future restoration under an ideal king from the branch of Jesse (the line of David). God's coming to Jerusalem to save the remnant of Israel from its enemies and to gather in the dispersed exiles would be witnessed by all the nations, opening a new epoch in world history, and bringing an end to sin. In some eschatological writings, Israel's election is reinterpreted as an election *to a mission*. Israel was chosen in order to be "a light unto the nations" (see Isa 49:6)—the suffering servant who would bring a universal return to God (Isa 53).

Although God had punished Israel according to the terms of the conditional Sinaitic covenant, the prophets maintained that alienation from God was not and never would be final, because of the unconditional covenant with the patriarchs and the House of David. The sixth-century prophet Jeremiah saw the restoration of Zion under a Davidic king as the time in which a new covenant would be made with Israel—a covenant etched on the heart, encoded into human nature. In the meantime, a relationship with God was possible even outside the land of Israel.

The fall of Jerusalem brought an abrupt end to the national and territorial foundation of Israel's culture and religion. The Israelites were now confronted by a great test: Could their faith in Yahweh survive the loss of their national culture, their temple and land? Certainly many Israelites traded Yahweh for Marduk and assimilated into their new surroundings. But others did not. For these others, the words of the ancient prophets held a special consolation. Even uprooted and scattered, Israel could remain Yahweh's people able to serve him—in the absence of cultic forms—with justice, mercy, and humility. The prophetic contribution to the formation of Judaism was significant. The emphasis on God's desire for morality and righteousness above all else became a fundamental theme of all of later Judaism.

Themes of the Wisdom Tradition

Ancient Near Eastern Wisdom is a genre of literature characterized by the praise of human intelligence applied to practical understanding. The intellectual tradition of scribal schools, teachers, and elders, Wisdom contains traditional advice and is universal and humanistic in its orientation. Israelite Wisdom literature, as found in the books of Proverbs, Job, and Ecclesiastes, is a part of this larger Ancient Near Eastern tradition. Eventually, the Wisdom tradition combines with the Deuteronomic-covenantal tradition, to create a deterministic theology of retributive justice. The book of Proverbs in particular maintains that the righteous and the wicked of the world receive what they deserve in life. If a person suffers, he has surely sinned and should accept his punishment without complaint. This formulaic piety is challenged in two other wisdom books of the Bible: Job and Ecclesiastes. In Job we find the idea that suffering is not always explicable and is not always a sign of sin. Likewise, the righteous are not always rewarded, for God is not a moral accountant. Righteousness is an absolute virtue in and of itself, the obligation of humankind even in the absence of temporal or eternal reward. Even more explicitly than Job, Ecclesiastes attacks the principle of divine providence and distributive justice that is so central to the Deuteronomic-convenantal and Wisdom traditions (see Document 7).

The richness of the Hebrew Bible lies precisely in its juxtaposition of radically diverse points of view. This diversity is of great importance for the development of later Judaism. As religious and spiritual needs arose or shifted, as historical events presented new challenges, Jews turned to their biblical heritage and found a vast and varied set of resources that fueled the adaptation and continued growth of their tradition.

CHAPTER 4

FROM BIBLICAL ISRAEL TO SECOND TEMPLE JUDAISM

The six hundred years of Jewish history referred to as the Second Temple period (520 B.C.E.–70 C.E.) saw dramatic change in the politics, society, culture, and religion of Judea and the Jewish communities of the diaspora. Biblical Israel became Second Temple period Judaism which, despite its great variety, was characterized by some specific commonalities.

Biblical Israel was a tribal society led by kings and prophets, dwelling on its ancestral land. Membership in this society was determined largely by birth or a simple process of absorption. Such "naturalization" often happened through intermarriage, for example. Israelites engaged in communal sacrifices and worship of Yahweh at a Temple controlled by priests.

By contrast, the Judaism that emerged in the Second Temple period was defined less as a tribally based nation, and more as a cultic community that revered a common Scripture. While membership was still guaranteed by birth, by the end of the period foreigners could gain access to Jewish identity through a more or less formal rite of conversion. The Davidic monarchy was gone (though the ideal of a Davidic king retained its grip on the national imagination), and prophets in the classical model were displaced by apocalyptic visionaries. In addition, a new type of leader emerged—the scribe, whose authority was based not on hereditary office or privilege (like kings and priests) or divine effluence and charisma (like prophets), but on knowledge of the sacred ancestral traditions. While the priest-controlled sacrificial cult remained of central importance to the community, other forms of piety gained in significance, including prayer and study of the Torah. The Torah reached its canonical shape in this period. At the same time, other religious writings, expressing new ideas arising from the interaction with non-Jewish cultures, were produced at a significant rate.

In this period, Yehud (known as Judea after Alexander's conquest), was ruled by a series of empires that granted local populations a considerable degree of autonomy. The transformation from biblical Israel to Second Temple Judaism was facilitated by imperial support for the local institutions that would become the key markers of Jewish identity—specifically, the Temple in Jerusalem and the Torah. One scholar has identified a distinctive worldview that emerged in this period due in large part to the adoption of the Torah as the constitution of the Jewish community in Judea. The main convictions of that worldview were that the one God entered into a covenant with the people of Israel and promised blessing and protection in exchange for obedience to his Torah (instruction) and faithful worship in his one Temple. Reward and punishment were tied to Israel's fulfillment of the terms of the covenant.

At the same time, a rather different set of ideas surfaced in some Jewish literature of this period, particularly in apocalyptic writings (see below). These ideas may be seen as an attempt to answer perplexing questions concerning the fate of Israel: When and how would Israel be freed from the dominion of idolaters? Why did the wicked flourish while the righteous faithful suffered or were martyred? Many writings of this period were filled with messianic expectation focusing on an ideal, anointed king (messiah) of the house of David who would deliver Israel from subjugation to its enemies and restore harmony between Israel, God, and the nations.

THE PERSIAN PERIOD

In 538 B.C.E., a decree by Cyrus of Persia, attested in archaeological and biblical sources, granted the Judean exiles permission to return to Jerusalem and rebuild their Temple. Though many remained in Babylonia forming the nucleus of a Jewish diaspora in the east, many others returned. The Second Temple was completed between 521 and 515 B.C.E., an event seen by many as fulfilling the words of the prophet Jeremiah, who had predicted an end to the exile after seventy years (2 Chr 36:22). There was great friction, however, between the Jews who had remained in Judea at the time of the exile and the returning exiles who, though few in number, enjoyed imperial support. These self-styled "children of the exile" referred to the local Judeans as "peoples of the land"—a derogatory term that questioned the latter's very status as Jews. Conflicts over Jewish identity and the boundaries of the Judean community were bitter during this period.

In keeping with their policy of creating stability through local, religious, and legal reform, later Persian emperors promoted the establishment of the Torah as the authorized law of the Jews. This task is associated with two figures whose chronological sequence is uncertain—Ezra and Nehemiah. Ezra, a Babylonian Jew from a priestly family described as a scribe expert in the Torah of Moses, was commissioned by the Persian emperor to supervise the Temple, establish the Torah of Moses in the Judean province, appoint scribes and judges, and administer civil and moral order. As the Persian-appointed governor of Yehud, Nehemiah instituted a number of economic and social reforms.

According to the biblical books that bear their names, Ezra and Nehemiah sought to regulate and unify Jewish life in the Restoration community. They instituted some radical reforms aimed at strengthening the religious identity of the Judahites and preventing the decline of exclusive Yahwism by enforcing a policy of social and religious separatism. Their most radical act was the dissolution of foreign marriages and insistence on a genealogical standard for Jewish identity. Ezra objected to marriages between the returning exiles and the "peoples of the lands"—foreigners, but possibly also Judeans who had remained in the land during the exile and who, according to the book of Ezra, had adopted many of the customs and religious practices of their neighbors. He described these unions as a great sin and called upon the exiles to divorce their foreign spouses and expel from the community children born of such unions. The prohibition of intermarriage with any foreigner and the refusal to assimilate foreigners within the community was an innovation on Ezra's part. The Torah prohibits marriage with certain, but not all, foreigners and in any event allows for the assimilation of, and marriage to, foreigners who renounce idolatry and agree to the terms of Israel's covenant with Yahweh.

Ezra called a public assembly to present an extended public reading of, and communal rededication to, the Torah of Moses—which probably consisted of something like the Deuteronomic and priestly traditions. The biblical account describes the pledge of all the people who "join with their noble brothers, and take an oath with sanctions to follow the Teaching of God, given through Moses the servant of God, and to observe carefully all the commandments of the Lord our God, His rules and laws" (Neh 10:30).

There then follows a long list of obligations to which the people commit themselves. Significantly, the ban on intermarriage and the observance of the Sabbath top the list as central covenantal obligations.

Many scholars believe that this was the moment when the Torah, backed by Persian imperial power, became the official and authoritative norm for Israel. In this period, Judaism took the decisive step toward becoming a religion of Scripture. The zeal of Ezra and Nehemiah with the sponsorship of the Persian imperial authority, helped to preserve—or more properly, create—a national and religious identity for Jews at a time when their numbers were small and they were surrounded by enemies. However, the reforms of Ezra and Nehemiah met with resistance, as evidenced in various postexilic sources that protest the policy of extreme separatism, and the bans on intermarriage and conversion. Isaiah 56:1–7 reassures foreigners who have joined themselves to God that they will be welcome in the holy Temple to worship and offer sacrifices. The postexilic book of Ruth is the story of a foreign woman who chooses to join the community of Israel. Welcomed by those who know of her righteous and compassionate deeds, Ruth will become the great-grandmother of Israel's most famous and beloved king David. One cannot imagine a story standing in greater contrast to Ezra's policy of separatism and nonassimilation of foreigners than the book of Ruth. The assimilation of foreigners at this time was widely viewed as possible, and we have much evidence that non-Jews became Jews and that Jews felt no compunction about marrying them, despite Ezra's campaign to the contrary. For example, the powerful and influential Tobiads were originally Ammonite, but adopted Jewish identity and were fully assimilated by the Ptolemaic period.

The Torah of Moses may have become the unchallenged norm and source of authority for Jews in the Persian period, but this did not in itself result in a uniform or monolithic set of Jewish practices and beliefs. It simply meant that practices and beliefs were perceived as authentic to the degree that Scriptural warrant could be found for them. Various techniques of scriptural interpretation arose, enabling widely divergent Jewish groups to claim authenticity for their practices and beliefs. The Second Temple period spawns a variety of Jewish subgroups—Pharisees, Sadducees, Essenes, and more—each claiming scriptural or divine authority for its interpretation of the common heritage of the nation. Thus, although Ezra succeeded in unifying Israel around a common text, he did not succeed in unifying Israel around a common interpretation of that text.

HELLENIZATION AND THE JEWS

In addition to being rejected by many Jews, the extreme separatism promoted by Ezra was downright impractical in the Hellenized east of the ensuing centuries. During this period, the pressure on native populations to "be Greek" was tremendous. Many Jews saw the advantages that could be derived from adopting elements of Greek culture or from reconstituting their cities as Greek cities. Thus, despite the tendency of contemporary scholars to describe this period as one in which Hellenism and Judaism stood in opposition to one another, the fact is that most Jews found a way to negotiate the claims of Jewish identity and Greek culture comfortably.

In various ways and to varying degrees, Jews participated in Greek life and opened themselves to prevailing cultural, religious, and intellectual trends—all the while identifying themselves as Jews. Certainly, there were differences of opinion, sometimes fierce, concerning those elements of Jewish culture and tradition that were negotiable and those that were not, or those elements of Greek culture and tradition that could be accommodated and those that could not. But most Jews did not view the adoption of elements of Greek culture as per se inconsistent with the preservation of a native culture and identity. As a result, Second Temple Judaism is an extraordinarily complex phenomenon, with Jews from different regions and walks of life manifesting their negotiated Jewish identity and practicing their Judaism in quite different ways—despite what has been called by one scholar the integrating ideology of one God, one Temple, and one Torah. In the rest of this chapter we examine several major varieties of Judaism in the Second Temple period.

The Encounter with Greek Philosophy

Hellenistic Jewish writers wrote in Greek and appropriated Greek arguments and philosophical ideas in the defense of biblical religion and its claims. They used philosophical arguments to defend the rationality of the Jewish laws, often attacked as irrational (for example, the laws of impurity) or as preventing Jewish interaction with the rest of the world (for example, the dietary laws). The most overt borrowing of Hellenistic concepts and terminology occurred among Jews in the diaspora, particularly in the city of Alexandria, Egypt. A Greek translation of the Bible, known as the Septuagint (mid-third century B.C.E.), was produced for the large and thriving Jewish community in Alexandria. Translating the Bible into Greek facilitated the importation of Hellenistic concepts into biblical religion. Many biblical terms were translated with Greek terms that possessed additional connotations absent from the Hebrew original. For example, the translation of the Hebrew word *torah* (meaning instruction) with the Greek term *nomos* (which took on the meaning of written law) narrows the meaning of the original significantly, while the translation of Hebrew *nefesh* (meaning throat, breath, or life force) with the Greek term for "soul" assumes a body–soul dualism otherwise absent in the Hebrew Bible. Similarly, words like "sin" and "salvation" acquired new spiritualized connotations when read in Greek—connotations not clearly present in the original Hebrew (see below).

An important Hellenistic Jewish thinker and writer was Philo of Alexandria (estimated dates 20 B.C.E. to 50 C.E.). Philo received a broad Greek general education while remaining deeply loyal to the Jewish nation and Jewish tradition. Philo used philosophical terms to describe God's autonomy and immutability even as he maintained the biblical notion of a creator God with providential concern for the universe. He adopted the Stoic idea of a divine Reason, or Logos, that confers intelligibility upon the world. Logos, which unifies the various powers of God, is also the highest intermediary between God and the world. Philo identified Logos with Wisdom, which is described in Prov 8:22 as the "first born son" of God. (This identification of Logos as God's first-born son will be important for early Christianity.) Logos, as the agent through which God's activity is manifest in the world was also understood by Philo as embodied in the Torah, the teaching by which humans are to live.

Characteristic of Philo's thought is a body–soul dualism and an ascetic deprecation of the physical world often found in schools of thought deriving from Platonism. The soul, made in the image of the divine Logos, is entombed in the body and yearns for release from the body and reunion with God. Philo argues that at its deepest level the Pentateuch of Moses describes the path of the soul's salvation for all humankind: The soul descends into the world where it is captured and held by the body, the charms of the senses, and physical pleasure. By extricating itself from their clutches through learning and wisdom it readies itself for union with the mind of God. This can happen in fleeting ecstatic experiences in life, but happens ultimately at death, when the body—the shell encasing the soul—is stripped away and the soul now liberated or "saved" achieves a permanent state of immortal bliss.

Many of these ideas seem far distant from biblical thought. Yet, Philo found these ideas in the biblical text through allegorical reading. Allegory is a reading strategy premised on the belief that one can move beyond the literal ("corporeal") meaning of language to a level of abstract truths and ideas. The Stoics, for example, read Homer as allegory, demonstrating that Homer's stories were symbol systems pointing to deeper philosophical and ethical truths. In a similar manner, the concrete biblical notion of salvation from one's enemies is read by Philo as an allegory for the salvation of the soul from the prison of the body, from corporeality and sensuality. Philo employed allegory to interpret the concrete laws and commandments of the Torah as pointing to spiritual truths. While the laws and commandments must still be literally obeyed, their higher purpose, Philo believed, is the conveyance of these spiritual and philosophical truths.

THE RISE Of APOCALYPTICISM

The primary strands of biblical religion—the Deuteronomic-convenantal strand and the priestly-cultic strand—are blended in the Persian period into a kind of ideological mainstream that has been referred to by one scholar as "covenantal nomism."[i] It is the fundamental conviction of covenantal nomism that the one universal God through the giving of his Torah, has bound himself in covenant with his people, Israel, who must study and obey his teachings and worship him in the Jerusalem temple under the supervision of his chosen priests. Obedience to the terms of God's holy covenant will be faithfully rewarded while disobedience will be duly punished.

Yet, common human experience stood as a challenge to this picture. The period of the Restoration and the centuries following were a time of disappointment and disillusionment. The Restoration was not the glorious reestablishment of the nation in its land under a Davidic king that the prophets had promised. War, strife, and the dominion of foreign nations had not ceased; the God of Israel had not been universally recognized. Although the Maccabean revolt brought a century of independence under

---

i. Seth Schwartz, *Imperialism and Jewish Society, 200 B.C.E. to 640 C.E.* (Princeton: Princeton University Press, 2001), p. 66.

native Jewish rulers, the Hasmoneans were not universally loved and were in any event defeated by the Romans, who appointed Herod—a Judaized Idumean—to rule in Judea. The promises of the prophets and the divine retributive justice of the Lord seemed a long time in coming.

The problem of evil and the delayed justice of God were central themes of the apocalyptic worldview that developed in this period. Although the apocalyptic worldview was an outgrowth of prophetic eschatology, it had deep mythological roots and exhibited the influence of Persian and Hellenistic thought. Apocalypticism imagines a dualistic universe in which forces of good and evil—angels and demons, darkness and light—are pitted against one another. While earlier prophetic eschatology asserts the importance of human effort in bringing about the hoped-for change in historical time, apocalyptic eschatology is fatalistic, assuming the impotence of humans in the larger cosmic struggle between good and evil forces.

In apocalyptic thinking, the forces of evil have gained control, filling the world with suffering and wickedness, and forcing God and his loyal retinue into retreat. The apocalyptic idea that the world is the domain of Satan or demons is found in some of the letters of Paul in the New Testament. Apocalyptic eschatology is marked by a great urgency borne of the conviction that the final battle between good and evil is coming. The wicked will be punished and the righteous will be rewarded with a blessed heavenly existence. To ensure that one will be judged righteous one must be cleansed of sin and stand ready to follow the appointed messiah on the Judgment Day. A Jew depicted in the gospels and known as John the Baptist preached a typical apocalyptic message when he cried, "Repent, for the Kingdom of God is at hand!" and offered a baptism of repentance for the forgiveness of sins.

The book of Daniel is the only fully developed apocalyptic book in the Hebrew Bible. It was composed at the time of the Maccabean revolt (160s B.C.E.) when Jews were suffering persecution at the hands of the Syrian king, Antiochus IV Epiphanes. The author disguises references to contemporary historical events by placing his hero, Daniel, in the Babylonian exile of the sixth century. Many features characteristic of apocalypses are found in Daniel including the use of symbolic and often bizarre imagery, such as a series of beasts and monsters to represent the succession of wicked foreign kingdoms; a list of catastrophes that signal the coming of the end; the division of humankind into two mutually exclusive groups—the righteous minority and the wicked majority; the depiction of God as an enthroned king who brings all history to a crashing halt destroying the wicked and rewarding the righteous; and a doctrine of life after death, in the form of personal immortality and/or a general resurrection of the dead.

Daniel 12 postulates a resurrection of the dead as compensation to those who died under the Syrian persecution—a clear attempt to deal with the injustice that mars this world. Remain faithful, the author urges, and know that this great evil and suffering will be set right by God not in this world, but in an ultimate and cataclysmic triumph of life and faith over death and evil. And know that it will be soon. With this message the book of Daniel emphasized God's firm control over history and so bolstered loyal Jews who faced indignities, torture, and even death because of their faith. Daniel 12 is the only passage of the Bible to explicitly affirm life after death. It is a marked break from the general conviction of the Hebrew Bible that human life is limited to this world, that the fundamental concern of humans and God is morality in this life and not immortality in another.

Apocalyptic literature has been described as a literature of despair and hope. It is a literature of despair because its basic premise is that this world holds out no promise for the righteous. It is a literature of hope because it affirms that God will intervene in human history and set everything right, interrupting the natural order and destroying the world as we know it in order to rescue the righteous and humiliate the wicked. The apocalyptic worldview is imbued with a sense of crisis. It offers assurance of salvation to those alienated from the power structures of this world and suffering for their religious convictions. The final vision is one of Zion victorious, the righteous rewarded, Zion's enemies and the wicked annihilated.

SECOND TEMPLE JEWISH MOVEMENTS IN JUDEA

The nonmythological covenant ideology and the apocalyptic worldview with its advanced angelology and demonology were part of the intellectual ferment of the Second Temple period, standing in dialectic tension with one another, complementing and even interpenetrating one another. Various Jewish groups emerge in Judea in this period, each drawing to different degrees and with different emphases on these two ideological complexes to create a unique ideological profile.

Scholars have used the word "sect" to describe the distinct groups that arise in Second Temple Judaism, but this term is not entirely appropriate, implying as it does a normative orthodoxy from which organized splinter groups separate. We cannot speak of a single normative Judaism at this time; we may speak of a larger *Jewish society*, within which diverse movements arose. These groups certainly viewed themselves as distinct from other groups and may have marked that distinction through different modes of dress, behavior, and thought, but most were not strongly separatist.

The motivations for the formation of diverse movements within Jewish society are complex and varied, but divisions crystallized around certain focal issues and institutions—particularly the Temple and the Torah. The Temple and its sacrificial service were critically important symbols for all ancient Jews. Performed properly, the Temple rituals and sacrifices would attract and maintain the presence of God, ensuring blessings and bounty for the community. But a series of political realities compromised the integrity of the Temple leadership in the eyes of many. The Hasmonean usurpation of the high priesthood and Herod's transformation of the position from a hereditary and lifelong office to an annual appointment were viewed by some as unacceptable deviations from God's instruction. In addition, different standards of ritual and sacrificial purity led to conflict. Ritual purity was required of those who offered sacrifice, entered the Temple, or officiated within. Some Jews practiced an extreme form of ritual purity that went far beyond the biblical prescriptions. These Jews were angered by what they considered to be the laxity of those in control of the Temple and boycotted the Temple as long as their own higher standards were not in force.

Sadducees, Pharisees, Essenes, and Others

The Jewish historian Josephus (d. ca. 100 C.E.) mentions three main Jewish movements beginning in the late second century B.C.E.—the Sadducees, the Pharisees, and the Essenes. We have two additional sources of information about these movements—the Christian New Testament and the writings of later Jewish rabbis. Unfortunately each of these three sources has significant limitations. Josephus' presentation is slanted toward the interests of the Roman audience for whom he wrote and by his own political agenda. The Christian New Testament is a polemical work with strong theological and ideological reasons for discrediting first-century Jewish movements. It paints the Pharisees in particular as villains and hypocrites. Rabbinic writings contain some old and authentic traditions about Jewish movements in the late Second Temple period, but these traditions passed through a lengthy process of oral transmission and editorial revision before reaching the written form we possess. Due to the nature of our sources, any reconstruction of the major movements in Second Temple period Judea is necessarily tentative.

The Sadducees (Hebrew, Zadokim) appear to have originated in opposition to the Hasmoneans as a party that believed the priesthood belonged to the Zadokite line within the priestly fold. They appear to have been associated with the Temple leadership and are described by Josephus as wealthy and powerful. The Pharisees emerged also in the Hasmonean period as a kind of political interest group promoting certain goals for Jewish society. Josephus describes the differences between Sadducees and Pharisees as doctrinal in nature: the Sadducees denied immortality and reward and punishment after death while the Pharisees believed the souls of the righteous pass to other bodies after death; the Sadducees believed in a determinative fate with no free will while the Pharisees affirmed the interplay of fate and free will. Another point of disagreement was over the nature and source of Jewish law. The Pharisees were skilled in jurisprudence and claimed to possess in addition to written Scripture, a body of unwritten ancestral traditions—oral teachings, laws, and interpretations that adapted the Bible to the needs of a new age. The Sadducees rejected the notion and authority of ancestral teachings.

In stark contrast to Josephus' testimony, rabbinic sources detail disputes between Pharisees and Sadducees that center on matters of law, ritual purity, the Temple cult, tithing, Sabbath observance, and the interpretation of Scripture. The Pharisees were probably a kind of educated, voluntary association with members drawn from all walks of life that promoted the observance of Sabbath laws, purity, and tithing—all important in maintaining Jewish identity. They practiced a kind of table fellowship (*havurah*) of persons who aspired to a higher level of purity in connection with consuming food. The Pharisees hoped for a Jewish community dedicated to the covenant, as they interpreted it, and sought to transform daily activities into sacred or semisacred occasions. The word Pharisee is from the Hebrew word "parush" meaning "separated." The name may derive from the fact that the Pharisees separated themselves to some degree from those who were less observant of the laws of purity and tithing.

For all their differences over questions of authority and leadership the Pharisees and Sadducees were both involved in the community. Other groups gave up on Jewish society, rejected the existing leadership, and withdrew to form small holy communities. According to Josephus, the Essenes formed separatist associations throughout the country. Admission to their community required a three-year period of preparation and probation and culminated in the taking of oaths, including an oath to be obedient, to guard the secrets of the sect (including the names of the angels), and to "hate forever the unjust and fight the battle of the just." The community followed a rigorous discipline centering on ritual and moral purity. Property was in some way communal and members practiced celibacy, though Josephus mentions a second order of Essenes that did marry. Dress was simple and daily communal meals included prayer and recitation of Scripture. Essenes believed in the immortality of the soul and were possibly dualists.

Excavations at Qumran in the Judean desert near the Dead Sea have turned up what may be the remains of a settlement inhabited, with some interruption, from the mid-second century B.C.E. to 68 C.E. Though some question whether the site was home to a community of any kind, others maintain the site was inhabited by a group of separatists. They point to documents discovered in caves near the site (the famous Dead Sea Scrolls) that attest to practices and beliefs that resemble those of the Essenes. Some of these writings denounce the practices of other Jews, including marriage practices, calendar (these writings promote a solar calendar rather than a lunisolar calendar), Sabbath and festival observance, and purity practices. Other writings testify to an Ezran separatism that rejects the assimilation of gentiles through marriage or conversion.

According to some scholars, this sect believed that the Temple was controlled by wicked and corrupt men who had taken power illegitimately. Believing themselves to be the true Israel, they settled in the wilderness in order to establish a pure and holy society until God saw fit to return them to a purified Temple. Many of the sect's writings are characterized by a dualistic apocalypticism according to which the end of days was near. Divinely inspired leaders (or messiahs) would soon appear to lead the final battle between the Sons of Light (the Qumran sectaries) and the sons of

Darkness (their enemies), and the righteous remnant would be restored. The sectarians read the prophetic books of the Bible as coded references to these historical events, as predictions that the dawning of the Last Day was imminent.

A host of other smaller groups arose in this time of social, political, and economic unrest prior to the revolt of 66 C.E. Some had an unconquerable desire for liberty and refused to be ruled by any but God. Through their preaching they aroused crowds against the Herodians and the high priests appointed by them, leading in some cases to acts of zealous violence. Judas the Galilean urged the people not to pay taxes to the empire. His grandson Menahem seized a mountaintop Roman fortress on Masada. Masada was the last Jewish holdout in the war against Rome. On the eve of the Roman capture, the Jews at Masada under the leadership of Eleazar ben Jair, chose suicide rather than submission to any human master.

Holy men were numerous in this period also and often attracted bands of followers that were perceived by the Romans as a social and political threat. In the 20s C.E. John the Baptist aroused suspicion because of his ability to attract followers by preaching the apocalyptic message of the imminent arrival of the kingdom of God. Another such holy man was Bannus who led an ascetic desert existence. Other charismatic Jews provoked violent repression from the Romans, such as Theudas (who was killed along with his followers in the 40s). Jesus of Nazareth and James, the brother of Jesus in Jerusalem, may also be counted among these charismatic figures. Apocalyptic beliefs crystallized around Jesus—some believed he was the one who would bring the end of evil and usher in the final rule of the kingdom of God. He and his followers developed a reputation for controlling and exorcising demons. Like many other charismatic Jewish figures able to draw a large crowd, Jesus was deemed dangerous and put to death by the Romans.

CONCLUSION

Judaism in the late Second Temple period was a rich and variegated phenomenon developing in active conversation with and deeply influenced by the ambient cultures of Egypt, Persia, Syria, Greece, and Rome. The rise of many sects in the Second Temple period was also the symptom of a larger trend: the authority of hereditary leaders (kings and priests, favored by the Sadducees) was being challenged by other types of leadership based on charisma (holy men) or on learning and wisdom (Pharisees). Learned scribes and sages might come from any level of Israelite society. Among these scribes and sages—particularly among the Pharisees—the most important relationship was the relationship between teacher (*rav* or *rabbi*) and disciple, and at the heart of Pharisaic Judaism lay Torah study.

CHAPTER 5

FROM SECOND TEMPLE JUDAISM TO RABBINIC JUDAISM

The period from 70 to 640 C.E., commonly referred to as the Talmudic period, sees the eventual emergence of classical rabbinic Judaism which will inform all subsequent forms of Judaism in some way—even those that resist or attempt to reform it. Rabbinic Judaism did not spring up overnight and once its main contours were in place it did not quickly gain ascendancy. The rabbinic movement of the first century was a small, peripheral movement and centuries would pass before rabbis exercised a significant degree of influence and authority over a large portion of the Jewish population.

The revolts against Rome in 66–70 C.E. and 132–135 C.E. decimated the Jewish population and the ranks of the priestly and scribal elites. The failure of the revolts doubtless engendered alienation and even abandonment of Judaism. For many Jews, the collapse of the Temple and related institutions dealt a serious blow to the authority of the Torah and its interpreters. Jewish society disintegrated and Judea, renamed Syria Palestina after the Bar Kokhba revolt, looked very much like any other Roman provincial society. Political power and legal authority were concentrated in the hands of the Roman governor and local city councils. Judges appointed by the Romans ruled according to an ad hoc mixture of Greco-Roman, eastern and local law. In the cities and large villages, many Jews took on the religious, cultural, and social norms of their Greco-Roman neighbors. Public life and culture were predominantly pagan in character and pagan iconography is found in the art and architectural decoration of Jews of this period. For many, Judaism was just one part of a larger identity that was essentially Greco-Roman in character.

The destruction meant the decimation of several pre-70 groups. Those whose power and authority were based in the Temple were undercut. The Sadducees and Essenes fade from view in our sources, as do the descendants of the Herodians. Priests survived and maintained some prestige but the high priest was no longer a functioning authority. Messianic nationalism simmered for some decades after the first Roman War (66–70 C.E.), finally exploding in the Bar Kochba Revolt (132–135 C.E.). However, with the crushing defeat of Bar Kochba, messianic nationalism and eschatological fervor were muted, finding expression primarily in liturgical, mystical, and magical/theurgical contexts and in the new Christian movement.

There was, however, one small movement bearing some sort of relationship to pre-70 scribes and Pharisees, which preserved and developed a Torah-centered Judaism through the first centuries C.E. In the postdestruction decades, it seems that this movement of proto-rabbis centered around certain key figures such as Yohanan ben Zakkai and later Gamliel II, whose grandfather is mentioned in New Testament sources as a Pharisaic leader in the time of Jesus. Teachers, judges, and holy men, these early rabbis may have enjoyed some prestige in matters of tithing, purity, and piety, but in general they were marginal and relatively powerless. Recent archaeological finds, including caches of private legal papyri, suggest that Jews generally handled their everyday legal affairs not through rabbinic courts but through Roman courts. Synagogue excavations from this period indicate that rabbis were also not influential in the administration and operation of early synagogues.

Scholars note that the position of the rabbis slowly changed in the third century, perhaps as a result of Patriarchal patronage.[i] The Patriarch was the chief representative of the Jews to the Romans. The Patriarch at the turn of the third century was R. Judah I or R. Judah ha-Nasi (the Prince, or Patriarch),[ii] a wealthy and well-connected landowner whose authority appears to have been widely recognized. In the late second and

---

i. Seth Schwartz, *Imperialism and Jewish Society, 200 B.C.E. to 640 C.E.* (Princeton: Princeton University Press, 2001), p. 113. The description of Jewish society in the postdestruction era and the rise of the rabbinic movement contained in this chapter follows Schwartz' revisionist account closely.

ii. In this book, R. is used to abbreviate Rabbi, Rav, and Rabban—honorific titles for rabbinic sages. The name Rabbi standing alone refers to Rabbi Judah ha-Nasi.

third century, Jewish communities in the diaspora increasingly looked to the Patriarch to represent and advocate for their interests in the imperial court. As diaspora Jews sent funds from abroad, the Patriarch's wealth, prestige, and power grew. By the end of the fourth century the patriarch was legally recognized as the head of the Jewish community throughout the empire, holding a higher rank in the imperial senate than did provincial governors. To the extent that the patriarch supported the activities of rabbis in the third and fourth centuries—appointing them as judges and religious functionaries—their influence and prestige also increased.

R. Judah I's promulgation of the Mishnah (see later), a collection of rabbinic teachings and disputes on all matters of agricultural, religious, civil, criminal, and personal status law, was surely an important boost to the rabbinic movement and the development of rabbinic institutions, such as the study house (or *bet midrash*). In addition, the rabbis won some influence through their own abilities as preachers, as teachers of Torah, and as holy men (they were reputed to perform miracles, bring rain, and heal the sick). Nevertheless, it seems that the rabbis lacked much real jurisdiction. The Theodosian Code of 398 granted Jewish leaders authority over religious law (liturgy, dietary rules, and the like) but all other matters (marriage, divorce, civil and criminal proceedings, inheritance) were handled by the imperial courts. Moreover, the main centers of rabbinic activity were the cities of Tiberias and Sepphoris. Since very large numbers of Jews lived in the Upper Galilee and Golan, the rabbis likely had very little to do with them.

Following the Christianization of the Roman Empire (a process begun by the Emperor Constantine in the early fourth century), Jews were no longer one tolerated religious group among many tolerated groups. As Greco-Roman paganism slowly disappeared, Jews soon became the only significant non-Christian minority in the Christian state and their situation gradually deteriorated. The Patriarch, once a great dignitary of the empire, lost much of his prestige as church influence made itself felt at all levels of government, and when the Patriarch Gamliel VI died in 425 C.E. no new patriarch was appointed. The emperors promoted religious uniformity and while Jews were Roman citizens, citizenship was increasingly identified with orthodox Christianity. Hostility to Jews and Judaism in Christian writings intensified in these centuries and discriminatory legislation, forced conversions, and seizures of synagogues occurred.

Increasingly marginalized and ultimately excluded from the patronage networks that characterized the empire, Jews faced the choice of integration through conversion to Christianity, or adherence to Judaism and, as a result, further withdrawal from the surrounding society. At the same time, imperial legislation legally recognizing Jewish leaders dependent on the patriarch (who was in turn dependent on the emperor) created an alternate Jewish patronage structure. Paradoxically then, Jews were both marginalized and empowered by the Christianization of the empire.

Despite the disabilities and hostilities they faced, many Jews from the late fourth century onward chose to constitute themselves as religious communities, forming around a synagogue. The years 350–550 C.E. in Palestine are known as the great period of church construction; but they are also known, not coincidentally, as the great age of synagogue construction, despite the fact that the construction of synagogues had been declared illegal. Synagogues of the previous two centuries, like churches of the time, tended to be located in private houses in cities. But in the fourth and especially fifth and sixth centuries synagogues, like churches, became monumental structures built in villages throughout Palestine.

The formation of local and religiously significant Jewish communities and the rapid diffusion of synagogues throughout Palestine in late antiquity were not attributable to or connected with the activity of rabbis. Rabbinic texts even express occasional disapproval of specific liturgical practices, the use of representational art and other features of early synagogues. Gradually, however, rabbis began to regulate both synagogues and local Jewish communities. Rabbinic literature of the fourth and fifth centuries reflects a rabbinic effort to move outward so as to influence a larger segment of the general population. This effort coincides with a similar effort on the part of Christian leaders. Rabbis at this time began to preach in synagogues and by the sixth century they served their communities more broadly as religious functionaries, charity collectors, and teachers. By this time the Torah scroll had acquired a central place in the synagogue with zones of sanctity around it. The ritual reading of the Torah each week and its translation into Aramaic became the main rite of the synagogue service. The development of a liturgy in conjunction with the rise of *piyyut* (a type of elaborate liturgical poetry) was symptomatic of an increasingly professionalized service. Since *piyyut* was constructed around the set liturgy prescribed in rabbinic writings and often summarized and alluded to rabbinic exegesis and laws, the rise of *piyyut* in synagogues may be seen as evidence for the rabbinization of liturgical practice in the Palestinian synagogue in the sixth century. Rabbinic circles in this period (fifth to seventh century) also assembled the major works of midrash (biblical interpretation and commentary).

Despite the explosion of religious literary production (*piyyut* and *midrash*), *legal* creativity had come more or less to an end in Palestine, as signaled by the closure of the Palestinian Talmud, a compendious commentary on the legal traditions of the Mishnah, toward the end of the fourth century. It was in Babylonia that study of the legal traditions continued apace and in the ensuing centuries Babylonia would emerge as the intellectual and spiritual center of rabbinic Judaism.

The Babylonian Jewish community, which claimed descent from the ten northern tribes of Israel exiled in 722 B.C.E., was the only major concentration of Jews outside the Roman Empire and outside the sphere of Hellenistic culture and society. Major centers in the Talmudic period were the northern city of Nisibis and the southern cities of Nehardea, Sura, Pumbeditha, and Mahoza. In the early third century, Rav (a disciple of R. Judah ha-Nasi) brought the Mishnah to Babylonia where it became the basic text of the rabbinic curriculum. The Babylonian Talmud mentions some formal gatherings of sages, but it was not until the end of the Talmudic period that rabbinic academies (*yeshivot*, sing. *yeshivah*) with an elaborate institutional structure, were established. Throughout the Talmudic period, an Exilarch represented the Jewish community before the Sassanian king and exercised important judicial and economic authority. Relations between the sages and the exilarch soured significantly in the later period.

A RABBINIC MYTH OF ORIGINS

While the literary works produced by rabbinic sages of Palestine (Mishnah, Tosefta, Palestinian Talmud, Midrashic texts) and Babylonia (Babylonian Talmud) are critically important sources for the study of rabbinic Judaism, they are, naturally enough, quite rabbinocentric. They do not tell us much about the majority Jewish population of the first few centuries C.E. They *do* tell us about the small rabbinic movement, its perception of its own importance, and its aspirations for itself and for the Jewish people. Like the biblical narrative before it, the rabbinic "myth of origins" became foundationally important for subsequent Judaism and for that reason we rehearse its basic contours here.

While rabbinic texts do not explicitly identify Second Temple Pharisees as the immediate forerunners of the rabbinic sages, several early or proto-rabbinic characters are referred to as Pharisees in extra-rabbinic sources (in Josephus and the New Testament). Pharisaic views and concerns (e.g., tithing and purity) as depicted in rabbinic and nonrabbinic sources often correspond with the views and concerns of later rabbis. Some have suggested that the connection with Pharisees is muted in rabbinic sources because of a desire to avoid sectarian division after 70 C.E.

One predestruction sage valorized in rabbinic sources is Hillel the Babylonian, who flourished under Herodian rule. Rabbinic sources contain over 300 cases recording disputes between Hillel and Shammai or the disciple groups associated with them (the House of Hillel and the House of Shammai). While it is difficult to separate legend from fact, later rabbinic tradition credits Hillel with developing new methods of biblical interpretation and resolving various legal problems. More important, Hillel's prominence and authority are based on learning rather than social status or personal charisma. It was not until after the destruction of the Temple in 70 C.E. that the views of Hillel prevailed and the school of Hillel emerged as the leading school of Pharisaic Judaism, eventually representative of rabbinic Judaism generally. The leaders and patriarchs of the early rabbinic community traced their line through Gamliel to Hillel, implying or at least claiming some continuity between the pre-70 Pharisees and the later sages.

Many late rabbinic stories depict the rabbis (or "sages") as playing a central leadership role in the immediate postdestruction period. This, then, is how the rabbis write their own story. It was *they* who confronted the national tragedy and loss and persevered in the tradition. It was *they* who busied themselves with the reconstruction of Jewish life in the nation's darkest hour. The head of this forward-looking movement, they assert, was Yohanan ben Zakkai. According to rabbinic sources, Yohanan ben Zakkai escaped the Roman siege of Jerusalem in 68 C.E. and assembled a group of sages and disciples at Yavneh. The sages of Yavneh are credited in rabbinic sources with beginning the process of transforming Temple-centered biblical Israel into Torah-centered rabbinic Judaism (see Documents 8a–c).

Rabbinic sources describe Yohanan ben Zakkai and later Gamliel II as reconstituting the Sanhedrin and undertaking a series of enactments (*takkanot*) that transformed and preserved Judaism as a post-Temple, non-priestly creation. They are credited with drawing together the legal traditions and teachings of preceding generations and establishing normative practice (or *halakhah*) in accordance with the Hillelite school in most cases. While early rabbinic sources suggest an emphasis on laws of purity, tithing, and calendar-setting, later texts credit the Yavneh generation with: canonizing Scripture; composing obligatory daily prayers in imitation of the daily sacrifices in the Temple, as well as prayers and blessings for a variety of occasions; and transferring certain Temple observances—especially the ceremonies associated with the pilgrimage festivals—to the home and/or synagogue. Thus, even though the Passover lamb could no longer be sacrificed, a family observance of the Passover was possible and the non-Temple elements of the ceremony—the eating of unleavened bread and of bitter herbs—took on a heightened importance. The basic framework of the Passover Haggadah (the liturgy accompanying the Passover meal in the home) is believed to have been composed in the early rabbinic period.

Although the picture of reconstruction that emerges from rabbinic texts is surely idealized, and streamlined—representing as rapid, formal, unified, and widespread a process that was probably slow, informal, chaotic, and fairly marginal—it is true that within the space of two to three centuries, the main contours of rabbinic Judaism are in place and the rabbis, backed by the patriarch, are emerging as local leaders. Coming from all levels of society, these rabbis serve local communities as adjudicators, teachers, and advisors.

It is clear from rabbinic literature that the rabbis had no great love for Rome. Nevertheless, rabbinic texts do not seek to inflame zealous nationalism or rebellion against the hated regime. In the eyes of the rabbis, the disastrous Bar Kokhba revolt and the persecutions that followed in its wake only confirmed the dangers of political messianism and nationalism. The rabbinic program is one that focuses inward on the quest for piety and sanctity, in the belief that God will bring an end to the dominion of the idolaters when he sees fit. God's hand cannot be forced. The Jews will be restored, the Temple will be rebuilt—but in God's own time. The task of Jews until that time is dedication to God's Torah, the blueprint for the life of *imitatio dei* (imitation of God's ways). Torah is seen as the source of life and to abandon it is to live without divine protection and blessing. What precisely do the rabbis mean, however, when they speak of Torah?

THE TORAH OF THE RABBIS

The meaning of the term "Torah" expanded dramatically in the rabbinic period. In its most restricted sense, it continued to refer to the first five books of the Hebrew Bible containing early human and Israelite history, the record of God's covenant with Israel and the divinely revealed moral, legal, civil, and cultic rules of life for the community of Israel. In a second expanded sense it came to mean the Hebrew Bible as a whole—all of God's teachings as found not only in the Pentateuch, but also in the words of the prophets and the later writings. A third and still more greatly expanded meaning arose by the third century C.E. when Torah was used to refer to the entire body of interpretation and learning arising from meditation upon the revealed word of God, transmitted over generations and continuing in the present.

In order to distinguish these latter two usages, a distinction between the *Written* and *Oral* Torah arose. This idea of a dual Torah—one written and one oral—is first seen in rabbinic texts from the end of the third century C.E. In these texts, the term *Written Torah* designates the Hebrew Bible—the fixed, eternal, and immutable revelation of God preserved in writing, to which nothing may be added or taken away. The *Oral Torah* is the massive body of interpretation and explication of the Written Torah that, according to the rabbis, had been generated and transmitted, from teacher to student, over the centuries (see Document 9). Unlike the Written Torah, the Oral Torah is understood to be a living, ever growing body of tradition to which new interpretations and teachings were continually added. Its development and transmission in face-to-face oral exchanges between master (*rav*) and disciple are essential features of the Oral Law.

There is no single rabbinic understanding of the relationship between the Written and Oral Torah. In some accounts, the Oral Torah is said to have been an explicit part of God's revelation to Moses at Sinai. God taught Moses far more than he was able to include in the Written Torah. These additional teachings Moses taught orally to Joshua. This oral accompaniment to the Written Torah was then relayed to others by

Joshua, a process continuing down to the time of the rabbis themselves. Other rabbinic texts claim that certain interpretative rules were revealed with the Written Torah at Sinai and the Oral Torah was developed by means of the application of these rules over time. Still other texts speak of the Written Torah as a kind of nucleus from which Oral Torah would be developed. When God revealed the Torah to Moses, it contained all that future generations would derive from it through close study, much as a seed "contains" the tree that will grow from it through cultivation. The later derivations and interpretations that are developed through the process of study and interpretation of the Written Torah—a process that continues into the future—constitute Oral Torah.

Whether the Oral Torah is a body of teachings or a set of interpretative rules delivered by God to Moses and handed down over centuries, or something slowly emerging from continual study and interpretation of the biblical text by subsequent generations of scribes and rabbis, all rabbinic accounts of the Oral Torah agree on two points: First, the rabbis' Oral Torah is rooted—directly or indirectly—in God's revelation to Moses at Sinai just as all interpretations of a text are latent in that text. Second, without the Oral Torah, the Written Torah (or Bible) cannot be fully and properly understood.

The rabbinic conception of divine revelation is thus somewhat complex: there was a singular historical revelation at Sinai designed to serve the needs of every age. However, that original and perfect revelation must be continually unfolded through study and interpretation. This notion is captured by two rabbinic mottos. The first, "The Torah is from heaven," asserts the divine and perfect origin of the Torah, while the second, "The Torah is no longer in heaven," underscores the fact that the task of interpreting and applying the Torah is an on-going endeavor that has been given over to humankind.

According to the rabbis, God no longer sends prophets to convey his message or will to humans. Revelation continues but in a new mode. Through interpretation and study of God's one-time, eternal revelation at Sinai, the messages and teachings needed in each new age are revealed. Understanding the divine will is made available not by the charismatic and inspired prophet carrying a message from God, but by the interpreter of the Book, the scribe or sage who can search out new dimensions and hidden meanings in Scripture. Revelation continues in the process of interpretation (see Document 11).

The results of the interpretative activity of Palestinian and Babylonian rabbis are contained in a series of collective works—originally oral—that span centuries. The material found in these works can be divided into two main genres: halakhah and aggadah. Halakhah refers to the normative actions or rules by which rabbis conducted their lives. The word is often translated "law" and like the English term law, it can refer to a specific rule (a particular halakhah) or the entire legal system (the halakhah as a whole). The rabbis produced works that are primarily, but not wholly, halakhic in character. Aggadah (from the verb "to tell") refers to units of tradition that are not halakhic. Aggadah includes biblical exegesis, parables and legends, folktales and ethical teachings, and even recipes and practical advice. The rabbis produced works that are largely aggadic in character, but many halakhic works also contain aggadic elements and much aggadah is implicitly normative. For example, tales highlighting exemplary behavior are aggadic in literary style but may be morally normative. Halakhah and aggadah are thus the warp and woof of the fabric of rabbinic learning.

While rabbinic teachers may have consulted written notes, all rabbinic learning was conducted orally. In many respects, the rabbis shared in the culture of Greco-Roman paideia—a form of personal cultivation that entailed the study of canonical traditions and attachment to a particular pattern of life. In third- and fourth-century Palestine, rabbinic learning— like Christian rhetorical paideia—featured disciple-communities engaged in the oral transmission of teachings and patterns of pious behavior. As in philosophical and patristic schools of the period, learning occurred within the context of service to and attendance upon a master (or *rav*).

Sages were praised for their prodigious memories and the fear of forgetting one's learning was great. Nevertheless, over time the primary works of Oral Torah were also written down. The oldest compilation of rabbinic halakhah (normative traditions) that we possess is the Mishnah. Early versions of collections of teachings likely predate the Mishnah; one collection that reached its final form only after the Mishnah, is the Tosefta.

According to tradition, the Mishnah was edited by the great Patriarch, Rabbi Judah I around 220 C.E. The halakhic teachings of numerous sages from the first two centuries C.E. are gathered together in this encyclopedic work, which served as a kind of "script" for continued "performances" and amplifications of Oral Torah in the master–student exchange. Each sage mentioned in the Mishnah is a tanna ("repeater" of tradition). For this reason, we refer to the period from 70 to 220 C.E. as the tannaitic period, and to works and teachings of this period as tannaitic works or teachings.

The Mishnah is divided into six Orders—Agriculture, Festivals and Holy Days, Women/Personal Status Laws, Damages, Holy Things, and Purities. These orders are in turn divided into tractates dealing with specific topics (such as the Sabbath, Tithes, Oaths, Divorce, Menstrual Purity). There are a total of sixty-three tractates divided into chapters, which are further divided into paragraphs, each of which is referred to as a *mishnah* (lowercase "m"). This compendious collection covers all areas of life because, as we saw in our examination of the biblical covenant, God's blueprint for a holy society encompasses every aspect of life. God's laws govern the way one tends one's fields, buys and sells, settles disputes, marries and begins a family, worships and rejoices, contributes to charity, and interacts with one's fellow beings.

While it is true that the Mishnah discusses normative behavior in all areas of life, it is not easily classified as a law *code*. Basic legal definitions and requirements are not set out and tractates often pick up in the middle of a topic and deal with borderline and exceptional cases. Many topics with no practical application (such as details of the sacrificial cult) are treated extensively. There is also some aggadic material—occasional short narratives, bits of biblical exegesis, and gnomic sayings. More important, a great deal of the material contained in the Mishnah is presented in the form of unresolved disputes so that it is often quite difficult to know what the established law is. For example, one passage reads:

> We do not kindle [the Sabbath lamp] with oil of burning on the festivals. R. Yishmael says, "We do not kindle the Sabbath lamp with resin because of the honor owing to the Sabbath." But the sages permit all kinds of oils: sesame oil, nut oil, radish oil, fish oil, gourd oil, resin and naphtha. R. Tarfon says, "They kindle only with olive oil." (m. Shabbath 2:2b)

In this short paragraph, several distinct opinions are expressed. The rabbis permit a range of oils for lighting the Sabbath lamp, while R. Yishmael excludes one of these oils (resin), and R. Tarfon permits only olive oil! The Mishnah is characteristically full of controversies such as these, leading many scholars to conclude that the Mishnah was not intended as a law code but as a kind of textbook to be used in the training of rabbinic disciples. Indeed, already in the early third century, the Mishnah had become the central text studied in rabbinic circles in both Palestine and Babylonia. Certainly, the great prestige of its editor, R. Judah the Patriarch, contributed to the Mishnah's dissemination and adoption as the basis of the rabbinic curriculum.

Detailed study of the Mishnah occupied successive generations of sages and their disciples. A posttannaitic sage is known as an *amora*, and thus the period following the close of the Mishnah (220–400 C.E.) is known as the amoraic period. In this period, individual paragraphs of Mishnah would be analyzed carefully and the views of various *tannaim* explicated as fully as possible. For example, early amoraic sages might explore the reason for R. Yishmael's exclusion of resin, others might try to clarify obscure terms while later amoraic sages might move on to other concerns: deriving from the cases of the *mishnah* general principles of action or judicial decision making, expanding the collection of recorded precedents and exemplary court cases, drawing analogies between this case and cases in other areas of life, systematizing the views of individual rabbis, showing or finding the biblical bases for the Mishnah's determinations. The explanations and discussions of the Mishnah generated by these sages were ultimately woven together into superstructures of commentary and argument called *gemara* (which means study). The term "talmud" refers to the totality of Mishnah plus its *gemara* commentary.

Because the Mishnah formed the basic rabbinic curriculum in both Palestine and Babylonia, two Talmuds were produced. The Palestinian Talmud compiled by rabbis in northern Palestine was finalized before 400 C.E. The Babylonian Talmud, compiled by rabbis in Babylonia, is at least four times the size of the Palestinian Talmud and reached its final form as late as the seventh century C.E. Because scholars traveled between the two centers, traditions and teachings of Palestinian sages were transmitted to Babylonia and are found on nearly every page of the Babylonian Talmud, while some Babylonian teachings were transmitted to Palestine and are to be found in the Palestinian Talmud. The Palestinian Talmud covers the first four orders of the Mishnah, while the Babylonian Talmud covers the middle four orders, and two additional tractates.

The time difference between the two Talmuds accounts in large part for their very different characters. The Palestinian Talmud is fairly concise— almost too concise to be readily understood. It is composed primarily of brief comments, glosses, and explanations of the Mishnah around which it revolves. The Babylonian Talmud is far more elaborate and developed. In Babylonia, amoraic traditions of the third to fifth century C.E. were taken up by later anonymous editors (*stammaim*) in the sixth century C.E. and embedded in complex dialectical structures. Elaborations and digressions were added, creating lengthy and involved debates and discussions that often leave the mishnah far behind. Many of these discussions are literary and intellectual masterpieces, carefully crafted tours of a set of related rabbinic teachings, biblical verses, legal principles, hypothetical test cases, and aggadic material (about one-third of the Babylonian Talmud is aggadah). Although most of the material is presented in dialogue form (questions and answers, objections and rejoinders, refutations and counter-refutations), it is quite clear that Talmudic discussions do not generally record actual conversations, if only because the participants in these "debates" often derive from different time periods and geographical regions. Anonymous editors have brought a wide variety of source materials together in a piece of grand orchestration (see Document 12). Studied continuously, the Babylonian Talmud eventually eclipsed the Palestinian Talmud to become the classic text and exemplar of rabbinic Judaism, referred to simply as *the* Talmud.

In addition to the topically organized halakhic collections discussed above (Mishnah, Tosefta, the two Talmuds), the rabbis also produced works of midrash—exegesis of, and elaboration upon, biblical verses (see Documents 13a–c). There are several midrashic collections that can be divided into two main categories: halakhic and aggadic. Works of halakhic midrash are tannaitic (pre-220 C.E.), proceed verse by verse and feature exegesis of the legal sections of the Bible (beginning in Ex 12). There are halakhic midrashim (plural of midrash) for Exodus (the *Mekhilta*), Leviticus (*Sifra*), Numbers and Deuteronomy (*Sifrei*). Works of aggadic midrash are amoraic and focus on the narrative or nonlegal portions of the Pentateuch and the "five scrolls" (Song of Songs, Ruth, Lamentations, Ecclesiastes, and Esther). They are freer in both style and content than the halakhic midrashim, often weaving complex interpretive structures out of verses from widely disparate parts of the Bible. Some of these works may have their roots in homilies delivered in synagogues or within rabbinic circles, though many bear the earmarks of polished literary crafting. The aggadic midrashim teach, inspire, and console and are an important source for discerning the general worldview of rabbinic culture.

The study and interpretation of Torah was an intense and deeply religious expression. The minute examination of God's revealed word, the application of reason and logic to the discovery of God's will for humans regarding even the most mundane aspects of human life and every conceivable human activity were part of a serious effort to sanctify the most specific and concrete actions of the everyday world. Study was not the only mode of religious expression in rabbinic culture—certainly prayer, asceticism, and even martyrdom played an important role. Moreover, study was not the chief mode of religious expression for the common Jew. But in classical *rabbinic* Judaism, the mind—one's critical intelligence—was the chief vehicle for discovering and effecting God's will on earth and was thus a primary tool of piety. The application of one's critical intelligence to the study of God's Torah was not a hubristic assault on holy Scripture; it was seen as mandated by God himself. For the rabbinic elite, the intellect was the instrument by which the community would be sanctified and the penetrating use of the mind was what God desired and demanded of his creatures.

CHAPTER 6

TOPICS IN RABBINIC JUDAISM

RABBINIC JUDAISM

In the modern period, religions are often defined as belief systems centered on a creed. A creed is a fixed formula promulgated by an authoritative figure or body summarizing the essential dogmas of the religion and serving as an admission test for converts and as a loyalty oath for faithful adherents. A Christian is a person who believes Christian dogmas or confesses a particular Christian creed. However, in the ancient world, and even in certain traditions of the modern world, religion did not always center on beliefs. Religious traditions in antiquity were concerned with actions (how one lives) rather than creeds (what one believes).

In the Hellenistic period, *religio* referred to the ancestral customs and way of life believed to be enjoined by the gods for the betterment of human kind and the proper conduct of society at large.[i] If one wished to speculate on questions like free will, immortality, or the problem of evil and develop belief systems about such matters, one turned to the traditions of "wisdom" (in the Ancient Near East) or philosophy (in Greece and the Hellenistic Near East), not *religio*. Persons with widely different beliefs could join together in the practice of a common religion because religious

---

i. Shaye J.D. Cohen, *From the Maccabees to the Mishnah*, ed. Wayne A. Meeks (Philadelphia: The Westminster Press, 1989), p. 60. For a full, but accessible treatment of some of the ideas summarized in this chapter see Cohen's presentation of Jewish religion, pp. 60–103, 214–231 and the presentation of rabbinic religion in Robert Seltzer, *Jewish People, Jewish Thought* (New York: Macmillan Publishing Company, Inc., 1980), pp. 281–314.

communities were defined less by doctrine than by a prescribed way of life and mode of worship.

Whereas the early church was defined and held together almost entirely by a particular set of creedal convictions, Judaism's origins were not doctrinal and Jews did not need a catechism to create or establish an identity. Jewish identity in antiquity was based on membership in a historic people and/or participation in a distinctive ethnic-religious culture (including observance of the ancestral laws and customs of the covenant). Certainly, Jews were known to deny the gods of other nations and to assert that their god was the one god of the universe. Nevertheless, even outside observers in antiquity described the difference between Jews and Gentiles in terms of practice—a distinctive way of life—rather than theology or beliefs. Although various Jewish sects arose in the Second Temple period, the debates among these sects tended to focus on matters of practice rather than theology. The separatist literature found at Qumran criticized other Jews for their purity practices, Temple practices, their calendar, and their rules concerning interaction with Gentiles—not for their theological doctrines. Indeed, the diverse writings at Qumran suggest that a range of theological views were held by the authors of those works.

Formal creeds, and the discipline of theology in general, played little role in the maintenance of ancient Jewish identity and the construction of rabbinic Judaism. The early church fathers produced theological treatises, in which they carefully formulated entire systems of belief and developed arguments in defense of their philosophical validity. These treatises were often directed to persons outside the faith, and sought to persuade them of the truth of the writer's belief system. Rabbis of the Talmudic period simply did not produce theological writings of this type. The central focus of rabbinic thought was *halakhah* and rabbinic literature is overwhelmingly directed to an internal Jewish, or even rabbinic, audience.

Nevertheless, although the rabbis did not produce works of systematic theology they did reflect on issues of central concern to theologians—the nature of God, the nature of humanity, the ethical life, the problem of suffering and evil, reward and punishment, immortality, and resurrection. Their reflections on these matters are not presented systematically, but appear in the form of maxims, parables, stories, and biblical interpretations scattered throughout the anthological compilations that make up the rabbinic corpus. They can be discerned as the often unspoken principles guiding rabbinic discussions of civil, criminal, marital, and agricultural law. Do these reflections and principles taken together form a rabbinic theology? Not if by the term "theology" we mean a unitary system of doctrines developed and argued systematically. We would do better to speak of a rabbinic "worldview" or "religious outlook." This worldview is often complex and variegated. That is not surprising, considering that rabbinic writings contain the teachings and traditions of literally hundreds of sages over the course of several centuries.

In the following pages we will attempt to trace the general contours of this worldview, in all its complexity and variety. However, it should be noted that in so doing we are by definition isolating and foregrounding an aspect of rabbinic Judaism that, in the Talmudic period, was never an isolated and foregrounded activity. Judging from the rabbinic literature that has come to us from late antiquity, the rabbis did not often speculate on theological matters in isolation of some practical or exegetical concern. Thus, while it is rewarding to explore the religious worldview of the rabbis we must remember that for rabbinic Jews, this worldview was the organic background to the religious life, important precisely and only because it engendered obedience to God's commandments and commitment to the task of humankind in this world.[ii]

God: Faith, Heresy, and the Shekinah

Continuing an ancient practice, the rabbis prescribed the twice-daily recitation of a biblical passage known as the "Shema" after its opening word (Deut 6:4–9). The first paragraph of that passage reads:

> Hear (*Shema*), O Israel! Yahweh is our god, Yahweh alone. You shall love Yahweh your God with all your heart and with all your soul and with all your might. Take to heart these instructions with which I charge you this day. Impress them upon your children. Recite them when you stay at home and when you are away, when you lie down and when you get up. Bind them as a sign on your hand and let them serve as a symbol on your forehead, inscribe them on the doorposts of your house and on your gates.

---

ii. For a full, if dated, discussion of many of the themes summarized below, see Ephraim E. Urbach, *The Sages: Their Concepts and Beliefs*, trans. Israel Abrahams (Jerusalem: Magnes Press, 1979).

The passage opens with an affirmation of God's sovereignty and then ordains complete love for God and devotion to and immersion in his commandments. Successive paragraphs outline the rewards and punishments for obedience and disobedience respectively, and the obligation to meditate on God's commandments and his redemption. This central and daily recitation encapsulates the essence of rabbinic religion—to acknowledge God necessarily entails accepting upon oneself his commandments. For the rabbis, a heretic is one who denies God not so much in word or belief, but in deed and practice, by breaking the commandments and *acting* as if there is no God and no covenant. The rabbis refer to a heretic as an *apikoros*, from the Greek "Epicurus," since Epicurus' philosophy claimed *not* that there were no gods but that the gods were indifferent to humanity. For the rabbis, faith is not belief in a set of doctrines; but trust that there is a permanent relationship between God and creation, a relationship that places demands on humans.

But how can there be a relationship between an omnipotent, exalted creator God and the physical world? Monotheistic systems that view God as abstract and transcendent often try to bridge the gap between the divine and human orders, ensuring a vital intimacy and nearness to God. In Second Temple times, Jews populated the heavens with all sorts of intermediate angels who communicated with humans. Philo and Greek-speaking Jews saw God's reason, or Logos, as the intermediary between the divine and human realms. Christians believe that the Logos became flesh in Jesus Christ. Later, the Holy Spirit was believed to mediate between God and the Christian community. By contrast, the rabbis speak of the "*shekinah*"—the presence or "in-dwelling" of God. At first the *shekinah* referred to a manifestation of God in a particular place but later it came to mean the divine presence (particularly in its feminine aspect) everywhere. According to one tradition, there is no place upon earth devoid of the *shekinah* while according to another the *shekinah* is present whenever two or more persons share words of Torah. In some traditions it appears that God's in-dwelling, or *shekinah*, is linked to human conduct. Sin drives the *shekinah* from the earth, while righteous deeds draw the *shekinah* closer.

Rabbinic Anthropology

Platonic dualism appears in Second Temple period Jewish writings, particularly those by Greek-speaking Jews. The body–soul dichotomy assumed in these works is associated with an ascetic deprecation of sexuality and the physical world generally. In sharp contrast to Second Temple Jewish groups and early Christianity, rabbinic anthropology resists platonic dualism with its denigration of the bodily plane of existence. Rabbinic writings tend to define the human being as a body animated by a soul (an integrated composite) rather than a soul that is only housed (or trapped or entombed) in a body. The corporeal realm and the life and activities of the body are not unambiguously negative for the rabbis. The body is not base matter, an essentially corrupt and evil prison for the godlike and perfect soul.

Rabbinic Judaism takes seriously the biblical statement that humans—actual, embodied, male and female humans—were created in the image of God. In many teachings, the human body is the object of both admiration and care. Bathing and attention to the digestive process are referred to as pious deeds, and natural bodily functions are an occasion to bless the wisdom of the creator. Indeed, the daily liturgy contains a blessing for the processes of eating and eliminating.

In Genesis 1, God's first command to humans is to be fruitful and multiply. The biblical representation of human corporeality and sexuality as part of God's original intention for humankind motivates the rabbis' generally positive view of sexuality and marriage on the one hand, and their ambivalence toward asceticism on the other. While the rabbis saw reproduction as the primary purpose of sex, they also valorized the secondary purposes of pleasure, intimacy, and health. We see this in legal rulings that permit consensual sex even when it is not procreative (for example with a pregnant or a sterile wife). The Mishnah stipulates the frequency with which a husband is obligated to fulfill his "conjugal duty," in an effort to guarantee the sexual rights of the wife and to protect her from being neglected.

Despite individual teachings to the contrary, rabbinic texts on the whole praise marriage; according to diverse traditions a man without a wife is said to lack not only joy and blessing, but even atonement, Torah, and moral protection. An unmarried man is incomplete and, according to one rabbi, diminishes the divine image, since the image of God after which humans were modeled is both male and female (Gen 1:27). Nevertheless, although the biblical affirmation of corporeality and sexuality prevented the development of celibacy as an ideal in rabbinic culture, rabbis struggled to meet the demands of both family life and Torah study. The tension between Torah study and domestic life was particularly pronounced in the late Babylonian period when scholars often lived a great distance from places of study. The tension was at least partially resolved by the practice of early marriage followed by long periods of absence for study. Students who fulfilled their marital and procreative obligations at an early age were free to travel great distances to study Torah and would be absent for months at a time. Rabbinic stories suggest ambivalence about this practice, however, imagining the wives of these scholars as alternately uncomplaining and supportive or grief-stricken and despairing.

Biblical affirmations of human corporeality and sexuality and the rabbinic resistance to a dualistic denigration of the physical aspects of human existence, explain the rabbinic ambivalence toward asceticism. Many rabbinic sources continue an ancient understanding of self-affliction and fasting as important means of stimulating God's mercy and forgiveness of sin. Some urge self-restraint and avoidance of pleasures.

But on the whole, rabbinic writings oppose asceticism and self-affliction as dishonor and disrespect for God's creation. According to one tradition, a scholar may not practice fasting because he diminishes the work of heaven. Self-affliction and fasting are described in some texts as gratuitous and one text even suggests that fasting is nothing short of a sin, since it is God's intention that his creatures enjoy the bountiful world he has created for them. According to one third-century sage, a man will have to give account in the judgment day of every good thing he could have enjoyed but did not! The enjoyment of aesthetic pleasures entails appreciation and the rabbis ordain blessings, which in rabbinic Judaism are expressions of gratitude to God, for a wide range of aesthetic pleasures—upon seeing beautiful trees or persons, upon seeing the budding trees of spring, and more.

Rabbinic anthropology is not unaware of the human capacity for evil and a number of rabbinic teachings and stories deal directly with the psychology of evil. In a few texts humans are understood to have two inclinations or urges: the *yetzer hatov* (the good urge) and the *yetzer hara* (the evil urge). This is not a body–soul dualism because the good and evil elements are not the soul and body respectively, but two basic human instincts or urges that are at war with each other in the human self. Most rabbinic texts, however, reject even this ethical dualism and view humans as possessing a singular nature—one basic urge or passion (*yetzer*) that can be put to either good or evil account. The rabbis composed prayers asking for God's help in dealing with the *yetzer*—channeling or harnessing it for some good use, perhaps suppressing it, but rarely purging it. The *yetzer* is an essential part of human existence, motivating and empowering any number of useful endeavors such as marriage and procreation, and the competitive desire to excel in art or industry. Unfortunately, the *yetzer* can urge us further to illicit sex, adultery, violence, and other destructive behavior. In moderation, however, it ceases to be evil and becomes very good, that is, when it is in the service of life. Hence, the sages can actually urge people to employ both the good and evil inclinations in the service of God, for in so doing they transform the evil inclination into the good.

The *yetzer* is analogized to the yeast in dough. The proper amount of yeast makes the dough rise and take perfect shape. Too much yeast spoils the dough, and in fact can bring about rotting and decay. So, it is with the *yetzer*. In moderate amounts the *yetzer* is responsible for much good in the world, but when out of control it wreaks havoc. Rabbinic texts suggest that although God created the *yetzer hara'* in us, he also gave us the power to control it. While anger, impatience, lust, and idolatry fan the flames of the *yetzer hara'*, countermeasures can be taken to contain and channel it—most notably, the study of Torah.

The Ethical Life

The commandments are central to Torah and to rabbinic Judaism because the God of the Bible not only redeems but also commands his people. For the rabbis, the laws and commandments of the Bible are literal laws and commandments that demand obedience. Systematic allegorical readings of the commandments (see Chapter 4), as found in the works of Philo and the early church fathers, are not carried out by the rabbis. Allegorical reading assumes a dualistic distinction between the concrete or literal plane of the text and a deeper spiritual or symbolic meaning. Allegory was a tool by which some readers spiritualized biblical laws, decoding and then, in some cases, discarding the literal meaning in favor of a spiritual meaning. But any reading that undermines observance of the commandments is, in the rabbinic view, pernicious. This is not to say that the rabbis confined themselves to a plain reading of the text. On the contrary, the activity of midrash (rabbinic interpretation of Scripture) is a highly creative enterprise that can produce multiple, even contradictory readings of the Bible. But midrash is not allegory *in the classical sense,* because it does not spiritualize the commandments in a manner that diminishes or cancels their status as actual concrete commandments.

The rabbinic period is characterized by an enlargement of the sphere of the commandments (*mitzvot*; singular: *mitzvah*), which are celebrated as opportunities to serve God. According to rabbinic tradition there are 613 biblical commandments—248 positive commandments (injunctions to do a particular thing) corresponding to the number of bones in the human body and 365 negative commandments (prohibitions) corresponding to the number of days in the year. The idea communicated by this tradition is that Israel is surrounded by commandments in both physical space and time—all actions each day are subject to commandments that can be performed in the name of God. It is commendable to adorn or beautify the commandments and the very observance of the commandments can give a feeling a joy (the "joy of the *mitzvah*"). Joy arises when the commandment is performed for its own sake as an expression of love for God, and not for some other purpose, gain, or benefit.

Ideally, all commandments—major and minor—should be observed with equal diligence and enthusiasm. Nevertheless, the reality of persecution raised a critical question: Were all commandments of equal importance such that one should be prepared to lose one's life for them? In a famous Talmudic passage, the majority view is stated as follows: A Jew who is ordered to violate his law on pain of death is permitted to violate the law in all but three cases—incest, murder, and idolatry. A few rabbis were even more stringent and ruled that one should not violate any precept at all in public, and the Talmud contains legends of Jews killed for refusing to violate even minor precepts.

Immortality, Death and Suffering

We have already discussed the emergence of a belief in immortality in Second Temple Jewish writings. The late biblical book of Daniel posits an afterlife in which pious martyrs will be resurrected and rewarded. Rabbinic texts continue the assumption of an eternal reward for the righteous in a "world-to-come." Nevertheless, the rabbis also struggle to make sense of premature death and undeserved suffering.

The rabbinic understanding of death and its connection to Adam's sin is quite different from a normative Christian understanding. Rabbinic texts assert that the sin of Adam brought toil and death to humanity;

they do not espouse the Christian notion of "original sin" according to which all humans after Adam are born in sin (are inherently sinful) and stand in need of redemption. In Christianity, the sinful state into which humans are born can be overcome only through faith in Christ. In rabbinic Judaism, humans remain morally free. Adam's sin brought death, not a predestination to sin. Humans who exercise their moral freedom in a sinful manner can find atonement without an intercessory figure, through such means as repentance, Torah study, good deeds, and prayer. Some texts assert that death alone effects atonement for the deceased's life even in the absence of repentance and prayer.

Many rabbinic passages are devoted to a discussion of suffering and the attempt to explain it or make it more bearable and religiously meaningful. R. Akiva was known for his startling view that suffering can be a sign of divine love. Just as a father must chasten the child he loves so that he may grow and develop on the right path, so God must chasten the children he loves, protecting them from greater harm, and aiding their correct growth and development. Sufferings are sent as "chastenings of love" and have atoning value. R. Akiva's view of suffering is valorized, but at the same time, marginalized. The rabbis recognize that not every individual is capable of interpreting suffering as a divine chastening of love. For some, suffering simply crushes the spirit and alienates the individual from God. Such individuals need sympathy and help, not a lecture on the religious significance of their suffering.

Certainly, there are stories in which death is meted out to a sinner, as divine punishment for his evil deeds. But a premature or unpleasant death is not always to be taken as a sure sign of sin and some rabbinic texts acknowledge that attempts to justify such deaths often fail.

Redemption and Messianism

The biblical view of redemption was conditioned on upheaval. Catastrophe would usher in the new age in which the people of Israel would be redeemed from servitude to the other nations and the universal kingdom of God would be realized. The Redeemer was imaged as a human king (God's anointed, or messiah) of the house of David or occasionally as God himself.

In rabbinic texts, the belief in a future Davidic redeemer remained alive, but it was not characterized by the same sense of urgency and actuality. Although the rabbis hoped and prayed for the rebuilding of the

Sanctuary, the ingathering of the exiles, and the restoration of their nation under a Davidic king, they focused their energies on the life of Torah and the commandments. Some traditions curse those who calculate the end time because of the bitter disillusionment such predictions create. The messianic agitation that had contributed to two disastrous revolts against Rome is seen as dangerous. In many rabbinic texts, the messianic impulse is ethicized. Jews should pray, repent, and strive for moral perfection and righteousness as a means of meriting, even hastening, the coming of the messiah. God's messianic promise is conditioned on the moral life in an increasingly noneschatological, nonapocalyptic, ethically oriented view of redemption. Illustrating this position is a statement attributed to Rabbi Yohanan ben Zakkai: "If you are planting a plant and someone tells you 'Behold, the Messiah is here!'—finish planting the plant and *then* go forth to welcome him."

The Rabbi in Society

In Chapter 5, we traced the emergence of the rabbis from a marginal scholastic elite in Palestine to a prominent class in Palestinian and especially Babylonian Jewish society. The Babylonian rabbi was a new kind of leader. He was not a priest, a prophet, or a king, but he functioned in political, judicial, cultural, religious, and educational capacities. Rabbis of the later Talmudic period were lawyers and advisors, handling the small claims, legal questions, and religious affairs of the people. They were also religious scholars, studying the ancient traditions, and creating liturgical compositions and blessings. There is evidence that some engaged in mystical speculation, particularly around the mysteries of creation and theurgy. Finally, rabbinic literature depicts some rabbis as holy men, so righteous as to merit exceptional powers.

There is no doubt that the rabbis were a social, intellectual, and religious elite characterized by a belief in the supreme significance of the study of Torah. Rabbinic texts that tout the redemptive power of Torah study establish an ideal that would eventually find broader acceptance in Jewish society as a whole. By the end of the Talmudic period, study of the ancient traditions became a central part of Jewish education and worship outside the rabbinic academy—a hallowed activity even for those who could not devote themselves to full-time scholarship.

A Culture of Learning: Pluralism, Dialectics, and Normativity

In its classical form, the culture of learning fostered by the rabbinic movement is famous for multiple opinions, intense dialectics, and argumentation. To some degree these features are an accident of history. For much of the tannaitic period (70–220 B.C.E.), the rabbinic movement was a small, socially fragmented network of individuals lacking a central institutional framework. Individual masters and their students studied the ancient traditions, generating diverse legal opinions on a wide array of subjects. These diverse teachings were later gathered together in rabbinic texts (such as the Mishnah). Editors tried to impose order by harmonizing opposing views or by labeling some views as the majority opinion, and others as rejected. Nevertheless, the overall impression created is one of pluralism and controversy. One way of coping with the diversity of teachings and opinions is to accept and legitimate it by tying it to the nature of God's revelation. In the amoraic period, several fascinating traditions describe God's revelation as pregnant with multiple—even contradictory—meanings, all of which are valid. The diverse views of rabbinic scholars are said to reflect the multifaceted nature of God's Torah itself.

Whether this acceptance of pluralism is more ideal than real, is difficult to assess. Nevertheless, to assert the possibility of diverse interpretations of God's revelation even if only as an ideal has two important implications. First, intellectual inquiry and debate are more easily seen as supportive of, rather than antithetical to, the discernment of God's will and a pious life. In the later Talmudic period, argument is valued above all things as leading to the greater comprehension and dissemination of God's teachings, and the documents of rabbinic literature take the form of argument and debate. The high value placed on argument and dialectical skill in rabbinic culture is illustrated in a poignant legend about the Palestinian amora R. Yohanan who fell into a deep depression when his intellectual sparring partner, Resh Lakish, died. Resh Lakish's great virtue had been to bring twenty-four *objections* to every teaching uttered by R. Yohanan and through the ensuing dialectics and argumentation, Torah was advanced. The cultivation of Torah is best achieved in conversation with one who *disagrees*, who presses for reasons, who challenges and argues.

The second implication of the acceptance of pluralism is an ambivalence toward normativity. A distinction must be drawn here between matters of belief (subsumed under the rubric of aggadah) and matters of practical law (halakhah). Generally speaking, correct belief is less important to the rabbis than ethics and piety and later rabbinic statements assert that diverse opinions on speculative (aggadic) matters need not be adjudicated. However, in the realm of halakhah, the idea that God's multifaceted Torah engenders various equally valid interpretations sets up a genuine tension. How is one to establish communal norms of behavior if more than one interpretation of God's law is possible? If everyone were to follow his own interpretation of the law, would not chaos ensue? Several rabbinic traditions address the tension between pluralism and normativity in halakhah (see Documents 10a–d). The selection of one among a number of legitimate interpretations of God's law is effected by majority rule—a nod to normativity. But the defeated, or minority opinion is preserved and even studied, because it too is one facet of God's Torah and may be relied upon by future rabbinic authorities—a nod to pluralism. The greater emphasis on normativity in halakhah than in aggadah accounts for the popular characterization of classical rabbinic Judaism as an orthopraxy (requiring right praxis) rather than an orthodoxy (requiring right belief).

ELITISM

Rabbinic attitudes toward the common run of folk who do not share the rabbis' scholarly preoccupation with Torah are many and varied. The term 'am ha'arez (literally meaning "people of the land") is used in rabbinic sources to refer to such nonrabbinic Jews. However, the characterization and evaluation of the 'am ha'arez shifts dramatically over the course of the rabbinic period and between Palestine and Babylonia.

Tannaitic sources do not refer to the 'am ha'arez with any particular disrespect or vituperation. Interaction with the 'am ha'arez is expected, though too much intimacy is discouraged. It is only the chronologically last stratum of the Babylonian Talmud (the anonymous material of the final editors, post-500 C.E.) that espouses a contempt and disgust for nonrabbis that is completely absent from earlier Palestinian and Babylonian rabbinic sources. One scholar notes that it would be wrong to read these few hyperbolic texts as reflecting real social relations. The negative attitudes expressed in these late texts were probably intended for an audience of other sages and served as a means of self-definition and self-justification by contrasting the academic life of the sages with that of the outside world.

The powerfully negative rhetoric against the *'am ha'arez* possibly points to an increased sense of professionalization, elitism, and isolation from the general population among late Babylonian rabbis. Where Palestinian rabbis interacted with nonrabbinic Jews and even attempted to win disciples from among the nonrabbinic population, Babylonian rabbis tended to remain aloof from nonrabbis, interacting with them in primarily formal contexts.[iii]

The Rabbis and Non-Jewish Society

GENTILES

Confronting Gentiles on a regular basis in the land of Palestine, tannaitic rabbis felt compelled to set forth rules that would govern Jewish–Gentile interaction. These rules were elaborated upon by later generations of amoraim.[iv]

In rabbinic halakhah, the Gentile is imagined as an ethnic other *or* as a religious other. As an ethnic other, the Gentile is merely a non-Israelite or *goy* (member of a non-Israelite nation) to whom the laws of the Mosaic covenant do not apply. Because the Gentile is ignorant of the terms of the law, the Jew must be on guard against unintentional violations of the law in his interaction with a Gentile. One tractate of the Mishnah consists of regulations that make it possible to deal with Gentiles with the confidence that one is not violating any religious prescriptions. For example, one chapter contains a list of Gentile foods prohibited because of the possibility of mixture with, absorption of, or defilement by impure or forbidden substances (such as pork or blood), as well as a list of foods to which no such anxiety attaches.

The Gentile is also imagined as a *religious* other (idolater) who worships a deity or deities other than Yahweh. The Bible charges Israelites with

---

iii. For a fuller discussion of these ideas see Jeffrey Rubenstein, *The Culture of the Babylonian Talmud* (Baltimore: Johns Hopkins University Press, 2003), pp. 123–142 and Richard Kalmin, *The Sage in Jewish Society of Late Antiquity* (New York: Routledge, 1999), pp. 27–50.

iv. For bibliographic references and a full treatment of this subject see Christine Hayes, "The 'Other' in Rabbinic Literature" in *The Cambridge Companion to Rabbinic Literature* (Cambridge: Cambridge University Press, 2006).

the complete eradication of idolaters and idolatry from the land of Israel (Deut 7:1–5). Remarkably, despite some expressions of deep hostility and intolerance toward paganism, the Mishnah lacks any normative command to destroy pagans living in the land of Israel. As one scholar has argued, the tannaitic rabbis adopt a policy of passive resistance instead. Forced to accept the entanglement of Israelite and pagan society they adopt a twofold strategy of (i) distancing themselves from pagans through various avoidance mechanisms and (ii) creating a neutral space for legitimate interaction.[v] As regards the first strategy, the rabbis rule that a Jew must not benefit from or contribute to the existence of idolatry. As regards the second strategy, the rabbis create legal distinctions and categories that open the door for licit interactions. For example, pagan images need not be avoided if they are merely aesthetic rather than genuinely cultic. Other conceptual and legal distinctions create a neutral (noncultic) status or space in which Jews may interact with pagans and paganism.

The complex of rabbinic regulations concerning interaction between Jews and Gentiles—as both ethnic and religious others—are not designed to prevent all interactions between Jews and Gentiles or even to make such interaction difficult or cumbersome for Jews. Rather, these regulations are designed to prevent interaction *that would involve the observant Jew in a violation of the halakhah*. Setting out required standards and precautionary criteria, constructing legal distinctions and classifications, the rabbis negotiated a neutral space in which extensive commercial, business, and legal interactions—and even social contacts—between Gentiles and halakhically observant Jews could occur. Certainly there are some laws that bespeak a general distrust of Gentiles as dangerous and licentious, and warn against making oneself vulnerable to assault or injury at a Gentile's hands. On the whole, however, there is a tendency toward leniency and trust in the conduct of everyday life. Maintaining peaceful relations with Gentiles and avoiding their enmity are explicitly cited as relevant considerations in many legal rulings and determinations.

The rabbis do prohibit intermarriage between Jews and *unconverted* Gentiles. Nevertheless, the rabbinic position on intermarriage is not to be

---

v. Moshe Halbertal, "Co-existing with the Enemy: Jews and Pagans in the Mishnah" in G. N. Stanton and G. G. Stroumsa, eds., *Tolerance and Intolerance in Early Judaism and Christianity* (Cambridge: Cambridge University Press, 1998), pp. 163–168.

confused with the extreme separatism of Ezra or Second Temple groups as represented in some Qumran writings that prohibited both intermarriage and conversion (see Chapter 4). The rabbis reject Ezra's exclusively genealogical definition of Jewish identity and adopt a (primarily) moral-religious definition that creates a permeable group boundary and allows the assimilation of—and marriage to—converted foreigners. The genealogical or ethnic component of Jewish identity is muted but not entirely obliterated in rabbinic literature. Despite the rabbinic declaration that a convert is a Jew in all respects, the non-native origin of the convert is a relevant consideration in certain legal situations. Nevertheless, there is a broad tendency within rabbinic literature to remove the obstacles to full assimilation borne by persons of foreign descent—a tendency stronger in Palestinian sources than in Babylonian sources where a preoccupation with genealogy is more pronounced.

CONVERTS AND CONVERSION

Rabbinic law views involuntary conversion as illegitimate, but by the end of the rabbinic period, a process of voluntary conversion has became fully formalized and a conversion ceremony has been created. The ceremony assumes the initiative of the convert and an initial coolness on the part of the rabbinic authorities who interview him, in order to test the sincerity of his motives. Efforts are made to dissuade the potential convert by pointing out the many difficulties and disadvantages of life as a Jew. But should the convert persist, he is warmly accepted and taught a few of the commandments—so as not to be overwhelmed by the challenge of life lived under the Torah. This learning process continues until the convert is assimilated to his or her new way of life. One does not find in this rabbinic conversion ceremony the convert's confession of a formal creed or catechism.

There is some evidence for Jewish proselytism particularly in the first century of the Common Era, but rabbinic literature reflects little interest in or enthusiasm for this activity. Rabbinic abstention from active proselytizing reflects a certain ambivalence toward converts. There are individual traditions that express hostility to converts and question their sincerity. However, such views are distinctly in the minority, countered by numerous traditions that praise and bless the convert. The tannaitic work, Mekilta de-Rabbi Yishmael, contains a lengthy paean to the convert, and declares God's covenant with converts to be both unconditional and eternal.

CONCLUSION

By the end of late antiquity (early seventh century C.E.), the Jews were a diaspora people living in communities from Persia through Central Europe to Spain. These communities held certain features in common: The construction and maintenance of synagogues, a belief in the centrality of Torah, and a self-identification as members of a larger entity, Israel. A Jewish world had emerged whose shared symbols, texts, communal institutions, and practices marked it as distinct from the ambient non-Jewish world. These common features, combined with the rise of sages and the crystallization of rabbinic law, would create a socioreligious unity and interconnectedness across these many communities. This is not to say that there was no diversity among Jewish communities of this period, for indeed there was. It is simply to say that even as regional subcultures formed in the Middle Ages, certain standard features of Jewish life remained relatively constant.

CHAPTER 7

JUDAISM THROUGH THE AGES[1]

In the seventh and early eighth centuries, Muslim Arabs established a world empire that eventually reached from Persia in the east across North Africa and the Mediterranean to Spain in the west. The first Arab conquerors recognized the authority of the Jewish exilarch of Babylonia, who represented the Jews in the court of the caliph. Over time, the exilarch shared power with, and then was eclipsed by, the heads of the great rabbinical academies (*yeshivot*) of Iraq. These academies developed into institutions of advanced study and scholarship. Rulings issued in the name of an academy head (*gaon*) were a form of legislation that would eventually be viewed as binding throughout the diaspora.

The Muslim conquest did not extend into Central Europe, so that France, Germany, eastern Europe, and northern Spain remained under Christian control. Jews in the medieval period lived either under Muslim rule or under Christian rule. Jewish life under Muslim and Christian rule differed dramatically.

JEWS UNDER MEDIEVAL ISLAMIC RULE[ii]

Jews and other religious minorities under Arab rule were guaranteed religious toleration, judicial autonomy, and the protections of law as long as

---

i. For students interested in a fuller account of Judaism through the Ages than this brief survey can provide, see the relevant chapters in Robert M. Seltzer, *Jewish People, Jewish Thought* (New York: Macmillan Publishing Co., 1980).

ii. For an excellent and detailed comparison of Jewish life under medieval Muslim and Christian rule, see Mark R. Cohen, *Under Crescent and Cross: The Jews in the Middle Ages* (Princeton: Princeton University Press, 1994).

they recognized the supremacy of the Islamic state. These *dhimmi* (dependent peoples) had to conform to the terms of the Pact of Omar (ca. 800 C.E.) which enshrined their second-class, but nonetheless protected, status. On the whole, Jews adapted very well to the Islamic regime and the political, economic, and social changes it brought. Moreover, by adopting the Arabic language, Jews came into contact with forms of expression and cultural attitudes that led to a new phase of Jewish intellectual creativity. Beginning in the ninth century, the Islamic world was home to a revival of interest in Greek science, philosophy, and secular literature. Muslim jurisprudence and theology flourished amid a brilliant flowering of scholarship and the arts that reached its Golden Age in tenth- and eleventh-century Muslim Spain. Jews like Hisdai ibn Shaprut (915–970 C.E.) and Samuel ha-Nagid of Granada (993–1056 C.E.), served in the courts of the Muslim authorities, and combined an appreciation of general culture, natural science, and literary elegance with refined taste in secular and religious poetry, fidelity to rabbinic Judaism, and a lively interest in Jewish theology and philosophy. The early twelfth century was the climax of the Golden Age of Andalusian Jewry, producing outstanding Sephardic poets, philosophers, biblical commentators, theologians, and Talmudic scholars. A fine example is the Spanish philosopher and poet, Judah haLevi (1075–1141 C.E.).

Like their Muslim counterparts, leading intellectuals from these Sephardic Jewish communities (communities under Islamic rule) were interested in the rational clarification of religious beliefs and the systematic presentation of their faith. Some sought to defend Judaism against attacks by philosophically trained antagonists. In tenth- and eleventh-century Iraq, Saadiah ben Joseph, the Gaon of the *yeshivah* of Sura, defended rabbinic Judaism against the attacks of the Karaite movement (an anti-rabbinic movement of Jews who criticized Talmudic law and ridiculed the anthropomorphisms of midrashic literature). The most prominent medieval Jewish philosopher—Rabbi Moses ben Maimon (known by his acronym, the Rambam or as Maimonides, 1135–1204 C.E.), addressed his major work of philosophy, *Guide of the Perplexed*, to a student who had acquired only enough philosophic wisdom to leave him perplexed about his religious faith. The *Guide* is a masterful synthesis of Jewish thought and Aristotelianism and provides a philosophic interpretation of Scripture. Maimonides was also a great halakhist whose fourteen-volume classification by subject matter of the entire Talmudic and post-Talmudic halakhic literature (the *Mishneh Torah*) is a tour de force.

JEWS IN MEDIEVAL CHRISTIAN EUROPE

Jews were an anomaly in the rigidly hierarchical feudal structure of Medieval Christian society in France and Germany (an area known in Hebrew as Ashkenaz). Through special charters that granted the privilege of residence—generally in specified streets or neighborhoods—in return for financial and other obligations, Jewish communities secured the right to run their own affairs and maintain their own social and religious institutions, such as a charity box and sick fund, school, synagogue, council, court, public ritual bath, kosher butcher, and so on.

The Church's regulations concerning the Jews aimed at their subjugation and in 1215 C.E. Jews were ordered to distinguish themselves by special dress or a yellow badge in order to warn others of their "pernicious influence." Barred from many crafts and trades by Christian artisan guilds, some Ashkenazic Jews moved into moneylending. The characterization of Jews as demonic was fuelled by both religious and economic hatred, and led to the dual phenomena of expulsions and massacres in Christian Europe, generally preceded by a confiscation of all property and cancellation of all Christian debts to Jews. Jews were expelled from France in 1182 and 1306 and from England in 1290. The most devastating massacres were in Germany in 1298 (wiping out 140 Jewish communities), 1336, and 1348–1349 when the Black Plague was falsely attributed to Jews poisoning the wells of Europe.

In Christian Spain, anti-Jewish violence and degrading legislation led some Jews to convert, but in 1480, King Ferdinand and Queen Isabella established the Spanish Inquisition (a religious court charged with rooting out heresy) to investigate the charges that these Conversos (or Marranos) were secretly practicing Jewish ceremonies. Brutally tortured, thousands were burned at the stake. In 1492, Ferdinand and Isabella issued an edict making Judaism illegal in Spain. An estimated 100,000–150,000 Jews were expelled in the summer of 1492. Many went to Portugal only to be forcibly baptized five years later.

Ashkenazic Jewish communities under Christian rule did not share in the revival of classical culture that flourished in the Muslim-ruled world. However, Ashkenazic intellectuals also valued the tools of reason and applied strict standards of logic and argumentation in their close study of traditional texts—Bible and Talmud. Important centers of rabbinic scholarship appeared in the tenth century in the Rhineland cities of Mainz and Worms, and in France in Troyes and Sens. The first major literary figure of Ashkenazic Jewry was Solomon ben Isaac of Troyes (1040–1105 C.E.) known by his acronym, Rashi. His commentaries on the Bible and the Talmud became fundamental texts of an Ashkenazic Jewish education, and are still the standard commentaries for traditional Bible and Talmud studies.

The Ashkenazic ideal emphasized traditional Jewish learning and stood in contrast to the Sephardic admiration for universal culture, the study of science and philosophy, and the writing of secular as well as religious Hebrew poetry. Yet both communities produced great and comprehensive codes of Jewish law, the most influential being the Shulchan Aruch of R. Caro (1488–1575), a Sephardic Jew.

Folk Religion and Jewish Mysticism

While rabbinic Judaism and the study of Talmud preoccupied many middle- and upper-class Jews, particularly in Ashkenaz, folk religion—featuring practices and beliefs that diverged from central and standard features of classical rabbinic Judaism—is clearly attested in the medieval period. Nonrabbinic and even rabbinic Jews believed in demons and angels, and engaged in magical practices involving the Tetragrammaton and other secret names for God, even as rabbinic halakhah condemned such practices. The intense rationalism of medieval Jewish philosophy and Talmudic studies was also countered by the rise of Jewish mysticism, emphasizing immediate, personal, and suprarational experience of God. Jewish mystical pietists in twelfth- and thirteenth-century Germany (known as Hasidei Ashkenaz) combined passionate and selfless love of God, exacting and altruistic ethical standards and attention to heartfelt prayer, with ascetic practices, theurgy involving the mystical power of the letters of God's name, and a belief in demons. In twelfth-century Provence and thirteenth-century Spain, mystical/theurgical forms of Jewish religiosity would combine with classical rabbinic Judaism to produce the Kabbalah.

The Kabbalah conceived of God not just as a simple unity but as a structured organism with a specific inner configuration of ten attributes (*sefirot*; singular: *sefirah*) emanating from the *Ein Sof*, the unknowable and infinite "root of all roots" that is God. Evil is believed to be the direct result of an imbalance or rupture among the *sefirot*, an imbalance provoked by human sin, and set right by good deeds, fulfillment of the commandments, prayer performed with full intention (*kavvanah*) and mystical contemplation that can lead to *devekut* (cleaving to God). This process of cosmic repair, that restores the flow of divine light to earth, is known as *tikkun*. Thus, in Kabbalah, human sin locks God in a state of disrepair from which he must be redeemed by human action (an inversion of the Christian myth of sinful man requiring redemption by God). Other kabbalistic beliefs include reincarnation, the transmigration of souls, and the valorization of sexual intercourse as a sacrament mirroring the union among the divine *sefirot*. Many of these ideas are found in *The Zohar*, by the Spanish kabbalist Moses de Leon (late thirteenth century).

The Kabbalah contains a strong element of mythological thinking, especially in its depiction of God as an organic process affected by and affecting the mundane world. At a time when Jews were increasingly the powerless victims of hatred and persecution, standing outside the political mainstream, passive observers of the drama of general society, the Kabbalah provided an important counter-scenario. It depicted human life as transitory but supremely important because the health and inner harmony of God and the universe depended on the actions of each and every person. Evil and disharmony could be overcome through halakhic observance, ritual, and prayer.

The Kabbalah spread quickly and in sixteenth-century Safed in the Galilee, a young mystic named Isaac Luria (1534–1572 C.E.) reformulated this esoteric system in a manner that placed a heightened emphasis on messianic redemption. The religious practices of Lurianic Kabbalah included midnight prayers to mourn the destruction of the Temple, public confession of sins and intense asceticism. Another offshoot of Kabbalah that arose around an itinerant folk healer named Israel ben Eleazar or the Baal Shem Tov ("Master of the Good Name," 1700–1760) was eighteenth-century Hasidism. This movement captured the hearts of Jews in Russia, Poland, parts of Hungary, and Rumania. The message of the Hasidic masters was: that God is present and directly accessible in the world; that God is experienced and worshipped *not* in sorrow and ascetic suffering; that even the most irretrievable evil is capable of and longs for redemption; and that each Jew has an essential role to play in the transformation of the mundane into the holy. The new Hasidic pietism drew on the Kabbalah in a way that overcame its esoteric character. The Kabbalah was popularized: Its psychological and social aspects were emphasized while its speculative and messianic elements were muted.

Rabbinic authorities were openly hostile to Hasidic followers, criticizing their fervor and ecstatic worship and their willingness to deviate from strict norms as religious emotion dictated. They disliked the figure of the *zaddik*, or charismatic righteous man, who held supreme religious authority, and was seen as a medium of revelation. But Hasidism was becoming entrenched in the Jewish communities of Poland and the Ukraine. It split into smaller groups, each led by a local charismatic *rebbe* intimately involved in the lives of his followers, so that by the early nineteenth-century Hasidic dynasties had formed. In Lithuania, Lubavich or Habad Hasidism emphasized a distinctive blend of Kabbalistic speculation and rabbinic learning. Ironically, despite Hasidism's unorthodox antitraditionalist roots, it has come to represent orthodoxy (even ultraorthodoxy) in contemporary Jewish life.

MODERN JEWISH IDENTITY—RELIGION OR ETHNOS?

In the modern world, the religious and national elements of Jewish identity were torn asunder, challenged, and transformed, giving rise to a widening spectrum of Jewish ideologies, philosophies, and organizations seeking to define what it is to be Jewish. The religious component of Judaism was challenged by the secularization of society that occurred in the modern period and profoundly affected all religions. The national component of Jewish identity was challenged by the emergence of nation states. The term "nation" in the modern period no longer referred to small ethnic groups (e.g., the Jewish people). It now referred to a political entity with a government, all of whose residents were citizens. Emancipation from the disabilities and exclusions of feudal Europe left many nineteenth-century Jews wondering why they should continue to identify with the Jewish people when they could finally be full citizens of Germany, France, Holland, or other European states. Not only did their Jewish identity seem obsolete, it subjected them to persistent social discrimination. Many modern Jews chose to assimilate, often through conversion.

Many others, however, asserted that Jewish identity was not primarily ethnic or national in character, but religious. To be Jewish was to be a member of a religious denomination. One could therefore be a loyal German national, French national, English national—of the Jewish *religion*. For these Jews being modern meant acculturating, that is, adapting to and acquiring the culture of the fatherland, while retaining Jewish identity in so far as their religious faith was concerned.

The illustrious German-Jewish thinker Moses Mendelssohn (1729–1786 C.E.) was representative of those who made the transition from ghetto to modernity without breaking away from the Jewish people (acculturation without assimilation). He held a vision of Enlightenment Jewry participating in the cultural life of the wider world and continuing in the tradition of their forebears—a "double yoke" placed upon them by Providence.

But many Jews wondered why they should keep up this double duty, this Jewish particularism? This question, plus concerns over the rationality of Jewish belief and practices, sparked ideological controversies in mid-nineteenth-century German Jewry that led to the three modern forms of Judaism: Reform, modern Orthodoxy, and Conservative (or Positive-Historical) Judaism. Reformers wanted to remake Judaism as a fully modern religion consistent with German-Christian patterns of worship and decorum. Services were conducted in German, not Hebrew; sermons and choral singing were introduced and all references to Jewish national identity were removed from the liturgy. The Reform thinker Abraham Geiger (1810–1874) urged the rejection of outmoded practices and rituals not consistent with what he perceived to be the living, vital core of Judaism.

Traditionalists denounced these reforms as violations of the halakhah. An eloquent spokesman for the modern orthodox opponents of Reform was Samson Raphael Hirsch (b. 1808). Hirsch promoted a harmonious synthesis of loyalty to Jewish religious practice and openness to secular European civilization. Hirsch criticized the reformers for diminishing Judaism's duties for the sake of the convenience and comfort of modern Jews rather than elevating Jews to a Judaism newly comprehended and fulfilled with utmost energy.

Positive Historical Judaism led by Zecharias Frankel (1801–1875) was a European movement that opposed Reform's sweeping innovations on the one hand, and the modern orthodox view of Jewish tradition as largely unchanging. It became the basis of the Conservative movement in the United States.

While the three movements had different views on the need for modernization, the nature of revelation, and the importance of Jewish peoplehood/ethnicity, all were optimistic about the future of Judaism. But a large-scale resurgence of open hostility toward the Jews in the 1870s and 1880s shook this faith in the ultimate integration of Jews into modern civilization. Modern anti-Semitism was essentially a postemancipation backlash against Jewish success upon entering into mainstream European society, a sign that Jews were still considered alien. Some European Jews who had tried to see their Judaism as a religion only, and not as one aspect of a larger ethnic culture, wanting instead to be German, French, Dutch citizens of the Jewish faith, began to feel they had deluded themselves. A wide range of parties and movements sprang up all emphasizing Jewish nationalism (often to the exclusion of religious tradition) in one way or another. In 1882, Leon Pinsker urged Jews to emancipate themselves by creating a separate Jewish homeland. In 1897, Theodor Herzl convened the First Zionist Congress in Basle, Switzerland, which called for a Jewish national home in Palestine recognized by international law. In the wake of Russian pogroms and continued anti-Semitism in Europe, successive waves of Jewish immigrants entered Palestine, founding agricultural settlements and establishing an association of armed watchmen, a new Jewish city (Tel Aviv), a network of Jewish schools, a variety of modern Jewish political parties, mutual aid societies, and a periodical press. The ground was being laid for a modern Jewish homeland in Palestine. The horrific events of World War II and Hitler's extermination of six million European Jews (the Holocaust) fueled the drive for a Jewish state and in 1948, the state of Israel came into being, despite strong Palestinian and Arab resistance.

Post-Holocaust Theology

The experience of the Holocaust radically transformed Jewish life and called into question the three pillars of Judaism: God, Torah, and Israel. Some Jews, like Richard Rubenstein, asserted that the only honest response to Hitler's death camps was the rejection of God and an open recognition of the importance of religious ritual, symbolism, and community in creating value and nourishing life. Emil Fackenheim concurred that attempts to explain the Holocaust as punishment for sin, as an opportunity for martyrdom, or as a test of faith were inadequate and obscene. Nevertheless, Fackenheim insisted that the Holocaust did not prove God is dead. Indeed, post-Holocaust Jews must reaffirm their commitment to the God of Israel, for to despair of the God of Israel was to aid Hitler in the accomplishment of his demonic goal to eradicate Jews and Judaism from history.

MAJOR TRENDS IN MODERN JEWISH THOUGHT

Jewish thought in the modern period was influenced by trends in general philosophy, first the work of Immanuel Kant in the eighteenth century, and later the existentialist movement of the nineteenth and twentieth centuries. Existentialism was a philosophical movement that emphasized concrete and personal experience of the world over abstract and static rational theories about the world. The theology of Franz Rosenzweig (1886–1929) owed much to the influence of existentialism. In his book *The Star of Redemption*, Rosenzweig criticized philosophy's effort to reduce the universe to one single underlying essence, in defiance of our experience of the world as complex. In truth, he argues, we experience three main constituent elements of the universe—humans, world, and God. Biblical religion brings the three into correlation. The world is dependent on God's creative power. God reveals himself to humans in love. The revelation of God's love awakens a response in humans expressed in their redemptive love of others in the world.

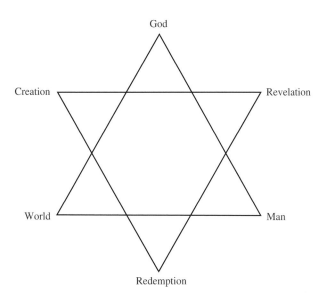

Franz Rosenzweig's Star of Redemption.

The leading twentieth-century Jewish existentialist is Martin Buber (1878–1965) who developed his "philosophy of dialogue" in the 1923 work *I and Thou*. Buber describes two primary attitudes that the self may adopt toward the world. The first he calls I-It, in which the self (I) remains detached from the other (a person or other entity) which is objectified. But in an I-Thou encounter two subjects stand over against one another totally present, responding unpredictably, and immediately with their whole beings. The main source of evil in human existence is an overabundance of the I-It, and balance must be restored through true dialogue in which subjects encounter one another as equals. For Buber, God is the eternal Thou known not through objective reasoning, but through I-Thou encounters—not only with God himself but also with persons, animals, nature, and even works of art. These encounters with the Eternal Thou are revelation, and through them one is brought to affirm the meaningfulness of life.

Abraham Yehoshua Heschel (1907–1972) was another Jewish thinker concerned about the impersonality of modern life and the sterility of formal theology. For Heschel, the crisis of modernity could be overcome by living in a holy dimension, experiencing the mysterious divine presence that suffuses the world, approaching our lives with a sense of wonder and awe. Because halakhah's fundamental demand is the sanctification of every aspect of life, the life of halakhic observance is particularly attuned to the presence of the ineffable.

An important American Jewish thinker of the twentieth century was Mordechai Kaplan whose book *Judaism as a Civilization* (1934) criticized existing Jewish movements (Orthodox, Conservative, and Reform) and called for a reconstruction of Jewish life. Kaplan's Reconstruction movement defines Judaism as an *evolving religious civilization*: A civilization, because the Jewish people possesses a full religious *and* secular heritage of literature, law, art, music, philosophy, ethics, and more; religious, because the special genius of Jewish civilization is in its articulation of the religious dimension of human life; and evolving, because Judaism grows and changes through time, with tradition serving as a guide and not a master.

A more recent and transdenominational movement, known as Jewish Renewal, emphasizes the spiritual vitality characteristic of Hasidism while embracing modern values—such as gender equality, racial equality, and the affirmation of other faith-communities—as well as commitment to social action and world healing.

CONCLUSION

From an ancient Israelite heritage, the religion of Judaism emerged in late antiquity and spread to the four corners of the earth. Through the Middle Ages and into the modern period, Judaism has developed into a complex tradition exhibiting great regional diversity. Nevertheless, common to most varieties of Jewish religious expression is the determined struggle to maintain faith in the basic goodness of creation and human beings, in the meaningfulness of earthly existence, and in the power of moral action to sanctify human life. Occasionally, it is a struggle that falters, more often it is a struggle that defines and nourishes, even as it tends to no clear resolution.

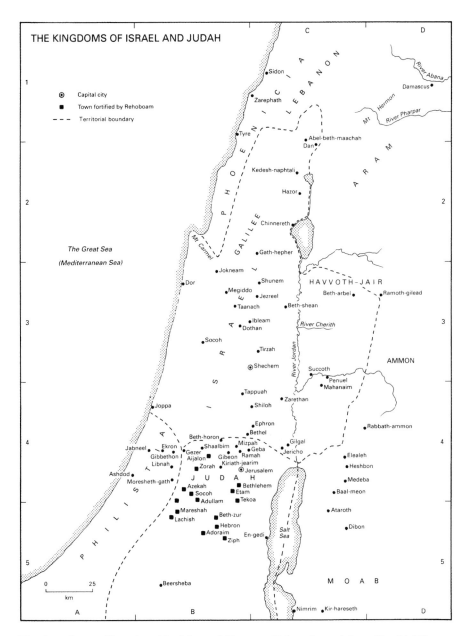

The kingdoms of Israel and Judah ca. 860 B.C.E. Taken from *Atlas of Jewish History*, Dan Cohn-Sherbok, © 1994 Routledge. Reproduced by permission of Taylor and Francis Books UK.

The Black Obelisk of Shalmaneser III of Assyria (859–825 B.C.E.) depicts scenes of tribute being brought by the representatives of various countries including king Jehu of Israel. © The Trustees of the British Museum.

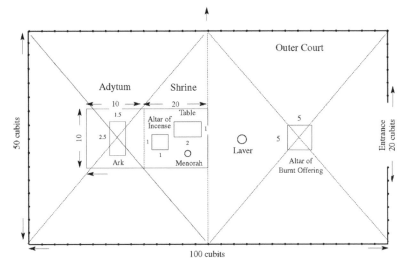

Outer Court

Adytum   Shrine

| 10 → | ← 20 → |
| 1.5 | Table |

Altar of Incense

Menorah

Ark

Laver

Altar of
Burnt Offering

50 cubits

Entrance
20 cubits

100 cubits

Schematic diagram of the Israelite sanctuary as described in the Pentateuch. Taken from *LEVITICUS: A Continental Commentary* by Jacob Milgrom, copyright © 2004 Augsburg Fortress. Used by permission.

Cave Number 4 in a cliff overlooking wadi Qumran, one of eleven caves to yield the manuscripts and manuscript fragments known as the "Dead Sea Scrolls." These materials were the library of a separatist community that occupied the area from the second century B.C.E. until the war with Rome in the first century C.E. Courtesy of Library of Congress.

The Cyrus Cylinder, fifth century B.C.E. The cylinder's inscription describes events from the reign of Cyrus, King of Persia, including his decree allowing the Israelites to return to their place of origin. © The Trustees of the British Museum.

Model of Herod's Temple. Taken from *Introduction to the Hebrew Bible with CD-ROM* by John J. Collins, copyright © 2004 Augsburg Fortress. Used by permission.

Panel from the Arch of Titus, built near the Roman forum in 81 C.E. to commemorate Titus' capture and sack of Jerusalem in 70 C.E. The scene depicted here shows a triumphal procession bearing treasures from the Jerusalem Temple, including the seven-branched golden candlestick (*menorah*). akg-images.

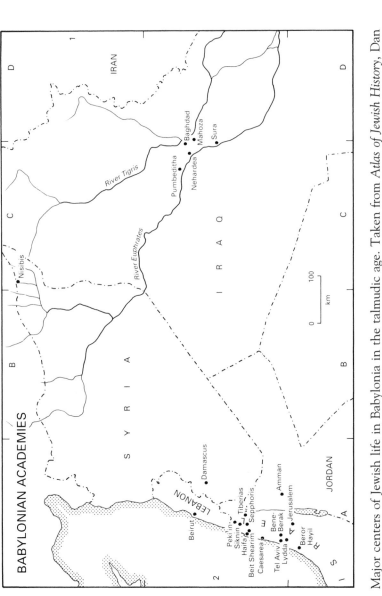

Major centers of Jewish life in Babylonia in the talmudic age. Taken from *Atlas of Jewish History*, Dan Cohn-Sherbok, © 1994 Routledge. Reproduced by permission of Taylor and Francis Books UK.

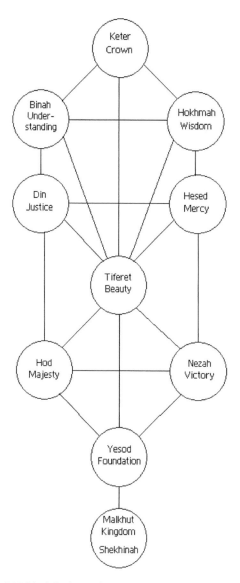

The ten sefirot of Kabbalah (Jewish mysticism). Courtesy of Benjamin Della Rocca.

Table 1 The twenty-four canonical books of the Hebrew Bible (TaNaKH). Abbreviations for each book are provided in brackets.

TORAH ("Instruction")
    1. Genesis (Bereshit) [Gen]
    2. Exodus (Shemot) [Ex]
    3. Leviticus (Vayiqra) [Lev]
    4. Numbers (BaMidbar) [Num]
    5. Deuteronomy (Devarim) [Deut]

NEVI'IM ("Prophets")
  A. Nevi'im Rishonim ("Former prophets")
    6. Joshua (Yehoshua) [Josh]
    7. Judges (Shophetim) [Jud]
    8. 1 and 2 Samuel (Shmuel) [1 Sam; 2 Sam]
    9. 1 and 2 Kings (Melakhim) [1 Kgs; 2 Kgs]
  B. Nevi'im Aharonim ("Latter Prophets")
    10. Isaiah (Yeshayahu) [Isa]
    11. Jeremiah (Yirmiyahu) [Jer]
    12. Ezekial (Yehezqel) [Ezek]
    13. The Twelve (Tere Asar)
        Hosea (Hoshea) [Hos]
        Joel (Yoel) [Joel]
        Amos (Amos) [Amos]
        Obadiah (Ovadyah) [Obad]
        Jonah (Yonah) [Jon]
        Micah (Micah) [Mic]
        Nahum (Nahum) [Nah]
        Habakkuk (Havakkuk) [Hab]
        Zephaniah (Tsephanyah) [Zeph]
        Haggai (Haggai) [Hag]
        Zechariah (Zekharyah) [Zech]
        Malachi (Malakhi) [Mal]

KHETUVIM ("Writings")
    14. Psalms (Tehillim) [Pss]
    15. Job (Iyyov) [Job]
    16. Proverbs (Mishle) [Prov]
    17. Ruth (Rut) [Ruth]
    18. Song of Songs (Shir haShirim) [Song]
    19. Ecclesiastes (Qohelet) [Eccl]
    20. Lamentations (Ekhah) [Lam]
    21. Esther (Ester) [Est]
    22. Daniel (Daniel) [Dan]
    23. Ezra-Nehemiah (Ezra-Nehemyah) [Ezra; Neh]
    24. 1 and 2 Chronicles (Divre haYamim) [1 Chron; 2 Chron]

Table 2 The orders and tractates of the Mishnah and Talmuds showing the number of chapters in each tractate, the tractate's sequence within the two Talmuds, and the presence or absence of gemara commentary.

Order	Mishnah Tractate Name Number of Chapters Topic	Babylonian Talmud Sequence G=gemara	Palestinian Talmud Sequence G=gemara
Zera'im	Agricultural Laws		
	1. Berakhot (9) – Benedictions	1G	1G
	2. Pe'ah (8) – Gleanings of the Field	2	2G
	3. Demai (7) – Doubtfully Tithed Produce	3	3G
	4. Kila'im (9) – Forbidden Mixtures	4	4G
	5. Shevi'it (10) – Sabbatical Year	5	5G
	6. Terumot (11) – Priestly Portions	6	6G
	7. Ma'aserot (5) – Tithes for Levites and the Poor	7	7G
	8. Ma'aser Sheni (5) – Second Tithe	8	8G
	9. Hallah (4) – Dough Offering	9	9G
	10. Orlah (3) – Fruit of Young Trees	10	10G
	11. Bikkurim (3) – First Fruits	11	11G
Mo'ed	Festivals and Sacred Times		
	1. Shabbat (24) – The Sabbath	1G	1G
	2. Eruvin (10) – Sabbath Limits	2G	2G
	3. Pesahim (10) – Passover	3G	3G
	4. Shekalim (8) – Half-Shekel Offering	11	5G
	5. Yoma (8) – Yom Kippur (Day of Atonement)	9G	4G
	6. Sukkah (5) – Festival of Sukkot	10G	6G
	7. Betsah (Yom Tov) (5) – Festival Laws	4G	8G
	8. Rosh haShanah (4) – New Year Festival	7G	7G
	9. Ta'anit (4) – Fast Days	8G	9G
	10. Megillah (4) – Purim	12G	10G
	11. Mo'ed Katan (3) – Intermediate Days of Festivals	6G	12G
	12. Hagigah (3) – Festival Sacrifices	5G	11G
Nashim	Women		
	1. Yevamot (16) – Levirate Marriage	1G	1G
	2. Ketubot (13) – Marriage Contracts	2G	3G
	3. Nedarim (11) – Vows	5G	4G
	4. Nazir (9) – Nazirites	6G	6G
	5. Gittin (9) – Divorce	4G	5G
	6. Sotah (9) – Suspected Adulteress	7G	2G
	7. Qiddushin (4) – Marriage	3G	7G

Nezikin	Damages (Civil Law)		
	1. Bava Qamma (10) – Damages	1G	1G
	2. Bava Metsi'a (10) – Civil Law	2G	2G
	3. Bava Batra (10) – Property Law	3G	3G
	4. Sanhedrin (11) – Courts	5G	4G
	5. Makkot (3) – Punishment of Flogging	6G	5G
	6. Shevu'ot (8) – Oaths	7G	6G
	7. Eduyyot (8) – Attested Legal Teachings	9	–
	8. Avoda Zara (5) – Idolatry	4G	7G
	9. Avot (5) – Sayings of the Fathers	10	–
	10. Horayot (3) – Erroneous Court Decisions	8G	8G
Qodashim	Sacrifices		
	1. Zebahim (14) – Animal Sacrifices	1G	–
	2. Menahot (13) – Meal Offerings	2G	–
	3. Hullin (12) – Slaughter of Profane Animals	4G	–
	4. Bekhorot (9) – Firstborn Animals	3G	–
	5. Arakhin (9) – Vows of Valuation	5G	–
	6. Temurah (7) – Substitution of Offerings	6G	–
	7. Keritot (6) – Penalty of Extirpation	7G	–
	8. Me'ilah (6) – Misappropriation of Sacred Offerings	8G	–
	9. Tamid (7) – Daily Sacrifices	10G	–
	10. Middot (5) – Dimensions of the Temple	11	–
	11. Qinnim (3) – Bird Offerings	9	–
Toharot	Purities		
	1. Kelim (30) – Impurity of Vessels	2	–
	2. Ohalot (14) – Impurity of Tents	3	–
	3. Nega'im (14) – Scale-Disease	4	–
	4. Parah (12) – The Red Heifer	5	–
	5. Toharot (10) – Ritual Purification	6	–
	6. Miqva'ot (10) – Ritual Baths	7	–
	7. Niddah (10) – Menstrual Impurity	1G	1G
	8. Makhshirin (6) – Liquids Conveying Susceptibility to Impurity	8	–
	9. Zavim (5) – Genital Fluxes	9	–
	10. Tevul Yom (4) – Impurity after Immersion before Sunset	10	–
	11. Yadayim (4) – Impurity of the Hands	11	–
	12. Uqtsin (3) – Impurity of Some Plant Parts	12	–

BIOGRAPHIES: LITERARY AND HISTORICAL FIGURES

INTRODUCTION

Conventional biographical sketches of central figures in the emergence of Judaism from ancient Israel cannot be written due to the nature and limitations of our sources. Scholars hold radically opposed views on the historical usefulness of the biblical traditions. Some dismiss the patriarchs, the matriarchs, and the central characters in the story of the Exodus and entry into Canaan as the fabrications of a much later era. Even those who maintain that the stories have ancient roots acknowledge that they are literary rather than historical compositions.

The increasing historical verification provided by extra-biblical sources after the turn of the first millennium B.C.E. affords a greater confidence in the actual historical existence of key figures (such as the kings of Israel and Judah, prophets like Jeremiah and the later priest-scribe Ezra). Nevertheless, extracting reliable biographical information from the biblical materials concerning these figures is, again, fraught with difficulty. In the Hellenistic period we have good information on Philo and even better information on Josephus—both of whom authored works that have been preserved for us. But rabbinic figures present familiar problems—our information about Hillel, Shammai, R. Akiva, R. Ishmael, and other sages comes from sources that are not historiographical in nature.

Because conventional biographies of the key figures in biblical Israel and later Judaism are in most cases not possible, we offer here a summary of the *literary representation* of several important figures. For biblical characters, we describe the character's depiction in the Biblical text followed by a brief description of his or her depiction in postbiblical tradition and classical Judaism.

These sketches are presented in chronological order, beginning with the most legendary and literary figures—the patriarchs and matriarchs of the Hebrew Bible— and ending with figures whose actual existence is more certain but whose biographical details remain, for the most part, unavailable or unverifiable.

PATRIARCHS AND MATRIARCHS: ABRAHAM, SARAH, ISAAC, REBEKAH, JACOB, LEAH, RACHEL

The patriarchs and matriarchs are the founding fathers and mothers of biblical Israel and, ultimately, the Jewish people. The Hebrew Bible and later Jewish tradition limit the title "patriarchs" (*avot*) to Abraham, Isaac, and Jacob and the title "matriarchs" (*imahot*) to Sarah, Rebekah, Leah, and Rachel. The patriarchs are represented as descendants of Noah's son Shem through Eber, nomads originating in Ur and moving with their flocks of asses to Haran, Canaan, the Negev, and Egypt.

Abraham. Originally called Abram ("exalted father"), Abraham (popularly understood to mean "the father of multitudes") appears as a semi-nomadic tent dweller whose wanderings took him through the central hill country of Palestine and the Negev. With his numerous flocks, silver, gold, slaves, and private army, Abraham is depicted as a figure of some stature negotiating alliances and dealing with powerful figures and kings. He is most strongly associated with the divine promises of nationhood and a national territory in Canaan—promises solemnized in what has come to be known as the Abrahamic Covenant and symbolized by the mark of circumcision that is instituted with Abraham. The biblical stories depict Abraham as an exemplar of faith because he believed in God's promises despite their seeming absurdity, and as a model of obedience because he stood ready to bind and sacrifice his son Isaac at God's command. Postbiblical Jewish tradition builds on these themes, representing the Binding of Isaac as only the last in a series of ten trials establishing Abraham's faith and obedience. In the midrash, Abraham is portrayed as the first monotheist and "friend of God," a zealot for Yahweh who destroyed the idols in his father's house as the first battle in a campaign against idolatry. A true and faithful follower of Yahweh, Abraham is said to have obeyed all of the commandments, even though they had not yet been revealed through Moses. Legends praise him for his hospitality to strangers and success in proselytizing. In rabbinic tradition, Abraham is referred to as both priest and prophet.

Sarah. Wife of Abraham and mother of Isaac, Sarah (at first Sarai, meaning "princess") is the first of Israel's four matriarchs, three of whom struggled not only to conceive but subsequently to secure the inheritance of the divine promise for a particular son. Her introduction in Genesis 12 is accompanied by a pronouncement of her barrenness. Whether this datum is intended to magnify the virtue of Abraham's belief in the divine promise of progeny or conversely to explain his readiness to deliver Sarah to foreign kings (Pharaoh and King Abimelech of Gerar) and procure offspring by other means, is unclear. In any event, Sarah's barrenness prompts her to offer her Egyptian handmaid Hagar to Abraham (such surrogacy was common in the Ancient Near Eastern and Egypt) who bears a son (Ishmael) in Sarah's stead. Later, Sarah miraculously conceives, as had been previously promised by a divine visitor, and gives birth to Isaac whose name, a play on "laughter," reflects Sarah's laughing response to the divine visitor's prediction that she would bear a son. Hagar's high-handed treatment of Sarah creates tension and leads ultimately to the expulsion of the slave-girl and her child. In postbiblical Jewish tradition, Sarah is extolled for her extraordinary beauty. She is described as a prophetess and is said to have joined Abraham in extending hospitality and in proselytizing. Many traditions attribute her death to shock upon hearing of the Binding of Isaac.

Isaac. The second of the patriarchs, born of Abraham and Sarah when they were one hundred years old and ninety years old respectively, Isaac—whose name is derived from the root for "laughter"—is understood to be the fulfillment of the divine promise of progeny to Abraham. It is Isaac who inherits the blessings of the Abrahamic covenant. Little is reported of Isaac—no details of his childhood are given other than his birth and the feast celebrated on the occasion of his weaning. Like Abraham, Isaac was a semi-nomad, though his wandering was confined to southern Canaan. The central episode in Isaac's life is reported in Genesis 22, when Abraham takes Isaac on God's command, to Mount Moriah (held by tradition to be the site of the future Temple) to offer him as a sacrifice. Isaac is bound to an altar but spared at the last moment when an angel intervenes. His passive character is evident in the story of his betrothal and marriage to the lively and active Rebekah. In his declining years, blind and enfeebled, Isaac is tricked by his wife and younger son Jacob and inadvertently gives the blessing and birthright of his elder son Esau, to Jacob. Postbiblical tradition emphasizes Isaac's virtue by imagining his willing submission to the sacrificial knife. Although the sacrifice was not carried out, numerous traditions assert that merit accrued to Isaac and his descendants for the deed. Likened to the Passover offering, Isaac's virtual sacrifice is cited as the reason for God's election of the Israelites, his forgiveness of the sin of the golden calf and other acts of beneficence. Because God's mercy is aroused by the sight of Isaac's ashes heaped up on the altar, the Binding of Isaac is mentioned in prayers of penitence and figures centrally in the liturgy for Rosh HaShanah (New Year's Day) ushering in the ten-day period of repentance that culminates in Yom Kippur (the Day of Atonement).

Rebekah. The sole wife of Isaac, mother of twins Esau and Jacob and sister of Laban, Rebekah appears from the first as an energetic and purposeful woman. Seeking a wife for his son Isaac, Abraham sends his gift-laden servant to kin in Aramaean territory to the east. There the servant encounters Rebekah, who impresses him with her hospitality and industry. She agrees to the marriage and returns with the servant to Canaan. Like other biblical matriarchs, Rebekah is barren for many years, conceiving only after Isaac's prayer on her behalf. Experiencing great pain during the pregnancy, Rebekah is told by God that twins struggle in her womb. Each will become a great nation and the elder will serve the younger. This story may serve to explain Rebekah's preference for Jacob and her scheme to trick Isaac into giving the blessing of the firstborn and the inheritance of the divine promise to Jacob rather than Esau. Rebekah protects Jacob from Esau's wrath by sending him to her brother Laban, ostensibly to seek a wife. In postbiblical tradition, Rebekah is praised as a prophetess, insightful enough to understand that the birthright should fall to Jacob rather than the wicked Esau.

Jacob. The younger son of Isaac and Rebekah and twin brother of Esau, Jacob—whose name is changed to Israel after a nighttime struggle with a divine being—is the eponymous ancestor of the Israelites. The identification of Jacob, the individual, with Israel, the nation, begins in the account of his uterine struggle for primacy. Jacob emerges from the womb holding on to the heel of his brother Esau as if to supplant him (the name Jacob is a play on both "heel" and "supplant"). Isaac prefers Esau while Rebekah prefers Jacob and joins him in one of two schemes to acquire his brother's birthright. Disguised as Esau, Jacob tricks his blind father into giving him the blessing of the first born, an act which arouses a murderous enmity in Esau. Jacob flees to the home of his maternal uncle Laban in Aramaean territory experiencing a dream theophany on the way in which God reiterates the patriarchal promise of progeny, land, blessing, and protection. Laban proves to be as much of a trickster as Jacob, and after twenty years of service to his uncle, Jacob returns to Canaan, with his retinue of wives (Leah and Rachel), concubines (Bilhah and Zilpah), children, flocks, and household belongings. Reconciled with Esau, the remaining days of Jacob's life are filled with tragedy, from the death of his beloved wife Rachel, to the rape of his daughter Dinah, and the events precipitated by the great enmity between his favorite son Joseph and his other sons.

In postbiblical Jewish tradition, Jacob's life is read as symbolic and even predictive of the nation's later history. Those who opposed Jacob are read as figures for the enemies of the nation of Israel—Esau and Laban are understood to be Rome, in both its pagan and Christian versions. Some traditions glorify Jacob as the quiet man, the tent-dweller who devoted himself to a life of learning, and denigrate Esau, the crude and dissipated idolater and shedder of blood. Nevertheless, in addition to apologetics, one can find criticism of Jacob in rabbinic literature. His deception of Isaac, his treatment of Esau, his disdain for Leah, his marriage to two sisters, and his unseemly favoritism for Joseph draw disapproving comment. For all his moral and very human complexity, Jacob is described in rabbinic tradition as the greatest of the patriarchs, elevated by God to a position just a little below the angels.

Leah. Daughter of Laban (Rebekah's brother) and elder sister of co-wife Rachel, Leah is married to Jacob when her father substitutes her for Rachel on the latter's wedding night. Biblical stories reflect the competition between the sisters to provide sons for their husband Jacob, either personally or through the agency of servant-girls offered as concubines. The offspring of Jacob by Leah, Rachel, and the servants—Zilpah and Bilhah—are the progenitors of the twelve tribes of Israel. Leah, the elder sister with distinctive eyes (whether they are weak or sensitive and tender is unclear) is unloved, but like many unloved biblical wives she is fertile and gives birth to Reuben, Simeon, Levi, Judah, Issachar, Zebulun, and a daughter Dinah. Her servant Zilpah gives birth to Gad and Asher. The two hereditary institutions of priesthood and monarchy can be traced back to two of Leah's sons—Levi and Judah, respectively. In postbiblical tradition, Leah's distinctive eyes draw considerable comment, as does the fact that she was the instrument by which Jacob received measure for measure punishment for deceiving his father by disguising himself as his elder brother.

Rachel. Daughter of Laban (Rebekah's brother) and younger sister of co-wife Leah, Rachel is married to Jacob. Jacob and Rachel meet at a well and share the only romantic love between man and woman to be explicitly mentioned in biblical narrative. Jacob works for his uncle Laban for seven years in exchange for Rachel's hand in marriage. On the wedding night, Laban substitutes Rachel's elder sister Leah, and grants Rachel to Jacob only when Jacob agrees to work an additional seven years. Beautiful and beloved, Rachel is barren for many years. Frustration over her state is exacerbated by the great fertility of her sister and on one occasion she impulsively demands that Jacob give her children or she will die. Rachel gives her servant Bilhah to Jacob as concubine, and Bilhah gives birth to Dan and Naftali. Finally, Rachel gives birth to Joseph. Jacob decides to return to his homeland. Unbeknownst to Jacob, Rachel steals and hides her father's household gods and thus becomes the unintended object of Jacob's curse against the thief. As the journey continues, Rachel dies giving birth to Benjamin and is deeply mourned by her husband. Jacob's deep love for Rachel is transferred to her children, a fact that creates rivalry and open enmity between the sons of Rachel (Joseph and Benjamin) and Jacob's other sons. In postbiblical literature, we find the idea that Rachel agreed to the substitution of Leah on her own wedding night so that the elder sister should not be ashamed. Picking up on Jeremiah 31:15 ("A voice is heard in Ramah; Lamentation, and bitter weeping—Rachel weeping for her children; She refuses to be comforted for her children, because they are no more"), several traditions develop the idea of a grieving Rachel winning divine mercy for her orphaned children.

PERIOD OF THE EXODUS AND ENTRY INTO CANAAN: MOSES, AARON, MIRIAM, JOSHUA

Moses. As noted in the introduction, the historicity of Moses cannot be ascertained. We therefore confine ourselves to a brief summary of the life and character of Moses as it is presented in the Bible and in postbiblical and rabbinic literature. The son of Amram and Yocheved of the tribe of Levi, Moses was born in Egypt during a period of oppression of the Hebrew slaves by Pharaoh. The story of Moses' birth and exposure to the Nile river contains generic motifs found in the birth story of Sargon of Akkad, Cyrus of Persia, and the god Horus. Yet, the ascription of foreign birth to a national hero and the presence of numerous Egyptian names among the early Levites (the name Moses is itself Egyptian), suggests some historical basis for the traditional association of Moses with Egypt. Moses is raised in the house of Pharaoh after being rescued from the Nile by Pharaoh's daughter. Several incidents in his youth foreshadow his role as liberator of the oppressed. When he sees a Hebrew slave being beaten he intervenes and kills the aggressor, a deed that causes him to flee to Midian in the desert. There he drives off some rough shepherds harassing a group of women drawing water from a well. He marries one of the women—Zipporah, daughter of the Midianite chieftain variously identified as Reuel, Hobab, and Jethro. While tending flocks in Midian, Moses experiences a theophany. He sees a bush that burns but is not consumed, and hears a voice that commands him to redeem Israel from Egypt. In this narrative, God identifies himself as Yahweh, leading scholars to associate Moses with the introduction of Yahwism proper. The antiquity of Yahweh-worship and the association of Yahweh with a mountain (Horeb/Sinai) are difficult historical questions. But according to the biblical narrative, Moses is understood to be the first messenger of Yahweh sent with signs to effect his will.

The Exodus story features a battle of wills between Moses and Pharaoh, with Moses finally leading the Israelites across a miraculously divided Sea of Reeds to safety. The Israelites journey to Mount Horeb/Sinai where Moses serves as the intermediary in the conclusion of a covenant between Yahweh and the newly formed nation. He is said to write down the detailed terms of the covenant and also to deposit a copy of the Decalogue carved on stone tablets in a special Ark of the Covenant. Moses continues to receive additional ritual, religious, and moral injunctions and later consults God in four difficult cases in which the law is not clear. In addition to his role as the mediator of God's laws and warnings to Israel, Moses is credited with establishing several central Israelite institutions: The administrative organization of the people into units of tens, fifties, hundreds, and thousands governed and judged by appointed officers in accordance with the advice tendered by his father-in-law Jethro; the construction of the tabernacle (portable Sanctuary); the establishment of the system of sacrifical worship; the inauguration of the Israelite cult and cultic calendar; and the investiture of the priesthood.

Critical scholarship points to the many inconsistencies and chronological difficulties that inhere in the traditions regarding Moses. Certainly, legal, cultic, and traditional materials of diverse origin have been assembled and represented as issued by God to Israel through the mediation of Moses. This literary conceit—ascribing all of God's revealed teachings to a single moment and mediator—undergirds the later tendency of postbiblical and rabbinic Judaism to represent new teachings and legal developments as the natural unfolding of the original revelation to Moses at Sinai.

The relationship between Moses and Yahweh is the most intimate divine-human relationship to be found in biblical narrative. Though he is not referred to in the Pentateuch as a prophet, Moses is described as Yahweh's servant and as a man of Yahweh. As Yahweh's servant he carries the divine word to the nation, rebuking them when they have erred and exhorting them to obey the terms of the covenant. Conversely, as the representative of the nation he intercedes on Israel's behalf, praying for mercy and turning back Yahweh's jealous wrath when it threatens to destroy the people. Moses alone enters the cloud encasing Yahweh to speak with him and the biblical text eulogizes him by saying that "Never again did there arise in Israel a prophet like Moses—whom the Lord singled out, face to face . . . for all the great might and awesome power that Moses displayed before all Israel" (Deut 34:10, 12). Yet for all his heroism and virtue, Moses is clearly a human and a flawed one at that, denied entry into the Promised Land for having exhibited impatience or lack of faith at an incident recounted in Numbers 20:1–13.

In postbiblical writings, Moses is portrayed in line with the ideological commitments of later authors and communities. Philo describes Moses as king, legislator, priest, and prophet—a divine man of extraordinary learning and reasoning capacity, with superhuman physical, mental, psychological, and spiritual gifts. For Josephus, Moses exemplified the classic features of the virtuous man, ruled entirely by reason and never by the passions (such as fear, jealousy, or anger). Josephus represents Moses as the most ancient and exalted lawgiver, the inspiration of later Greek philosophers and lawgivers. Pseudepigraphic works claim Mosaic authorship to establish the authoritativeness of their teachings (e.g., *Jubilees*, which purports to be a revelation to Moses over and above the "first law" recorded in the Pentateuch). In rabbinic writings, Moses' role as a teacher and sage is highlighted above all. Dubbed "Moshe Rabbenu" (Moses our rabbi, or teacher), Moses is described as the scholar *par excellence* and the vast corpus of rabbinic teachings are understood as deriving from the original revelation to Moses at Sinai. Rabbinic texts avoid ascribing divine or even semi-divine powers to Moses perhaps in reaction to the Christian divinization of Jesus.

Aaron. Brother of Moses, son of Amram and Yocheved, Aaron is the eponymous ancestor of the priestly Aaronites (priests claiming descent from Levi through Aaron). Aaron was Moses' mouthpiece before Pharaoh. Although he performs wonders in Pharaoh's presence through the power of God and joins Moses in bringing some of the plagues, he is clearly subordinate to Moses, a minor participant in the final stages of the Exodus and during the formation of the covenant at Sinai. During Moses' absence while receiving the Torah from Yahweh, Aaron yields to the popular demand for a golden calf to worship. He is spared death only through Moses' intercession. Despite this lapse, Aaron is appointed first high priest in Israel, a position that will be passed to his son Eleazar and on to descendants of Aaron in perpetuity.

Aaron is involved in two further serious incidents. In the first, he and his sister Miriam challenge Moses' exclusive claim to speak in the name of Yahweh. In the second, Moses and Aaron are criticized for monopolizing leadership. A rebellious faction headed by Korah, challenges Aaron's exclusive control of priestly rituals, but Aaron is vindicated by Yahweh. Like Moses, Aaron dies before entering the Promised Land, as punishment for disobeying God at the waters of Meribah. Some critical scholars have suggested that the character of Aaron is an idealized retrojection by later authors wishing to establish an authoritative biblical precedent for the Aaronite priesthood; nevertheless, the antiquity of the institution of priesthood in Israel is well supported by early texts.

Much of postbiblical literature on Aaron struggles to reconcile his involvement in the sin of the golden calf with his appointment as high priest. Legends make much of Aaron's love for and pursuit of peace, reflected in the proverbial statement attributed to Hillel (first century C.E.): "Be of the disciples of Aaron, loving peace and pursuing peace, loving one's fellow men and bringing them near to the Torah" (m. Avot 1:12).

Miriam. Sister of Moses and Aaron, Miriam exercised leadership during Israel's journey to Canaan following the Exodus from Egypt. She led the women of Israel in a joyous celebration following the successful crossing of the sea—dancing and singing praises to Yahweh. Identified as a prophetess, she had authority as a spokesperson. In the book of Numbers, Miriam and Aaron challenge Moses' exclusive claim to speak in the name of Yahweh, a rebellion for which Miriam is punished with temporary "leprosy" (Num 12). In postbiblical tradition, Miriam was identified as the sister who persuaded Pharaoh's daughter to find a Hebrew wet-nurse for Moses, thus reuniting the infant with his mother. Legend has it that a miraculous well (known as Miriam's well) accompanied the Israelites in their wilderness travels, on account of Miriam's merits.

Joshua. Son of Nun of the tribe of Ephraim, Joshua is depicted in biblical texts as Moses' successor, leading the Israelites into the Promised Land and overseeing the distribution of the land to the tribes of Israel. Joshua first appears as a warrior fighting against the Amalekites. He next appears as Moses's attendant, accompanying him as he ascends and descends Mount Sinai and standing guard at the Tent of Meeting, when Moses would speak with Yahweh. Joshua and Caleb were among the 12 spies sent to reconnoiter the land of Canaan. Only they opposed the negative report of the other spies, so only they were privileged to enter the Promised Land. On Yahweh's instruction, Moses appointed Joshua as his successor, transferring his wisdom and authority by laying his hands upon him. The book of Joshua recounts Joshua's role in conquering the land and apportioning the tribal allotments.

The Joshua materials are historically very problematic. There is little archaeological evidence for the conquest as described in the book of Joshua, leading some scholars to doubt the existence of Joshua altogether. Others concede that the literary account is not entirely reliable and reflects later interests and ideology but still credit Joshua with an early leadership role. Without adjudicating this debate we can assess the role and function of Joshua in biblical and later tradition. Many passages model Joshua on Moses. Like Moses, Joshua leads the people across a body of water that parts miraculously (in the season of Passover, no less). He encounters Yahweh in a theophany strongly resembling the theophany at the burning bush and he mediates a covenant renewal ceremony. In other respects, the portrait of Joshua mirrors the portraits of later kings, especially King Josiah. Thus, Joshua is a transitional figure in the story of Israel's leadership. In rabbinic tradition, Joshua is deemed as a prophet worthy to succeed Moses.

KINGS: DAVID, SOLOMON

David. Youngest son of Jesse of Bethlehem, David rose to become the second and greatest king of Israel, reigning from ca. 1005 to 965 B.C.E. Although a reliable reconstruction of a "historical David" is not possible, the biblical sources provide a rich literary portrait of a complex and extraordinary man. The biblical book of Ruth contains a genealogy that links David to a Moabite woman (Ruth) on the one hand and the union of Judah and his Canaanite daughter-in-law Tamar on the other. The line of David continues through all the kings of Judah, and the New Testament reports that Jesus is descended from David.

David's beginnings are humble—as an insignificant shepherd inexperienced in warfare he is singled out by the prophet Samuel and anointed as king. The spirit of the Lord is said to rush upon him mightily, symbolizing the transfer of power and favor from King Saul to David. In the royal court, David plays music that soothes the troubled king, and becomes the latter's armor bearer. In another story, David proves his military worth by defeating Goliath, the champion of the Philistines, with only a slingshot and stones. David's successes earn him the love of Saul's children Michal (whom he marries) and Jonathan. But Saul's jealousy is kindled and he plots against David even as David's fortunes continue to rise. David is forced to flee, eventually taking refuge among the Philistines who hire him as a mercenary. During this period he finds support among the disaffected and distressed. Saul's supporters continue to pursue David despite two remarkable incidents in which David chooses to spare Saul's life. From his base in the town of Ziklag, David curries favor with the notables of Judah hoping to win their support in his struggle against Saul. When Saul is killed in a battle against the Philistines on Mount Gilboa, David and his band go to Hebron where he is anointed as king and reigns for seven and a half years. However, his attempts to rule over all the Israelite tribes are foiled by a rival king—Ish-bosheth the son of Saul. When the latter is murdered, David is anointed for the third time, this time as king of both Judah and Israel. He captures the centrally located city of the Jebusites, establishing it as his capital—Jerusalem—and ruling from there for some thirty-three years.

David enjoyed a series of military successes over the Philistines, Moabites, Aramaeans, Edomites, and others. According to the biblical text his kingdom was extensive, stretching from the "river of Egypt" in the west through much of the Transjordan and approaching the Euphrates in the east, though modern scholars have cast doubt on the reliability of this claim. David established a centralized state modeled in part on Canaanite cities and appointed administrative officials. He brought the Ark of the Covenant to Jerusalem and built an altar to Yahweh on the threshing floor of Araunah the Jebusite in order to turn the city into a sacred capital for the nation. Although he hoped to build a House for the Lord, the task was left to his son. Instead, David is told through his prophet Nathan, that Yahweh has promised David a sure "house" (a dynasty) that will last forever. The promise of a ruler of the house of David as king in Israel is known as the Davidic Covenant and is the basis for the later belief that Israel's messiah will be a Davidide.

David's later life is marked by sin and family tragedy, beginning with his sexual liaison with a married woman Bathsheba, whose husband Uriah is killed at David's behest. The child of this union dies, as punishment for David's sin, but a subsequent child—Solomon—will eventually rule as David's successor. In the meantime, however, tensions build among the northern (Israelite) tribes as a result of David's imposition of a permanent central authority and dynasty in Jerusalem. The law of the king, with its taxes and corvée (a levy of forced labor), its standing army and civil bureaucracy is contrary to older tribal traditions. A series of crises ensue, including a rebellion led by David's son, Absalom. Absalom has himself crowned at Hebron and David is forced to flee. Following Absalom's death, David is restored to power only to confront another rebellion led by a Benjaminite named Sheba (2 Sam 20). A final contentious struggle for the throne between his sons Adonijah and Solomon mar David's declining years.

In postbiblical tradition David is praised as a skilled musician (the composition of the psalms is ascribed to him), a poet, and a godly king. Already the book of Chronicles presents an idealized portrait of David as devoted to God, omitting any mention of his major flaws and sins. Rabbinic texts emphasis the unique status of David's monarchy, specifically, its eternal nature. Rabbinic legends make much of David's extraordinary physical strength, poetic genius, musical skill, and his knowledge of Torah and halakhah. Some texts criticize David, particularly for his affair with Bathsheba, but others acquit him of all blame.

Solomon. Son of King David and Bathsheba, Solomon is anointed as the third king of Israel in David's lifetime even though he is the tenth of David's seventeen sons. There are no references to Solomon outside the biblical text, and scholars differ sharply in their view of the historical merits of the biblical material. While Solomon's reign (ca. 965 to 928 B.C.E.) is certainly idealized as a golden age, the basic portrait of a prosperous and peaceful nation engaged in diplomacy rather than expansionism seems plausible. Solomon's reign commences with the bloody elimination of opponents and enemies. His kingdom is said to be extensive, affording control over lucrative trade routes and bringing in tribute in the form of precious metals, cloth, spices, and horses. Illustrating this point is the famed visit of the Queen of Sheba and her retinue with camels laden with spices, gold, and precious stones. Under Solomon, Israel enjoyed great prosperity and close relations with other kingdoms, sealed by the king's many marriages to foreign women, numbering in the hundreds. Solomon undertook construction of public buildings and fortifications as well as a magnificent Temple and palace complex in Jerusalem, emphasizing the divine election of both the House of David and the city of Jerusalem (Zion). Such projects led to an increased tax burden as well as the institution of the corvée and the duty of the citizenry to supply provisions for the royal court, including horses and chariots. Acts of rebellion against the House of David broke out in the reign of Solomon's son Rehoboam leading ultimately to the secession of the ten northern tribes of Israel.

The Bible praises Solomon as a wise king and judge and postbiblical traditions credit Solomon with great works of poetry and wisdom literature. Rabbinic legends view the building of the Temple as his most important act, a deed achieved through all manner of miracles. Nevertheless,

Solomon is heavily criticized for his violation of the biblical laws regarding kings—the multiplication of wives who worshipped foreign gods, and the amassing of gold, silver, and horses—and for an excessive rationalism that led him to disregard laws whose purpose he could not fathom. According to these legends, Solomon's sins cost him dearly and he spent his final years as a mendicant. Jewish tradition maintains that he authored the Song of Songs in the passion of his youth, the book of Proverbs in the wisdom of his middle years, and Ecclesiastes in the despair of his old age.

DESTRUCTION AND RESTORATION: JEREMIAH, EZRA

Jeremiah. Born in the small village of Anathoth, 3 miles northeast of Jerusalem, Jeremiah was a major prophet in ancient Israel. Due to biographical and autobiographical passages in the biblical book that bears his name, we know more of his life than of any other prophet. Nevertheless, our information is still slim and a full biography is not possible. Jeremiah was born at a critical juncture in the history of Judah. The reign of King Manasseh had just come to an end, a reign in which Judah had been politically and religiously subservient to Assyria. The biblical account excoriates Manasseh for his introduction of pagan religious practices, and praises the young Josiah who ascended to the throne in 640 B.C.E. at the tender age of eight. The Assyrian empire was disintegrating in the face of numerous rebellions, and over the course of the next thirty years, Judah regained political and religious independence. This independence would be short-lived however, and after a brief Egyptian supremacy, the kingdom of Judah was destroyed by the Neo-Babylonians. Jeremiah was witness to these events.

Jeremiah was born to a wealthy priestly family which, scholars believe, was descended from Abiathar, a priest under David banished to Anathoth by Solomon. Jeremiah was called to prophesy in the thirteenth year of King Josiah (627 B.C.E.). Since he is described as a young boy (possibly twelve or thirteen years of age), he must have been born in ca. 640 B.C.E. While his prophecies are sometimes difficult to date, Jeremiah's active career as a prophet seems to have begun shortly after Josiah's discovery of a temple scroll in 622 B.C.E.—a discovery that led to the Josianic reforms involving the destruction of outlying altars, the centralization of worship in the Jerusalem temple, a covenant renewal ceremony, and a celebration of Passover. Jeremiah supported the reforms, but visions of destruction by an enemy poised to attack Judah from the north as delayed punishment for the sins of King Manasseh moderated his enthusiasm.

The next prophecy of certain date is the "temple sermon" delivered in the first year of King Jehoiakim (609 B.C.E.) shortly after the death of Josiah in the battle of Megiddo. In this sermon, Jeremiah expresses disappointment with the reforms of Josiah. He indicts the people for their sins and warns that they are under judgment. The sermon aroused vehement opposition from all quarters—the general populace as well as the national leadership. Jeremiah was banned from the Temple, arrested and nearly lost his life. After the battle of Carchemish in 605 B.C.E., the Babylonian threat was evident and Jeremiah resumed his prophesies of doom, pointing to the Babylonian king Nebuchadrezzar and his army as the agents of God's judgment. Unable to enter the Temple precincts, Jeremiah dictated his prophecies to his amanuensis Baruch ben Neriah, who then read them from a scroll in the Temple. King Jehoiakim called for the scroll and destroyed it. Jeremiah went into hiding and dictated the scroll again. When Jerusalem surrendered to the Babylonians in 597 B.C.E., Jeremiah viewed the deportation of the new young king Jehoiachin and leading nobles as confirmation of his warnings. In messages to the exiles, Jeremiah said that God was not confined to the Jerusalem Temple and could be reached through prayer and obedience even in a foreign land.

Jeremiah was convinced that the Babylonian empire was an irresistible power, the agent of God's just punishment of unrepentant Judah. In the years following the first deportation he urged complete submission to Nebuchadrezzar and railed against King Zedekiah's plans to rebel. When the Babylonians began their final assault on Jerusalem in 589 B.C.E., Zedekiah sought the word of the Lord from Jeremiah but the latter offered no encouragement, assuring the king that God was fighting for the Babylonians. Jeremiah was arrested and held in custody during the siege of Jerusalem. When the city fell, the Babylonians allowed him to stay in Mizpah with the new governor Gedaliah, but after the murder of Gedaliah a few weeks later, he was forced to flee to Egypt. His final words were spoken from Egypt.

Ezra. The historicity of Ezra has evoked controversies as deep as those surrounding the figure of Moses, to whom Ezra is often compared because of his putative role in reconstructing a postexilic Jewish community in Palestine. Some scholars consider Ezra to be the invention of the

Maccabean era, while others read the biblical books of Ezra and Nehemiah as the later elaboration of a basically historical tradition. The matter is further complicated by chronological problems in the sources that make it impossible to date Ezra with certainty. He appears to have some connection with Nehemiah, the governor of Judah in the fifth century, but whether he preceded or followed Nehemiah (465–425 B.C.E. or 405–359 B.C.E. are the common alternatives) is not clear. Ezra is described as both a priest and a scribe, expert in the Torah of Moses. Evidently, a man of some importance in Babylon, he assumed some sort of leadership role in the Jewish community in Jerusalem. To what degree he was a Persian functionary is debatable but his mission appears to have been the teaching and implementation of the Torah of Moses. Since the books of Ezra and Nehemiah contain references to a wide range of Pentateuchal traditions, it is thought that Ezra's "Torah of Moses" was much like the Pentateuch we currently possess. Ezra is particularly identified with efforts to quash intermarriage. In rabbinic tradition, Ezra is praised for rebuilding Judaism. It is said that he would have been worthy of receiving the Torah from God, had Moses not preceded him.

HELLENISTIC JUDAISM: PHILO, JOSEPHUS

Philo. Philo Judaeus was a Jewish philosopher from Alexandria (ca. 20 B.C.E.–50 C.E.). He was born into a noble family with connections to the Herodian dynasty, but little is known of his life. It is evident from his knowledge of classical literature, philosophy, rhetoric, and general science that he received training well beyond the Greek general education of the encyclia (literature, rhetoric, mathematics, music, and logic). His writings display an excellent command of Greek language and literary style. The source of his Jewish knowledge is less clear and it is thought that he did not know Hebrew, but read the Bible in its Greek translation (the Septuagint). He apparently attended Sabbath synagogue services and occasionally consulted learned members of the community about aggadic traditions. He undertook a pilgrimage to Jerusalem once in his life. Philo was a devout Jew who nevertheless took an active part in the social life of Alexandria, attending the theater, horse races, and banquets of the city. Following a series of anti-Jewish pogroms in Alexandria in 38 C.E., Philo headed a delegation of the Alexandrian Jewish community to emperor Caligula in Rome (40 C.E.). Although the mission failed, the increasing unrest was settled by Claudius who ascended the throne in 41 C.E.

Philo's writings may be divided into three general categories. The first consists of expositions of the Pentateuch as a legal code. In addition to biographies of biblical characters (the patriarchs, Moses) Philo wrote an exposition of the biblical commandments, classifying them under the various commandments of the Decalogue. The second category of works consists of philosophical interpretations of the Pentateuch. These works are allegorical treatments that ignore the plain narrative content of the Bible, reading it instead as a system of abstract philosophical-mystical concepts. The third category of writings consists of commentaries on Genesis and Exodus presented in a question and answer format. Philo also wrote treatises devoted to purely philosophical topics, as well as contemporary historical books. His works are strongly influenced by Stoicism, Platonism, and neo-Pythagoreanism.

Philo's writings were preserved by the Christian Church, some in Greek and some in Armenian translation. No Jewish source (other than Josephus) refers to Philo explicitly. While his influence on rabbinic Judaism was negligible, his influence on the Church fathers was great because of his systematic allegorical readings of the Hebrew Bible.

Josephus. A Jewish historian of the first century C.E., Josephus was born into an aristocratic priestly family in Jerusalem in 37 C.E. and died sometime after 100 C.E. Details of his life are reported in his autobiography (*Life*) and his account of the Jewish War against Rome (*The Jewish War*). As a youth, Josephus was learned in the law and aggadah and, at the age of 16, spent three years as a follower of Bannus, an ascetic who lived in the wilderness. When he was 27 years of age, Josephus was sent to Rome where he argued successfully for the release of certain captive priests. When the Jewish war broke out two years later Josephus became commander of the Galilee, the most important theater of war, though he was challenged in this position by John of Gishala. The continual strife was one factor in the Jewish failure against Vespasian's forces. After the decisive battle of Jotapata (67 C.E.), Josephus and forty of his men fled to a cave. There the men vowed to kill one another rather than be taken alive by the Romans. Josephus manipulated the casting of lots so that he was one of the two last men left alive. He convinced the other man to join him in surrendering to the Romans. Josephus was held prisoner in the Roman camp, where he seems to have come to the attention of Vespasian by predicting the latter's imminent ascension to the throne. When Vespasian was crowned emperor, Josephus was released. He traveled to Alexandria and later accompanied Titus as he laid siege to Jerusalem. According to Josephus' accounts, he made several attempts to convince the Jewish rebels to surrender peacefully but to no avail. In the final destruction, Titus allowed Josephus to remove a Torah scroll. Josephus subsequently settled in Rome, receiving Roman citizenship and a pension from the Flavian emperors (Vespasian, Titus, and Domitian). Acquiring the name Flavius Josephus, he lived in the palace and enjoyed general imperial favor, which he repaid by writing a history of the Jewish War that was supportive of the political goals of the emperor.

As a Jew living in the diaspora, Josephus saw gentile hatred of the Jews. Convinced that this anti-Semitism was fueled by ignorance, Josephus decided to write a Jewish history (*Jewish Antiquities*) that would prove the great antiquity of the Jews and underscore the many virtues of the nation's traditions. Relating biblical events, Josephus adapted his account to the tastes of his intended Gentile audience. For later events he employed various Hellenistic and Jewish-Hellenistic sources and writers. Other works include the *Life*, written in response to attacks on his character and conduct during the war, and *Against Apion*, a vigorous refutation of anti-Semitic propaganda. Josephus' literary talent has been highly praised, but his historical works exhibit the defects common among historians in antiquity. Nevertheless, Josephus' writings constitute an important source for our understanding of biblical and late antique Jewish history. For the most part, his writings were ignored by Jews, and have come down to us through the Christian church.

PHARISAIC AND RABBINIC JUDAISM: HILLEL, SHAMMAI, R. YOHANAN BEN ZAKKAI, R. GAMLIEL, R. AKIVA, R. ISHMAEL, R. JUDAH HANASI, RAV, SHMUEL, RAVA, ABBAYE

Note: R. is used to abbreviate Rabbi, Rav, and Rabban—honorific titles for rabbinic sages. The name Rabbi standing alone refers to Rabbi Judah haNasi, the patriarch who flourished at the turn of the third century C.E. Sages will be listed in chronological rather than alphabetical order.

Hillel. One of the leading sages of the Second Temple period, Hillel, flourished at the turn of the millennium and into the first century C.E. Born in Babylonia, Hillel came to Jerusalem where he was a student of Shemaiah and Avtalyon (reputed to be converts). Rabbinic sources trace his ancestry to David but the tradition is not reliable. Nor is the title "*nasi*" (Patriarch), which rabbinic sources apply to Hillel anachronistically. Hillel's halakhic teachings slowly gained prominence and in all but a few instances the halakhah follows the school of Bet Hillel rather than the school of Bet Shammai. Hillel's name is associated with certain economic reforms and he is idealized as a man of humility, piety, and gentleness. Because of his role in promulgating halakhah, Hillel is traditionally compared with Ezra—who also came from Babylonia to reestablish Torah.

Shammai. A leading sage of the Second Temple period and a contemporary of Hillel, Shammai flourished around the turn of the millennium (ca. 50 B.C.E.—30 C.E.). A builder by trade Shammai is best known in his debates with Hillel, debates in which he often takes a more stringent position and is, in general, defeated. In some rabbinic legends, Shammai is used as a foil for Hillel's greater piety and humanity.

R. Yohanan b. Zakkai. A first-century tanna who witnessed the destruction of the Temple, Yohanan is credited in rabbinic hagiography with helping to preserve and transform rabbinic Judaism at the end of the Second Temple period. No details of his life are provided in the sources other than the assertion that he was a student of Hillel. He is associated with the Galilee and later with Jerusalem where he is said to have taught "in the shadow of the Temple" and to have clashed occasionally with Sadducees and priests. A popular motif associated with R. Yohanan is the dialogue with Romans or non-Jews who raise problems from biblical passages or ask difficult questions about ritual practice. Yohanan's position during the war is unclear but rabbinic tradition contains four versions—legendary in character—of his escape from Jerusalem. According to these legends, Yohanan went to the emperor's camp and asked that the town of Yavneh (near modern-day Tel Aviv) and its sages, as well as R. Gamliel and R. Zadok, be spared. These stories express the conviction that R. Yohanan was responsible for the survival of Torah learning and the reestablishment of religious and national leadership after the destruction.

R. Gamliel. Descended from Hillel, Rabban Gamliel II, was a central figure at Yavneh beginning around the year 80 C.E. R. Gamliel is associated with several important *taqqanot* (rabbinic rulings) regarding religious practice particularly, and seems to have played a large role in formulating the *seder* ceremony for Passover. There are several legends in which Rabban Gamliel wields authority in a heavy-handed manner, humiliating and even excommunicating those who opposed him on substantive or procedural grounds. Other traditions indicate his openness to Greco-Roman culture and his children studied "Greek wisdom." He himself knew some Greek science and consulted astronomical charts when determining the calendar. He appeared to have had a representative role, traveling to Rome to intercede for the Jews of the Land of Israel. Although he is referred to as Nasi (Patriarch), this term is viewed as anachronistic.

R. Akiva. Born in Judea around the year 50 C.E., Akiva b. Joseph was a leading *tanna* whose influence on the halakhah was critical. The stories of his early life are the stuff of legend. They tell of his humble beginnings and ignorance, as well as his bitter enmity for scholars. Employed as a shepherd for the wealthy Kalba Savu'a, he married his employer's daughter Rachel which so angered Kalba Savu'a that he cut the young couple off. Akiva and Rachel lived in great poverty, but Rachel insisted that Akiva devote himself to Torah study, a task he undertook despite his advanced years. Akiva is said to have studied in Lydda and in Yavneh before becoming a teacher himself in Bene-Barak. According to the legends, Akiva absented himself for two dozen years, amassing thousands of students—all at the behest of Rachel, the ideal scholar's wife. When the revolt against Rome broke out in 132, Akiva apparently supported Bar Kosiba as the long-awaited Messiah who would throw off the foreign oppressors. Akiva was arrested for teaching Torah and was eventually flayed alive by the Romans. According to legend, he welcomed his martyrdom as an opportunity to fulfill the obligation of loving God with *all* one's soul.

Akiva's importance as a scholar is expressed in traditions that describe him as "*mesadder halakhot*" (one who arranges, perhaps clarifies, laws). Tradition also connects him with mystical study. His creative approach to the exegesis of Scripture has traditionally been contrasted with the more constrained and contextual exegesis of his contemporary, R. Ishmael. The corpus of tannaitic midrashic works have long been divided into two sets—those reflecting the methods and halakhic views of R. Akiva (the *Mekhilta* of R. Simeon b. Yohai on Exodus, the *Sifra* on Leviticus, *Sifrei Zuta* on Numbers—of which we have only excerpts and fragments—and *Sifrei* on Deuteronomy. The leading scholars of the next generation (R. Meir, R. Simeon b. Yohai, R. Yosi b. Halafta, R. Eleazar b. Shammua, and R. Nehemiah) were pupils of R. Akiva.

R. Ishmael. A *tanna* of the first half of the second century C.E., R. Ishmael b. Elisha was a younger colleague of R. Akiva. Descended from a priestly family, legend states that as a lad Ishmael was taken to Rome as a captive. R. Joshua ransomed him and became his teacher. Ishmael is associated with Yavneh. His primary disputes are with R. Akiva whose creative midrashic excesses are said to prompt exasperated protests from R. Ishmael. The principle that "the Torah speaks in human language" (i.e., that not every detail of the text's grammar, word choice, orthography, and syntax is interpretable) is attributed to R. Ishmael. However, the tradition that Ishmael developed thirteen exegetical principles is not reliable. The tannaitic midrashim that have traditionally been associated with the teachings and methods of R. Ishmael are the *Mekhilta de-R. Ishmael* on Exodus, the *Sifrei* on Numbers, and part of the Sifrei on Deuteronomy (1–54).

R. Judah haNasi. Flourishing in the latter half of the second century and early third century C.E., R. Judah haNasi is credited with the redaction of the Mishnah. R. Judah (often simply designated "Rabbi" in our sources) is associated with the town of Bet She'arim and later, Sepphoris. While some scholars maintain that the office of *nasi* or Patriarch was not fully established at this time (so that the title *nasi* is applied to R. Judah only anachronistically and retrospectively), it is nevertheless clear that R. Judah held a position of special prominence and authority, and enjoyed a measure of recognition by the Roman authorities. Numerous legends tell of his great wealth and close friendship with the emperor. According to rabbinic sources, the patriarchate grew in prestige and splendor under R. Judah haNasi. R. Judah had a contingent of bodyguards who punished opponents and contributed to the regal atmosphere of this new aristocracy of learning. In several stories, rabbis voice criticism of R. Judah—his method of making appointments, his opposition to teaching in public, his blunt hostility to the unlearned, his preference for Greek over Aramaic, his accommodations to Roman society and culture, and his efforts to centralize authority in his own hands, all come under attack.

Nevertheless, his many achievements won him a place in the pantheon of great Jewish sages. R. Judah is associated with many halakhic rulings intended to ease the financial and other burdens on Jews that resulted from the influx of non-Jews into the land of Israel. More significant, R. Judah is traditionally held to be the redactor of the Mishnah, a collection of halakhic traditions and disputes created by a process of careful selection, compilation, and editing. That this work became a canon, or standard of measure—due in no small part to R. Judah's prestige and personal authority—is indicated by the fact that traditions not included in the Mishnah are referred to as "outside" (*beraita*). R. Judah's work became the foundation for the further development of the halakhah by amoraim in both the Land of Israel and Babylonia. His pupils include prominent amoraim of the first generation (e.g., R. Hiyya and Rav).

Rav. Dating to the third century C.E. and heading rival "schools," Rav and Samuel are often referred to as the founders of the Babylonian Talmud, since their teachings begin so many of the discussions in that work. Rav was born Abba b. Aivu at Kafri in southern Babylonian and was also known as Abba Arikha ("Abba the Tall"). He traveled to Israel to study with his uncle Hiyya, who introduced him to R. Judah ha-Nasi. He learned the Torah of the Land of Israel with the last of the *tannaim* and is said to have brought the Mishnah of R. Judah ha-Nasi back to Babylonia around 219 C.E. He went first to Nehardea and its community of scholars where he was appointed market commissioner. When he refused to regulate prices, he had to leave Nehardea for Sura where he established a school. Talmudic and post-Talmudic sources anachronistically refer to this institution as a pre-eminent academy that attracted more than one thousand students, but this is surely hyperbolic praise. His authority is considered by subsequent tradition as equivalent to that of a *tanna*, and he was also a prolific aggadist. The school of Sura founded by Rav reflects the traditions of the Land of Israel. By contrast the school of Nehardea founded by Samuel reflects Babylonian traditions.

Samuel. The amora Samuel Yarhina'ah was born in the late second century C.E at Nehardea in Babylonia and studied with his father; any other teachers are unknown. Whether he ever studied in the Land of Israel is disputed. Although he was financially secure, he experienced family tragedy—his sons died young and two daughters were taken captive and ransomed. A third daughter married a Gentile who later converted. As the head of a *bet midrash / bet din* (school/court) in Nehardea, Samuel was a leading authority in many matters and upon Rav's death he became *the* leading Babylonian authority. He was close to the exilarch and according to rabbinic sources, made the acquaintance of the Persian King Shapur. He is most often associated with the principle that would govern Jewish communities in the diaspora for centuries: "The law of the land is the law [for Jews too]." Many rabbinic stories emphasize Samuel's business ethics and utter honesty as a judge.

Rava. Babylonian *amora* of the fourth century C.E, Rava and his colleague Abbaye are closely associated with the dialectical method of halakhic study that is the hallmark of the Babylonian Talmud. Rava (R. Abba b. Joseph b. Hama) lived in Mahoza. His teachers included R. Hisda (head of the school at Sura), R. Nahman b. Yaakov, and R. Joseph (head of the school at Pumbeditha). When his colleague Abbaye was appointed head at Pumbeditha following the death of R. Joseph, Rava established his own *bet midrash* (school) in Mahoza. When Abbaye died in ca. 338 C.E. many of the scholars of Pumbeditha moved to Mahoza. Rava was financially well off, and is said to have maintained close relations with the royal court, particularly with King Shapur's mother, Ifra Hormuz, and with the Persian authorities. Rava's debates with Abbaye fill the pages of the Babylonian Talmud. In these debates, Rava prevails in all but six instances in which the halakhah is according to Abbaye.

Abbaye. Babylonian *amora* of the late third to fourth century C.E, Abbaye (his true name is unknown) was born to a widow who herself died after giving birth. He was raised by an uncle, Rabbah b. Nahmani, and a foster mother of whom he was particularly fond. He succeeded R. Joseph as head of the school at Pumbeditha ca. 333 C.E., prompting Rava to return to Mahoza to open a *bet midrash*. Upon Abbaye's death in 338 C.E. many scholars in Pumbeditha joined Rava in Mahoza.

PRIMARY DOCUMENTS

Abbreviations: m. = Mishnah, t. = Tosefta, p. = Palestinian Talmud, b. = Babylonian Talmud

DOCUMENT 1. CREATION: GENESIS 1:1–2:4a

In the Ancient Near Eastern myth *Enuma Elish*, the world is created when Marduk, the god of the storm, battles Tiamat the primordial deep, represented as a ferocious water monster. Blasting an evil wind in Tiamat's face, Marduk slays her and then slices her carcass in two like a shellfish. Of one half, he creates the ceiling of the sky to hold back the monster's upper waters, and of the other he creates the foundation of the earth to press down and hold back the monster's lower waters. This division of the chaotic waters creates a "bubble" of space for the created world. Marduk next establishes heavenly bodies as stations for the great gods. When the gods complain to Marduk of their unending toil, he decides as an afterthought to create humankind to free the gods from menial labor. He fashions a human out of the blood of Kingu, the rebellious captain of Tiamat's army, and charges humans with serving the gods so that the gods might be free of all labor.

It has long been recognized that the creation account in Genesis 1:1–2:4 rejects this Ancient Near Eastern account by invoking and then demythologizing it. The Hebrew word for "deep [water]" (*tehom*) is etymologically cognate with the Akkadian word *tiamat* and appears here without the definite article ("with darkness over the face of Deep") as if it is a personal name. No longer a ferocious and defiant divinity, the primordial Deep appears simply as an inert watery mass. The wind that fells Tiamat in *Enuma Elish* is also present but demythologized as the wind of God that sweeps over the inert water. Most important, there is no divine antagonist and no cosmic battle. In Genesis, a single uncontested God by the power of his word imposes order on preexisting natural elements. In God's creation of an expanse—or space—between waters sealed above and below (vv. 6–7) we again hear echoes of *Enuma Elish*. After forming this water-encased "bubble" of space, the biblical God, like Marduk, sets up celestial bodies—sun, moon, and stars. But in Genesis these celestial bodies are not themselves divinities.

Creation takes place over six days and there is a discernible parallelism between the first three days and the last three days. Days 1, 2, and 3 prepare the needed conditions for the entities and creatures created on days 4, 5, and 6. Thus, on day 1 light and darkness are separated and on day 4 the heavenly bodies that give off light are created. On day 2 the firmament is established by separating the watery mass and on day 5 the inhabitants of the sky (birds) and water (fish) are created. On day 3 dry land is separated out from the sea and on day 6 the inhabitants of the land are created. Days 3 and 6 each have an additional element and the evident parallelism suggests that these should also be paired: on day 3 vegetation is created and on day 6 humans are created, implying that the vegetation is for the humans. Indeed, God states expressly that humans are to eat the fruit- and seed-bearing plants while animals are to eat the grasses and herbs. There should be no competition between humans and animals for food, and animals are not given to humans as food. Thus, according to Genesis 1 humans are vegetarian and the original creation is free of violence and bloodshed of any kind.

The biblical account presents humans as the pinnacle and purpose of creation, made in the image of God, rather than an afterthought produced as menials to the gods. The Hebrew word designating the creature created by God—the *adam*—is not a proper name (Adam) but a generic term meaning simply "the human," or more literally "the earthling" since the word *adam* derives from *adamah* meaning "earth."

On the seventh day following the six days of creation God ceases his labors and for this reason he blesses the seventh day and declares it holy, that is, belonging to God. Part of the purpose of this creation myth is to explain the origin of the seven-day cycle of the week and the observance of the Sabbath day.

Chapter 1 [1]When God began creating the heaven and earth[i]—[2]the earth being unformed and void, with darkness over the face of Deep [*tehom*] and a wind from God sweeping over the water—[3]God said, "Let there be light" and there was light. [4]God saw that the light was good and God separated the light from the darkness. [5]God called the light Day and the darkness he called Night. And there was evening and there was morning, a first day. [6]God said, "Let there be an expanse in the midst of the water, that it may separate water from water." [7]God made the expanse, and it separated the water which was below the expanse from the water which was above the expanse. And it was so. [8]God called the expanse Sky. And there was evening and there was morning, a second day. [9]God said, "Let the water below the sky be gathered into one area, that the dry land may appear." And it was so. [10]God called the dry land Earth, and the gathering of waters He called Seas. And God saw that this was good. [11]And God said, "Let the earth sprout vegetation: seed-bearing plants, fruit trees of every kind on earth that bear fruit with the seed in it." And it was so. [12]The earth brought forth vegetation: seed-bearing plants of every kind, and trees of every kind bearing fruit with the seed in it. And God saw that this was good. [13]And there was evening and there was morning, a third day. [14]God said, "Let there be lights in the expanse of the sky to separate day from night; they shall serve as signs for the set times— the days and the years; [15]and they shall serve as lights in the expanse of the sky to shine upon the earth." And it was so. [16]God made the two great lights, the greater light to dominate the day and the lesser light to dominate the night, and the stars. [17]And God set them in the expanse of the sky to shine upon the earth, [18]to dominate the day and the night, and to separate light from darkness. And God saw that this was good. [19]And there was evening and there was morning, a fourth day. [20]God said, "Let the waters bring forth swarms of living creatures, and birds that fly above the earth across the expanse of the sky." [21]God created the great sea monsters, and all the living creatures of every kind that creep, which the waters brought forth in swarms, and all the winged birds of every kind. And God saw that this was good. [22]God blessed them, saying, "Be fertile and increase, fill

---

i. A more accurate translation than the traditional "In the beginning" which implies an account of the beginning of all time, of ultimate origins. In fact, the story does not purport to tell us about the ultimate origins of things, but is interested in explaining how and why the world is as it is.

the waters in the seas, and let the birds increase on the earth." [23] And there was evening and there was morning, a fifth day. [24] God said, "Let the earth bring forth every kind of living creature: cattle, creeping things, and wild beasts of every kind." And it was so. [25] God made wild beasts of every kind and cattle of every kind, and all kinds of creeping things of the earth. And God saw that this was good. [26] And God said, "Let us make man in our image, after our likeness. They shall rule the fish of the sea, the birds of the sky, the cattle, the whole earth, and all the creeping things that creep on earth." [27] And God created man in His image, in the image of God He created him; male and female He created them. [28] God blessed them and God said to them, "Be fertile and increase, fill the earth and master it; and rule the fish of the sea, the birds of the sky, and all the living things that creep on earth." [29] God said, "See I give you every seed-bearing plant that is upon all the earth, and every tree that has seed-bearing fruit; they shall be yours for food. [30] And to all the animals on land, to all the birds of the sky, and to everything that creeps on earth, in which there is the breath of life, [I give] all the green plants for food." And it was so. [31] And God saw all that He had made, and found it very good. And there was evening and there was morning, the sixth day.

Chapter 2 [1] The heaven and the earth were finished, and all their array. [2] On the seventh day God finished the work that He had been doing, and He ceased on the seventh day from all the work that He had done. [3] And God blessed the seventh day and declared it holy, because on it God ceased from all the work of creation that he had done. [4] Such is the story of heaven and earth when they were created.

DOCUMENT 2. THE PATRIARCHAL PROMISE: GENESIS 12:1–9

The first eleven chapters of Genesis provide a cosmic and universal introduction to the story of Israel. According to the biblical story, the one supreme God who created a good earth for humans formed in his own image, was forgotten and spurned by those very creatures. Repeatedly in the first eleven chapters, humans turn their moral freedom to evil use. In Genesis 12, God begins again, this time singling out a lone individual—Abraham (originally Abram)—to whom he issues a command and makes a promise. Abraham is to leave his home and go to an unnamed land

God will show him and God will make of him a great nation, blessed among nations. Abraham obeys, and upon arriving in Canaan receives a further promise from God—the land of Canaan is assigned to Abraham's offspring. The themes of land and offspring will play a central role in the biblical account from this point forward. Moreover, the triple promise of land, offspring, and blessing may be seen as a reversal of the curses laid on Adam and Eve, who are exiled, bring forth offspring in great pain, and struggle with accursed, uncooperative soil (Gen 3:14–24).

God's choice of Abraham appears to be random, but later Jewish tradition credits Abraham's great faith as the key to his election. God is vague regarding Abraham's destination yet an unquestioning Abraham does as God commands. Likewise, in Genesis 15, Abraham's childlessness does not stop him from trusting in God's promise of countless progeny—a trust that God reckons to Abraham's merit (Gen 15:6).

Verse 6 of this chapter contains the interesting editorial comment that "the Canaanites were then in the land." This statement was clearly written at a time when Canaanites no longer occupied the land. Thus, it could not have been written by Moses because the Canaanites are represented as residing undisturbed in Canaan throughout Moses' lifetime. Retrospective verses like Gen 12:6 (e.g., Gen 13:7) have long been cited as evidence that Moses did not write the Pentateuch.

12 [1]The Lord said to Abram, "Go forth from your native land and from your father's house to the land that I will show you.

[2]I will make of you a great nation,
And I will bless you;
I will make your name great,
And you shall be a blessing.
[3]I will bless those who bless you
And curse him that curses you;
And all the families of the earth
Shall bless themselves by you."

[4]Abram went forth as the Lord had commanded him, and Lot went with him. Abram was seventy-five years old when he left Haran. [5]Abram took his wife Sarai and his brother's son Lot, and all the wealth that they had amassed, and the persons that they had acquired in Haran; and they set out for the land of Canaan. When they arrived

in the land of Canaan, [6]Abram passed through the land as far as the site of Shechem, at the terebinth of Moreh. The Canaanites were then in the land.

[7]The Lord appeared to Abram and said, "I will assign this land to your offspring." And he built an altar there to the Lord who had appeared to him. [8]From there he moved on to the hill country east of Bethel and pitched his tent, with Bethel on the west and Ai on the east; and he built there an altar to the Lord and invoked the Lord by name. [9]Then Abram journeyed by stages toward the Negeb.

DOCUMENT 3. ABRAHAM'S BINDING (*AKEDAH*) OF ISAAC: GENESIS 22:1–19

The theme of peril to and reaffirmation of God's promises to the patriarchs runs throughout the book of Genesis. Time and again the patriarchs are brought to the point of despair. Just when all seems lost, God intervenes to resolve the crisis and renew the promise. The supreme affirmation of the promise is the ceremonial formalization of the patriarchal covenant in Genesis 15, and the supreme threat to the fulfillment of the promise is the story of the binding of Isaac in Genesis 22. In this story, God tests Abraham with the most horrible of demands. The child of the promise— Isaac, born miraculously to Sarah when she was no longer of child-bearing age—is to be taken up a mountain and sacrificed to God by Abraham's own hand. God Himself had promised to make Abraham the father of a great people through his son Isaac, a fact that gives the story even greater power and pathos. Yet just as God once commanded Abraham to go (*lek lekha*) to an unnamed land he now commands him to go (*lek lekha*) to an unnamed mountain. Based on a passage in the book of Chronicles, the belief developed that this mountain (later named Mount Moriah) was none other than the Temple mount in Jerusalem.

One of the most riveting stories not only in the Bible but in world literature, this terrible and fascinating tale is a masterpiece of narrative skill and suspense. There is extreme economy in the descriptions of physical setting, character, and speech—the trademark of biblical narrative style. Rarely does the narrator comment upon or explain a character's thoughts or motives, and dialogue is kept to a minimum. Where this rule of verbal economy is broken and characters converse at some length, their speech is significant.

The biblical narrator's concealing of the motives of all of the story's main characters (God, Abraham, and Isaac) leads to ambiguity and the possibility of many interpretations. This indeterminacy makes Genesis 22 one of the most studied and interpreted texts of all time. Why is God testing Abraham? Does God really desire this sacrifice? What is Abraham thinking and feeling as he walks for three days with his son, bearing the wood and the fire for the sacrifice? Does he fully intend to obey this command, to annul the covenantal promise with his own hand or does he trust that God will intervene? Or is this a paradox of faith—does Abraham intend faithfully to obey this command, all the while trusting that somehow God's promise will nevertheless be fulfilled through Isaac? And what is Isaac thinking? Does he understand what is happening? Is he prepared to obey? He sees the wood and firestone in his father's hand and can deduce that a sacrifice is planned. He asks his father, "where is the sheep for the burnt offering?" but does he know the answer even as he asks? Does he hear the double entendre in his father's simple and solemn reply which in the unpunctuated Hebrew might be read: "The Lord will provide the sheep for the offering: my son." Does he acquiesce as he is bound to the altar, or does he struggle? The beauty of this narrative is its sheer economy, forcing generations of readers to imagine the innumerable possibilities, playing out the drama in countless ways—with an Abraham who is reluctant and an Isaac who is ignorant, or with an Abraham eager to serve his God to the point of sacrificing his own son and an Isaac who willingly bares his neck to the knife.

Known simply as the Akedah (or "binding"), this compelling story has figured prominently in later Jewish tradition and liturgy. Jewish prayer calls on God to remember the Akedah for the benefit of Abraham's descendants. Rabbinic texts describe the Akedah as the tenth and climactic test of Abraham's faith. Other interpretations focus on the virtue of Isaac, emphasizing that because he was a grown man he must have agreed to the slaughter—a prototype and example for future Jewish martyrs. In some late antique and medieval retellings of the story, Isaac is indeed sacrificed and it is his willingness to die that redounds to the credit of Abraham's descendants. In still other interpretations the test is a punishment meted out to Abraham for callously dismissing Hagar and Ishmael in the previous chapter. The Christian church appropriated the story as an allegory and prototype for the "sacrifice" of Jesus by his divine Father.

Some historians read this story as a condemnation of child sacrifice, which was likely practiced throughout the period of the monarchy, though not unopposed. Others ask whether Genesis 22 rejects or *assumes* the practice of child sacrifice.

> [1]Some time afterward, God put Abraham to the test. He said to him, "Abraham," and he answered, "Here I am." [2]And He said, "Take your son, your favored one, Isaac, whom you love, and go to the land of Moriah, and offer him there as a burnt offering on one of the heights that I will point out to you." [3]So early next morning, Abraham saddled his ass and took with him two of his servants and his son Isaac. He split the wood for the burnt offering, and he set out for the place of which God had told him. [4]On the third day Abraham looked up and saw the place from afar. [5]Then Abraham said to his servants, "You stay here with the ass. The boy and I will go up there; we will worship and we will return to you."
>
> [6]Abraham took the wood for the burnt offering and put it on his son Isaac. He himself took the firestone and the knife; and the two walked off together. [7]Then Isaac said to his father Abraham, "Father!" And he answered, "Yes, my son." And he said, "Here are the firestone and the wood; but where is the sheep for the burnt offering?" [8]And Abraham said, "God will see to the sheep for His burnt offering, my son." And the two of them walked on together.
>
> [9]They arrived at the place of which God had told him. Abraham built an altar there; he laid out the wood; he bound his son Isaac; he laid him on the altar, on top of the wood. [10]And Abraham picked up the knife to slay his son. [11]Then an angel of the Lord called to him from the skies; "Abraham! Abraham!" And he answered, "Here I am." [12]And he said, "Do not raise your hand against the boy, or do anything to him. For now I know that you fear God, since you have not withheld your son, your favored one, from Me." [13]When Abraham looked up, his eye fell upon a ram caught in the thicket by its horns. So Abraham went and took the ram and offered it up as a burnt offering in place of his son. [14]And Abraham named that site Adonai-yireh [the Lord will see], whence the present saying, "On the mount of the Lord there is vision."
>
> [15]The angel of the Lord called to Abraham a second time from the skies, [16]and said, "By Myself I swear, the Lord declares: Because you have done this and have not withheld your son, your favored one, [17]I will bestow My blessing upon you and make your descendants as

numerous as the stars of heaven and the sands on the seashore; and your descendants shall seize the gates of their foes. [18]All the nations of the earth shall bless themselves by your descendants, because you have obeyed My command." [19]Abraham then returned to his servants, and they departed together for Beer-sheba; and Abraham stayed in Beer-sheba.

DOCUMENT 4. THE COVENANT AND THE TEN COMMANDMENTS: EXODUS 19:1–9, 20:1–18

In the third month after the Exodus from Egypt, the Israelites arrive at the wilderness of Sinai and encamp at the mountain where Moses was first called by God to liberate the Israelites. As the scholar Nahum Sarna points out, thus far Israel has been the passive beneficiary of God's protection, but a new phase in Israel's history is about to commence: "God's redemptive acts on Israel's behalf require a reciprocal response on the part of Israel. The liberated multitude of erstwhile slaves must be united not only by a vital sense of a shared tragedy and a common experience of emancipation, but even more by bonds of perceived ideals—a vision of a new order of life, namely, the establishment of an essentially different kind of society from what had hitherto existed. The precondition for the fulfillment of this goal, indeed its instrumentality, is to be the forging of a special relationship between God and Israel. This relationship is to be sealed by a covenant, which would establish Israel as God's 'treasured possession,' as 'a kingdom of priests and a holy nation' " (*Exploring Exodus*, p. 130).

The covenant concluded at Sinai differs radically from the Noahide and Abrahamic (or patriarchal) convenants, in requiring obedience to a variety of commandments, laws, and moral ideals in exchange for the protection and patronage of God. The Mosaic covenant is both bilateral and conditional, and becomes the basis upon which later Judaism defines its special relationship with God. Later tradition praises the ancient Israelites for unanimously pledging obedience even before they had heard the terms of the covenant.

Modeled on Ancient Near Eastern prototypes, the covenant's preamble and historical background recounting God's former benefactions to Israel are found in Ex 20:1. The terms of the treaty are stipulated at length in the ensuing chapters. The covenant opens with the Ten Statements, more commonly known as the Ten Commandments or Decalogue. Unlike most of the subsequent legal material, the Decalogue is expressed in absolute or apodictic form, and articulates God's most basic and unconditional covenant demands. In the Ancient Near East broadly, laws were the product of human rulers albeit inspired by divinely endowed principles of justice and truth. But the biblical text depicts God as the direct author of the commandments and laws not only in Exodus but in the remaining books of the Pentateuch. This transforms the nature and purpose of law. The purpose of the laws is to create a holy people; obedience to the law is a religious duty and disobedience is not merely a crime but a sin (a violation of the will of God as expressed in his commandments).

The Decalogue is addressed to each member of the community and may be divided into two halves. The first five are duties to God and contain frequent references to "the Lord your God" as well as explanatory clauses to motivate their observance. Central among these duties is the obligation of exclusive loyalty to God (just as a sovereign who has benefited a vassal might demand his exclusive loyalty). The longest of these commandments concerns the observance of the Sabbath which is to be reserved for activities associated with God, not humans, as the quintessential expression of love for and loyalty to God. Honor and reverence for parents is seen as an extension of the honor and reverence owed to God. Reverence is defined in rabbinic tradition as obedience and respect, while honor is defined as the provision of food, clothing, and physical care, especially when infirm. The remaining five commandments—prohibiting murder, adultery, theft, false accusation and false testimony, and scheming to acquire another's property—are duties to one's fellow humans, but because they are required by God, their violation is also seen as a sin.

The Hebrew text does not number the commandments and the precise division into ten has been debated since antiquity—a debate that continues today and accounts for differences between the Ten Commandments of Jewish and Christian communities.

> [1]On the third new moon after the Israelites had gone forth from the land of Egypt, on that very day, they entered the wilderness of Sinai. [2]Having journeyed from Rephidim, they entered the wilderness of Sinai and encamped in the wilderness. Israel encamped there in front of the mountain, [3]and Moses went up to God. The Lord called to him from the mountain, saying, "Thus shall you say to the house of Jacob

and declare to the children of Israel: [4]"You have seen what I did to the Egyptians, how I bore you on eagles' wings and brought you to Me. [5]Now then, if you will obey Me faithfully and keep My covenant, you shall be My treasured possession among all the peoples. Indeed, all the earth is Mine, [6]but you shall be to Me a kingdom of priests and a holy nation.' These are the words that you shall speak to the children of Israel."

[7]Moses came and summoned the elders of the people and put before them all that the Lord had commanded him. [8]All the people answered as one, saying, "All that the Lord has spoken we will do!" And Moses brought back the people's words to the Lord. [9]And the Lord said to Moses, "I will come to you in a thick cloud, in order that the people may hear when I speak with you and so trust you ever after." Then Moses reported the people's words to the Lord . . .

. . . 20 [1]God spoke all these words, saying:

[2]I the Lord am your God who brought you out of the land of Egypt, the house of bondage; [3]You shall have no other gods besides Me.

[4]You shall not make for yourself a sculptured image, or any likeness of what is in the heavens above, or on the earth below, or in the waters under the earth. [5]You shall not bow down to them or serve them. For I the Lord your God am an impassioned God, visiting the guilt of the parents upon the children, upon the third and upon the fourth generations of those who reject Me, [6]but showing kindness to the thousandth generation of those who love Me and keep My commandments.

[7]You shall not swear falsely by the name of the Lord your God; for the Lord will not clear one who swears falsely by His name.

[8]Remember the Sabbath day and keep it holy. [9]Six days you shall labor and do all your work, [10]but the seventh day is a Sabbath of the Lord your God: you shall not do any work—you, your son or daughter, your male or female slave, or your cattle, or the stranger who is within your settlements. [11]For in six days the Lord made heaven and earth and sea, and all that is in them, and He rested on the seventh day; therefore the Lord blessed the Sabbath day and hallowed it.

[12]Honor your father and your mother, that you may long endure on the land that the Lord your God is assigning to you.

[13]You shall not murder.

You shall not commit adultery.

You shall not steal.

You shall not bear false witness against your neighbor.

[14]You shall not covet your neighbor's house: you shall not covet your neighbor's wife, or his male or female slave, or his ox or his ass, or anything that is your neighbor's.

[15]All the people witnessed the thunder and lightning, the blare of the horn and the mountain smoking; and when the people saw it, they fell back and stood at a distance. [16]"You speak to us," they said to Moses, "and we will obey; but let not God speak to us, lest we die." [17]Moses answered the people, "Be not afraid; for God has come only in order to test you, and in order that the fear of Him may be ever with you, so that you do not go astray." [18]So the people remained at a distance, while Moses approached the thick cloud where God was.

DOCUMENT 5. DEUT 6:1–9: "HEAR (SHEMA), O ISRAEL"

According to the biblical narrative, the Israelites spent forty years journeying through the desert, before arriving at the eastern shore of the Jordan River. As the nation stood ready to cross the river and claim possession of the land of Canaan, Moses delivered three speeches that constitute the bulk of the book of Deuteronomy. As a series of first-person addresses, Deuteronomy turns from simple narration to the highly charged rhetoric of public exhortation. Knowing that he will not cross into the Promised Land, Moses urges the Israelites to pledge exclusive loyalty to God and to obey his commandments faithfully that the nation might long endure in that blessed land flowing with milk and honey. Deuteronomy 6:4–9, a passage known after its first word as the *Shema* ("hear"), took on a special prominence for Jews of the late Second Temple period (Jesus refers to these verses as the "first" of all commandments; see Mark 12:29–30). The passage stands as the central pledge of loyalty and expression of love for God in the Jewish liturgy to the present time. In it, Moses urges the Israelites to love the Lord, the Lord alone, with all their hearts and souls and might.

Assyrian vassal treaties contained pledges of loyalty in which a vassal was urged to love the king, listen to his voice, and obey him. In Deuteronomy this political treaty form is borrowed and referred to God (see Chapter 2). And just as loyalty to the Assyrian overlord consisted in concrete service, so loyalty to God is no abstract concept. Here in Deuteronomy, loyalty to and love for God are given concrete expression by immersing oneself in God's teaching and by instructing one's children in that teaching (vv. 6–7). To love God is to recite his commandments from rising up to lying down (v. 7), and when moving about in the world (v. 7). Israel is to keep God's commandments constantly in mind and at hand (v. 8) so that she might long endure in God's land.

These verses are the basis for a number of obligations and ritual practices that arose in the Second Temple period (if not earlier), were formalized in the rabbinic period, and are common among observant Jews to the present day: the recitation of Deuteronomy 6:4–9 and related verses each morning and evening in fulfillment of verse 7; the obligation to teach Torah to one's children (v. 7), to wear *tefillin* (small boxes containing Deut 6:4–9 and related biblical verses) on the left arm and forehead during the morning and evening prayer in fulfillment of verse 8; and the obligation to inscribe these verses on the doorposts of one's home in fulfillment of verse 9 (today, a *mezuzah* is a small vessel containing Deut 6:4–9 and related verses that is posted on the doorframes of Jewish homes and some other buildings). *Tefillin* dating to at least the second century B.C.E. have been found at Qumran, as have *mezuzot* texts.

In their Ancient Near Eastern context, the Hebrew words *ahavah* and *avodah* refer to the "loyalty" and "service" of a vassal toward an overlord. In time, these words acquired a deep emotional content better translated as "love" and "worship." The twice-daily recitation of the *Shema* and its exhortation to love God with all one's heart, soul, and might are emotional highpoints in the daily liturgy followed by observant Jews, opportunities to express the individual's reverent yet intimate, even passionate, connection to God. According to one legend, when cruelly martyred at the hands of the Romans, R. Akiva (died ca. 132 C.E.) rejoiced that the time of his death coincided with the time for the recitation of the *Shema*, for by reciting the *Shema* with his dying breath he could finally fulfill the obligation to love God with *all* his soul. The tradition has arisen of reciting the *Shema*, not only in the midst of martyrdom, but on one's deathbed.

[1]And this is the Instruction—the laws and the rules—that the Lord your God has commanded [me] to impart to you, to be observed in the land that you are about to cross into and occupy, [2]so that you, your children, and your children's children may revere the Lord your God

and follow, as long as you live, all His laws and commandments that I enjoin upon you, to the end that you may long endure. [3]Obey, O Israel, willingly and faithfully, that it may go well with you and that you may increase greatly [in] "a land flowing with milk and honey," as the Lord, the God of your fathers, spoke to you.

[4]Hear, O Israel! The Lord is our God, the Lord alone. [5]You shall love the Lord your God with all your heart and with all your soul and with all your might. [6]Take to heart these instructions with which I charge you this day. [7]Impress them upon your children. Recite them when you stay at home and when you are away, when you lie down and when you get up. [8]Bind them as a sign on your hand and let them serve as a symbol on your forehead; [9]inscribe them on the doorposts of your house and on your gates.

DOCUMENT 6. THEMES OF CLASSICAL PROPHECY: MICAH 2:1–3; 3:1–4, 9–12; 4:1–7; 6:1–4, 6–8

Micah, from the small town of Moreshet 25 miles southwest of Jerusalem in Judah was the second southern prophet during the Assyrian crisis and the last of the eighth-century prophets. Unlike the city-bred Isaiah, Micah was a rural prophet prophesying between 740 and 700 B.C.E., often on behalf of the poor farmer. The book of Micah sounds many themes common to and representative of Israel's literary prophets. The prophet attacks the northern kingdom of Israel for idolatry, for which it will surely fall to the Assyrians. He condemns the people generally for their moral failings: Greedy landowners, dishonest merchants, a corrupt aristocracy are all the target of his denunciations (2:1–3, 3:1–4, 9–11) as are Judah's priests, judges, and false prophets (3:11–12). Where the prophet Isaiah is convinced of the inviolability of Jerusalem, Micah scornfully ridicules the belief that the sanctuary's presence in Jerusalem will protect the city from harm (3:12). On the contrary, he warns, God will destroy his city and his own Temple if necessary.

Micah 4:1–4 is an almost verbatim repetition of Isaiah 2:2–4 (which may indicate a circulation of units of literary prophecy among scribes). This passage tells of the future glory of Zion (= Jerusalem). Described in almost mythological terms, the mount of God's Temple towers above all other hills so that nations gazing upon it are inspired to ascend to the House of the God of Jacob and receive instruction in his Torah. There is a universalistic strand to these passages: in the future, God will arbitrate among the nations and an era of universal peace will ensue. Nevertheless the amalgamation of peoples is not here intended. The nations, cognizant of and accepting the word of the Lord from Jerusalem, continue to walk in the names of their gods (maintain their non-Israelite identity), while Israel walks in the name of the Lord, her God, forever (4:5).

In Chapter 6, Micah asserts the primacy of morality over cultic worship. The passage takes the form of a covenant lawsuit (or *riv*) in which God sues Israel for failing to abide by the terms of the covenant agreement. Verses 1–2 are the legal summons, in which the prophet acting as God's attorney summons the accused (Israel) and the witnesses (the mountains) who will hear God's case against Israel. The plaintiff's charge is presented in verses 3–4. Through his attorney (the prophet) God states his case: despite God's many benefactions and evident love for Israel, Israel has behaved appallingly. The defendant (Israel) has an opportunity to speak in verses 6 and 7, but with no case to plead she asks how she might effect reconciliation? How might she honor God—with sacrifices and offerings? The prophetic attorney's response in verse 8 is one of the most oft-quoted biblical verses and is praised in rabbinic tradition as the quintessence of all the commandments.

The book of Micah concludes with an assurance of God's forgiveness and eternal faithfulness to the patriarchal promises. The final verses (7:18–20) are incorporated in the liturgy for Rosh ha-Shanah (the New Year) and Yom Kippur (The Day of Atonement).

2 ¹Ah, those who plan iniquity
And design evil on their beds;
When morning dawns, they do it,
For they have the power.
²They covet fields, and seize them;
Houses, and take them away.
They defraud men of their homes,
And people of their land.
³Assuredly, thus said the Lord: I am planning such a misfortune
against this clan that you will not be able to free your necks from it.
you will not be able to walk erect; it will be such a time of disaster.

3 ¹I said:
Listen, you rulers of Jacob,
You chiefs of the House of Israel!
For you ought to know what is right,
²But you hate good and love evil.
³You have devoured My people's flesh;
You have flayed the skin off them,
And their flesh off their bones.
And after tearing their skins off them,
And their flesh off their bones,
And breaking their bones to bits,
You have cut it up as into a pot,
Like meat in a caldron.
⁴Someday they shall cry out to the Lord,
But He will not answer them;
At that time He will hide His face from them,
In accordance with the wrongs they have done.

⁹Hear this, you rulers of the House of Jacob,
You chiefs of the House of Israel,
Who detest justice
And make crooked all that is straight,
¹⁰Who build Zion with crime,
Jerusalem with iniquity!
¹¹Her rulers judge for gifts,
Her priests give rulings for a fee,
And her prophets divine for pay;
Yet they rely upon the Lord, saying,
"The Lord is in our midst;
No calamity shall overtake us."
¹²Assuredly, because of you
Zion shall be plowed as a field,
And Jerusalem shall become heaps of ruins,
And the Temple Mount
A shrine in the woods.

4 ¹In the days to come,
The Mount of the Lord's house shall stand
Firm above the mountains;
And it shall tower above the hills.
The Peoples shall gaze on it with joy,
²And the many nations shall go and shall say:
"Come,

Let us go up to the Mount of the Lord,
To the House of the God of Jacob;
That He may instruct us in His ways,
And that we may walk in His paths."
For instruction shall come forth from Zion,
The word of the Lord from Jerusalem.
³Thus He will judge among the many peoples,
And arbitrate for the multitude of nations,
However distant;
And they shall beat their swords into ploughshares
And their spears into pruning hooks.
Nation shall not take up
Sword against nation;
They shall never again know war;
⁴But every man shall sit
Under his grapevine or fig tree
With no one to disturb him.
For it was the Lord of Hosts who spoke.
⁵Though all the peoples walk
Each in the names of its gods,
We will walk
In the name of the Lord our God
Forever and ever.
⁶In that day—declares the Lord—
I will assemble the lame [sheep]
And will gather the outcast
And those I have treated harshly;
⁷And I will turn the lame into a remnant
And the expelled into a populous nation.
And the Lord will reign over them on Mount Zion
Now and for evermore.

6 ¹Hear what the Lord is saying:
Come, present [My] case before the mountains,
And let the hills hear you pleading.
²Hear, you mountains, the case of the Lord—
You firm foundations of the earth!
For the Lord has a case against His people,
He has a suit against Israel.
³"My people!
What wrong have I done you?
What hardship have I caused you?

Testify against Me.
[4]In fact, I brought you up from the land of Egypt,
I redeemed you from the house of bondage,
And I sent before you
Moses, Aaron, and Miriam . . . "

. . . [6]"With what shall I approach the Lord,
Do homage to God on high?
Shall I approach Him with burnt offerings,
With calves a year old?
[7]Would the Lord be pleased with thousands of rams,
With myriads of streams of oil?
Shall I give my first-born for my transgression,
The fruit of my body for my sins?"
[8]He has told you, O man, what is good,
And what the Lord requires of you:
Only to do justice
And to love goodness,
And to walk modestly with your God.
[9]Then will your name achieve wisdom.

7 [18] . . . Who is a God like You,
Forgiving iniquity
And remitting transgression;
Who has not maintained His wrath forever
Against the remnant of His own people,
Because He loves graciousness!
[19]He will take us back in love;
He will cover up our iniquities,
You will hurl all our sins
Into the depths of the sea.
[20]You will keep faith with Jacob,
Loyalty to Abraham,
As You promised on oath to our fathers
In days gone by.

DOCUMENT 7. ISRAELITE WISDOM TRADITION: ECCLESIASTES (QOHELET) 1:1–9; 2:13–17; 8:9–9:12

The books of Proverbs, Job, and Ecclesiastes (or Qohelet) belong to
the Wisdom genre of literature. The classic biblical book of Wisdom

is Proverbs. The book's short, two-line sentences value hard work and diligence; warn against overindulgence in sleep, sex and wine; and recommend honesty, kindness, loyalty, sobriety, and restraint. Wisdom is identified with fear of the Lord and the wise man knows that his good deeds will bring him happiness and success. The book is pervaded by a complacent, almost smug certainty, that the righteous and wicked of the world receive what they deserve in life; God's just providence and a moral world order are presupposed.

The book of Qohelet ("the one who assembles" in Greek, "Ecclesiastes") attacks the optimism and conventional piety of works like Proverbs and the Deuteronomistic corpus. The tone of the book is one of cynical detachment and skepticism, even melancholy. The theme sounded at the outset is the emptiness of human effort. All is futile: one generation goes, another comes and the earth remains the same forever. Nothing is permanent, all is fleeting. The only things that happen have happened before: the endlessly repeating cycles of nature and the endlessly repeating cycles of human life. In one of the most famous passages from the book, Qohelet expresses the idea that everything has its season or time, with the consequence that the effort of humans to alter or effect anything is meaningless. All things come to pass and return in endless cycles; we add nothing by our efforts.

The writer has tried everything in his search for something that is not vain or fleeting but permanent. He determines that wisdom is better than folly and ignorance, yet ultimately death obliterates everything and the fate of sage and fool are one and the same. The inexorable fact of death—beyond which there is nothing—makes life entirely meaningless, according to Qohelet. Even more explicitly than Job, Qohelet attacks the principle of divine providence and distributive justice. There is no principle of reward or punishment in this life (as evidenced by the fact that the wicked often prosper while the innocent suffer) or any other. But for all his despair and cynicism, Qohelet also sounds a positive note. He does not, after all recommend nihilism or suicide despite the lack of purpose or meaning in life. Rather, he states that every life has its moments of happiness, and these we should seize while we can (Qoh 9:7–10). We must not delude ourselves—there is no grand plan that we can see, no meaning to our toil, and no life in the hereafter that we are working toward. But one can still find happiness and love and with these one should be content. Striving after anything more is a striving after wind that leaves one weary and bitter. Accept the reality of death and enjoy what can be enjoyed in the short time one has—a recommendation that may rest on the insight that it is precisely the fact of death that makes life so precious. Whatever it is your power to do, Qohelet urges, do with all your might, for this is your one and only chance.

Qohelet is certainly an unusual book and its inclusion in the biblical canon was evidently a matter of some controversy. The pious postscript at the end of the book (Qoh 12:13–14 "The sum of the matter, when all is said and done: Revere God and observe His commandments! For this applies to all mankind: that God will call every creature to account for everything unknown, be it good or bad") may be a later editor's effort to conform the book to the conventional piety represented in works like Deuteronomy and Proverbs.

Tradition attributes the work to king Solomon, but internal evidence (the appearance of Persian words and late grammatical forms) points to a much later date, between the late sixth and third centuries B.C.E. The book of Qohelet is read on Sukkot, one of the three major pilgrimage festivals which commemorates both the completion of the fall harvest and the annual cycle of Torah readings.

> 1 [1]"Utter futility!" said Qohelet, "utter futility! All is futile! What real value is there for a man in all the gains he makes beneath the sun? One generation goes, another comes, but the earth remains the same forever.
>
> [9] . . . Only that shall happen which has happened, only that occur which has occurred; there is nothing new beneath the sun! . . . "
>
> 2 [13]I found that wisdom is superior to folly as light is superior to darkness; [14]a wise man has his eyes in his head, whereas a fool walks in darkness. But I also realized that the same fate awaits them both. [15]So I reflected: The fate of the fool is also destined for me; to what advantage then have I been wise? And I came to the conclusion that that too was futile, [16]because the wise man, just like the fool is not remembered forever, for as the succeeding days roll by, both are forgotten. Alas, the wise man dies, just like the fool! [17]And so I loathed life. For I was distressed by all that goes on under the sun, because everything is futile and pursuit of wind . . .
>
> 8 [9]All these things I observed; I noted all that went on under the sun, while men had authority over men to treat them unjustly. [10]And then I saw scoundrels coming from the Holy Site and being brought to burial, while such as had acted righteously were forgotten in the city.

And here is another frustration: [11]the fact that the sentence imposed for evil deeds is not executed swiftly, which is why men are emboldened to do evil—[12]the fact that a sinner may do evil a hundred times and his [punishment] still be delayed. For although I am aware that "It will be well with those who revere God since they revere Him, [13]and it will not be well with the scoundrel, and he will not live long, because he does not revere God"—[14]here is a frustration that occurs in the world: Sometimes an upright man is requited according to the conduct of the scoundrel; and sometimes the scoundrel is requited according to the conduct of the upright. I say all that is frustration.

[15]I therefore praised enjoyment. For the only good a man can have under the sun is to eat and drink and enjoy himself. That much can accompany him, in exchange for his wealth, through the days of life that God has granted him under the sun.

[16]For I have set my mind to learn wisdom and to observe the business that goes on in the world—even to the extent of going without sleep day and night—[17]and I have observed all that God brings to pass. Indeed, man cannot guess the events that occur under the sun. For man tries strenuously, but fails to guess them; and even if a sage should think to discover them he would not be able to guess them.

9 [1]For all this I noted, and I ascertained all this: that the actions of even the righteous and the wise are determined by God. Even love! Even hate! Man knows none of these in advance—[2]none! For the same fate is in store for all: for the righteous, and for the wicked; for the good and pure, and for the impure; for him who sacrifices, and for him who does not; for him who is pleasing, and for him who is displeasing; and for him who swears, and for him who shuns oaths. [3]That is the sad thing about all that goes on under the sun: that the same fate is in store for all. (Not only that, but men's hearts are full of sadness, and their minds of madness, while they live; and then—the dead!) [4]For he who is reckoned among the living has something to look forward to—even a live dog is better than a dead lion—[5]since the living know they will die. But the dead know nothing; they have no more recompense, for even the memory of them has died. [6]Their loves, their hates, their jealousies have long since perished; and they have no more share till the end of time in all that goes on under the sun.

[7]Go, eat your bread in gladness, and drink your wine in joy; for your action was long ago approved by God. [8]Let your clothes always be freshly washed, and your head never lack ointment. [9]Enjoy happiness

with a woman you love all the fleeting days of life that have been granted to you under the sun—all your fleeting days. For that alone is what you can get out of life and out of the means you acquire under the sun. [10]Whatever it is in your power to do, do with all your might. For there is no action, no reasoning, no learning, no wisdom in Sheol, where you are going.

[11]I have further observed under the sun that
The race is not won by the swift,
Nor the battle by the valiant;
Nor is bread won by the wise,
Nor wealth by the intelligent,
Nor favor by the learned.

For the time of mischance comes to all. [12]And a man cannot even know his time. As fishes are enmeshed in a fatal net, and as birds are trapped in a snare, so men are caught at the time of calamity, when it comes upon them without warning.

DOCUMENTS 8a–c. R. YOHANAN BEN ZAKKAI AND THE RABBINIC MYTH OF ORIGINS

The following three passages are legendary accounts of R. Yohanan b. Zakkai, an important figure in rabbinic historiography. According to the first story, R. Yohanan anticipated the destruction of Jerusalem, escaped the Roman siege, and saw to the preservation of Torah by assembling a group of sages and disciples at Yavneh (near modern-day Tel Aviv), with the emperor's permission. His sorrow at the destruction of the temple is palpable, and yet as the second story suggests, R. Yohanan b. Zakkai does not dwell on his grief. He simply asserts that an equally effective atonement—one that can serve until such time as the Temple is rebuilt—is still available. Through acts of loving-kindness and moral virtue Jews obtain atonement for their sins. They are thus no less capable of attracting and maintaining the divine presence in this post-Temple period than they were when the Temple stood. Reconstructing a life of Torah means developing practices, concepts, and institutions that would nourish Jewish life in the absence of the temple and in the midst of communal devastation. R. Yohanan b. Zakkai's pupil R. Joshua learns this lesson well. In the third story, R. Joshua encounters a group of ascetics who refuse to eat meat or drink wine since the destruction of the Temple. R. Joshua will not give in to nihilism despite the recent national trauma. This tale conveys the message that fixating on destruction paralyzes the community and brings life to a halt. Life goes on and one must move forward—remembering *without* despairing.

These texts are among the many stories redacted in rabbinic works of a much later date (fourth to seventh centuries C.E) that portray the rise of rabbinic Judaism as the work of noble (though not flawless) and determined sages acting with foresight and purpose on a large scale to renew and sustain Jewish life in the immediate postdestruction period (late first century C.E.). In fact, the rabbinic movement was most likely small, fractured, and insular in the late first century C.E. It would be some time before rabbinic Judaism acquired a large degree of prestige and authority among the general Jewish populace.

8a. Avot deRabbi Natan 4

When Vespasian came to destroy Jerusalem he said to them (the inhabitants), "Fools! Why do you want to destroy this city and [why do] want to burn the temple? What do I want of you except that you send me one bow or one arrow [to symbolize submission] and I will leave you?"

They said to him, "Just as we went forth against your two predecessors and killed them, so we will go forth against you and kill you."

When R. Yohanan b. Zakkai heard this he sent for the men of Jerusalem and said to them, "My sons, why are you destroying this city and [why] do you want to burn the temple? What does he ask of you but one bow or arrow and he will leave you?"

They said to him, "Just as we went forth against his two predecessors and killed them, so we will go forth against him and kill him."

Vespasian had men positioned within the walls of Jerusalem. They wrote down every word they heard on arrows and shot them beyond the walls, saying that R. Yohanan b. Zakkai was among the friends of the emperor.

R. Yohanan b. Zakkai spoke to them one day, then a second, and a third day, but they did not agree, so he sent for his students R. Eliezer and R. Joshua. He said to them, "My sons, arise and take me out of here. Make a coffin for me and I will lie down in it." R. Eliezer grasped its front and R. Joshua grasped its back. At twilight they carried him up to the gates of Jerusalem. The gatekeepers said to him, "What is this?" They said to them, "It is a corpse. Do you not know that one does not leave a corpse overnight in Jerusalem?" They said to him, "If it is a corpse, take it out."

They took him out and carried him until they reached Vespasian. They opened the coffin and he stood before him. He [Vespasian] said to him, "Are you Yohanan b. Zakkai? Ask, what shall I give you?" He said to him, "I ask nothing of you except that I may go to Yavneh and study with my disciples, and institute prayer there, and perform all the commandments." He said to him, "Go and do everything that you wish." He [R.Yohanan b. Zakkai] said to him, "Would you like me to tell you something?" He said to him, "Speak." He said to him, "Behold, you are about to become emperor." He said to him, "How do you know?" He said to him, "There is a tradition that the temple will not be delivered into the hand of a commoner but into the hand of a king, as it says, "The thickets of the forest shall be hacked away with iron, and Lebanon shall fall to the mighty one" (Isa 10:34).

It was said: Only one, two, or three days passed before there came to him a messenger from the city that the emperor died and they voted him to be emperor.

They brought him [Vespasian] a catapult and drew it up against the wall of Jerusalem. They brought him boards of cedar and he placed them in the catapult and he struck against the wall until he broke through. They brought him the head of a pig and he put it in the catapult and he shot it toward the entrails that were on the altar. At that time Jerusalem was captured.

R. Yohanan b. Zakkai was sitting and looking and trembling just as Eli sat and looked, as it says, "He found Eli sitting on a seat, waiting beside the road—his heart trembling for the Ark of God" (1 Sam 4:13). When R. Yohanan b. Zakkai heard that Jerusalem was destroyed and the temple burned, he tore his clothes, and his students tore their clothes, and they were sitting and crying and mourning.

8b. Avot deRabbi Natan 6

Once as R. Yohanan b. Zakkai was coming forth from Jerusalem, R. Joshua followed after him and beheld the Temple in ruins. "Woe unto us," R. Joshua cried, "that this, the place where the sins of Israel were atoned, is laid waste;" "My son," R. Yohanan b. Zakkai said to him, "be not grieved. We have another atonement as effective as this. And what is it? It is acts of loving-kindness, as it is said, *'For I desire mercy and not sacrifice'* (Hos 6:6)."

8c. b. Bava Batra 60b

Our Rabbis taught: When the Temple was destroyed for the second time, large numbers in Israel became ascetics, binding themselves neither to eat meat nor to drink wine. R. Joshua got into conversation with them and said to them: "My sons, why do you not eat meat nor drink wine?" They replied: "Shall we eat flesh which used to be brought as an offering on the altar, now that this altar is in abeyance? Shall we drink wine which used to be poured as a libation on the altar, but now no longer?" He said to them: "If that is so, we should not eat bread either, because the meal offerings have ceased." They said: "[That is so, and] we can manage with fruit." "We should not eat fruit either," [he said,] "because there is no longer an offering of first fruits." "Then we can manage with other fruits," [they said]. "But, [he said,] we should not drink water, because there is no longer any ceremony of the pouring of water." To this they could find no answer, so he said to them: "My sons, come and listen to me. Not to mourn at all is impossible, because the blow has fallen. To mourn overmuch is also impossible, because we do not impose on the community a hardship which the majority cannot endure ... The Sages therefore have ordained thus. A man may stucco his house, but he should leave a little bare ... A man can prepare a full-course banquet, but he should leave out an item or two ... A woman can put on all her ornaments, but leave off one or two."

DOCUMENT 9. THE TRANSMISSION OF TORAH

The first paragraph of Mishnah Avot, dating in its final form to the third century C.E., states that Moses received Torah at Sinai and transmitted it to Joshua, beginning a sequence of transmission that continued through the Elders to the Prophets, to the men of the Great Assembly (in the time of Ezra) among whom was Simeon the Righteous (third century C.E.). The transmission continued from Simeon the Righteous and his disciple Antigonus of Sokho through five pairs of teachers—the last being the famous pair Hillel and Shammai. Hillel and Shammai transmitted Torah to R. Yohanan b. Zakkai who lived at the time of the destruction

(70 C.E.) and who, in turn, transmitted Torah to five disciples. Each "link" in this chain of transmission is reported to have said three things— generally pithy aphorisms which are then cited (many are omitted here due to the constraints of space). Additional teachings are reported in some instances, and the teachings of R. Yohanan's five disciples as well as those of later sages continue in the ensuing paragraphs. It seems clear that the Mishnah speaks about the transmission of not only the Written Torah but also additional oral teachings that were conveyed from master to disciple.

The presentation of a chain of continuous teachings from Sinai to the rabbinic teachers and editor of the Mishnah itself, comports well with rab- binic pedagogical ideals according to which knowledge of Torah is gained only through personal discipleship. According to some scholars, the insis- tence that all rabbinic teachings remain oral underscores the centrality of the master–disciple relationship in the transmission of rabbinic culture—a phenomenon entirely consonant with the master–disciple relationship at the heart of Greco-Roman *paideia* (education).

The list of sages in m. Avot 1 has been compared to the *diadoche* texts of Greco-Roman philosophical schools—succession lists of recognized teach- ers of a particular school beginning with its founder. Such succession lists were also composed by early Christian writers from the second century C.E. on (e.g. Justin, Irenaeus, and Athanasius) as a kind of genealogy that legitimated authority.

Interestingly, the Mishnah's list leaves out the one group biblically appointed to teach Torah to Israel—the priestly class (Lev 10:11). This is most likely a pointed and purposeful omission. Instead, the leadership that emerges from this passage is rabbinic and many of the statements cited in the passage emphasize Pharisaic themes, such as the need for a "fence around the Torah" (the creation of additional laws to safeguard against inadvertent violations of biblical prohibitions), the importance of Torah study, and service to a master sage.

Scholars have long recognized a key interpolation in the middle of the material on Hillel. The interpolation, which appears here in italics, interrupts the chain of transmission from Moses through Hillel to R. Yohanan b. Zakkai and his students (these basic links in the chain appear in bold). The interpolation differs from the surrounding material in that it lacks the standard "X received from Y" formula, and consists of statements attributed to the immediate ancestors of R. Judah the Patriarch who is credited with editing the Mishnah (ca. 220 C.E.). These ancestors are R. Gamaliel (a contemporary of R. Yohanan b. Zakkai), his son Shim'on, and *his* grandson who is likewise named Shim'on and is also the father of R. Judah. Following this interpolation we pick up again with Hillel and continue the transmission of teaching to R. Yohanan b. Zakkai and his disciples. It would seem that R. Judah has inserted into this text a genealogy of the patriarchate in an effort to trace that office back to Hillel and so establish its legitimacy and authority.

Mishnah Avot (early third century C.E.), selections from Chapters 1 and 2:

Moses received the Torah at Sinai and handed it down to Joshua, and Joshua to the elders, and the elders to the prophets, and the prophets to the men of the Great Assembly.
The latter used to say three things: "Be deliberate in judgment, raise up many disciples, and make a (protective) fence around the Torah."

Simeon the Righteous was one of the last of the Men of the Great Assembly.
He used to say, "The world is based upon three things: The Torah, divine service and acts of loving kindness."

Antigonus of Sokho received from Simeon the Righteous.
He used to say, "Do not be like servants who serve the master in the expectation of receiving a reward, but be like servants who serve the master without the expectation of receiving a reward, and let the fear of heaven be upon you."

Yosi b. Yo'ezer of Zeredah and Yosi b. Yohanan of Jerusalem received from them [Simeon the Righteous and Antigonus of Sokho].
Yosi b. Yo'ezer used to say: Let your house be a meeting house for the sages and let yourself be covered by the dust of their feet and drink in their words with thirst.
Yosi b. Yohanan of Jerusalem used to say...

Joshua b. Perahiah and Nittai the Arbelite received from them [the foregoing pair].
Joshua b. Perahiah used to say...
Nittai the Arbelite used to say...

Judah b. Tabbai and Shimeon b. Shetah received from them [the foregoing pair].
Judah b. Tabbai used to say . . .
Shimeon b. Shetah used to say . . .

Shemayah and Avtalion received from them [the foregoing pair].
Shemayah used to say . . .
Avtalion used to say . . .

Hillel and Shammai received from them [the foregoing pair].
Hillel used to say, "Be one of the disciples of Aaron, loving peace and pursuing peace, loving one's fellow beings and bringing them near to Torah . . ."
. . . He also used to say, "If I am not for myself, who is for me; but if I am for myself alone, what am I; and if not now, when? . . ."
Shammai used to say, "Make your Torah [study] a regular habit. Speak little but do much, and receive all men with a pleasant countenance.

R. Gamaliel used to say . . .
Simeon his son used to say . . .
R. Simeon, son of Gamaliel used to say . . .
Rabbi [Judah the patriarch, son of the preceding] used to say . . .
R. Gamaliel, the Son of R. Judah the patriarch used to say . . .

Hillel also used to say . . .

R. Yohanan b. Zakkai received from Hillel and Shammai.
He used to say, "If you have learned much Torah, do not claim credit for yourself, because it was for this purpose that you were created."

R. Yohanan b. Zakkai had five disciples and they were these R. Eliezer b. Hyrcanus, R. Joshua b. Hananiah, R. Yosi the priest, R. Simeon b. Netana'el, and R. Eleazar b. Arakh . . .
They each said three things . . .

DOCUMENTS 10 a–d. CENTRAL FEATURES OF BABYLONIAN RABBINIC JUDAISM

The Babylonian rabbinic Judaism that emerged from late antiquity is characterized by certain features that continued through the medieval period and into the orthodox Judaism of the modern age. These include the institution of the yeshivah centered around the study of the Talmud; the valorization of argumentation, dialectic, and indeterminacy; and the ideal of endless study as a means to serve God. As early Christianity developed an orthodoxy that rejected dialectics and debate in favor of a single undisputed truth, Babylonian rabbinic Judaism divinized dispute and ambiguity and rejected the idea of a single knowable *logos*.

The turn to dialectics, indeterminacy, and ambiguity is thematized in sources from fifth- to seventh-century C.E. Babylonia. A few earlier rabbinic texts, like contemporaneous Christian texts, evince a suspicion of controversy as a threat to authority. In the first passage cited below from the Tosefta, the rise of controversy and dispute is blamed on students who were inattentive in their studies.

10a. t. Hagigah 2:9

> Once there were many disciples of Hillel and Shammai, who did not serve [their masters, i.e., study] sufficiently. There grew up many divisions within Israel, and the Torah became two Torahs.

In contrast to this text, other early sources and especially stories and discussions found in later strata of the Babylonian Talmud, abandon the idea of a single uncontested truth. These stories celebrate the polyphony and indeterminacy of God's revelation and locate the ideals of debate and pluralism in the formative period of Yavneh immediately after the destruction. Thus, Document 10b reverses Document 10a and asserts that controversy between the disciples of Shammai (Bet Shammai) and the disciples of Hillel (Bet Hillel) in the first century C.E. was not the result of inept students; rather it was a reflection of divine polysemy (conveying more than one meaning at once). As a consequence, even contradictory interpretations of the law can be declared the words of the living God. For practical purposes, of course, decisions regarding the interpretation of the law must be made. But such decisions are recognized as contingent. Although Bet Hillel merit that the law should be decided according to their view because of their pious demeanor and inclusive study methods, the words of their opponents are no less "correct."

10b. b. Eruvin 13b

> R. Abba stated in the name of Samuel: For three years there was a dispute between Bet Shammai and Bet Hillel, the former asserting, "The halakhah is in agreement with our views" and the latter

contending, "The halakhah is in agreement with our views." Then a heavenly voice came forth, announcing, "These and these are the words of the living God, but the halakhah is in agreement with the rulings of Bet Hillel." Since, however, both are the words of the living God what was it that entitled Bet Hillel to have the halakhah fixed in agreement with their rulings? Because they were kindly and modest, they studied their own rulings and those of Bet Shammai, and were even so [humble] as to mention the actions of Bet Shammai before theirs.

The retrojection of these ideals onto the Yavneh period continues in Document 10c, one of the most famous passages of the Babylonian Talmud. First the text:

10c. b. Bava Metsia 59a

[Regarding a certain kind of oven, R. Eliezer rules that it is ritually pure and the sages rule that it is ritually impure.]

It was taught: On that day, R. Eliezer responded with all the responses in the world, but they did not accept them from him. He said to them, "If the law is as I say, let the carob [tree] prove it." The carob uprooted itself from its place and went 100 cubits—and some say 400 cubits. They said to him, "One does not bring proof from the carob." The carob returned to its place.

He said to them, "If the law is as I say, let the aqueduct prove it." The water turned backward. They said to him, "One does not bring proof from water." The water returned to its place.

He said to them, "If it [the law] is as I say, let the walls of the academy prove it." The walls of the academy inclined to fall. R. Joshua rebuked them. He said to them, "When sages argue with one another about matters of law, what is it to you?" It was taught: They did not fall out of respect for R. Joshua, and they did not straighten up out of respect for R. Eliezer, and they are still inclined!

He said to them, "If it is as I say, let it be proved from Heaven." A heavenly voice went forth and said, "What is your problem with R. Eliezer, since the law is like him in every place?"

R. Joshua stood up on his feet and said, "It is not in Heaven" (Deut 30:12).

What is "It is not in Heaven?" R. Jeremiah said, "We do not listen to a heavenly voice, since you already gave it to us on Mt. Sinai and it is written there, Incline after the majority" (Exod 23:2).

> R. Nathan came upon Elijah. He said to him, "What did the Holy One do at the time [of R. Joshua's and R. Jeremiah's bold statements]?" [Elijah] said to him, He laughed and said, "My children have conquered me, my children have conquered me."

The first-century *tanna*, R. Eliezer is described as locking horns with the other rabbinic sages over the ritual purity status of a particular type of oven. R. Eliezer advances every argument he can think of but the sages are not persuaded. He then resorts to miraculous feats to prove his view, but as the other sages wryly observe, these are not arguments and have no power to persuade. Finally, a heavenly voice indicates that the law is indeed as R. Eliezer says. To this R. Joshua boldly responds that the Torah is not in heaven, but on earth where it is to be studied and interpreted by humans through the tools of rational discourse, argumentation, and majority rule.

The late editors of this story dramatically assert not only that the majority have authority over the minority but that the sages' rulings arrived at through reasoned argumentation can defeat God—the very author of the instruction whose interpretation and application is under debate! No miracle, not even a heavenly voice, can legitimate or ground the authority of a legal view because while the Torah may be *from* heaven, it is no longer *in* heaven. In other words, despite the Torah's divine origin, control over the interpretation and administration of the Torah has been ceded by God to admittedly fallible human beings who must follow proper legal processes of argumentation and majority rule. God has been locked out of the academy—or rather he is but one voice within the academy, a voice that can be overruled. God is depicted as reacting to this bold assertion of rabbinic legislative and interpretative authority with pleasure.

In the continuation of the story not cited here, R. Eliezer is punished with excommunication and subjected to some humiliation, presumably for failing to recognize that interpretation of God's instruction is determined by principles of rational argumentation and majority rule. Yet this overly harsh action is clearly disapproved by God, who strikes down R. Gamliel for issuing the excommunication. Majority rule is not a license for the expulsion and humiliation of the minority since "these and these are the words of the living God." It is merely a procedural mechanism for the good order of the community.

Pluralism, debate, and inclusiveness are central themes in Document 10d and once again R. Gamliel and his politics of exclusion are criticized.

This late Babylonian version of an older Palestinian original depicts R. Gamliel as a rather tyrannical head of the academy. Brooking no opposition, R. Gamliel humiliates those who propound halakhah that diverges from his own view. His public shaming of R. Joshua leads to a rebellion and R. Gamliel is ousted as head of the academy. His elitist admission policy is revoked, the doors are thrown open and benches introduced to accommodate the flood of newly admitted students. R. Gamliel fears that he was wrong to have denied access to so many and is comforted with a dream from God indicating that the new students are worthless. But, the narrator tells us, it was not so—God merely pitied R. Gamliel! In fact, the author notes, all pending matters in the academy were resolved at that time—testimony to the virtue of an open admission policy.

Tellingly, one of the matters to come before the academy following the deposition of R. Gamliel is the question of admitting an Ammonite into the community of Israel (Ammonites are one of two groups explicitly prohibited entry into the community by Torah law; see Deut 23:4). R. Gamliel opposes the acceptance of the Ammonite but R. Joshua skillfully argues for the lawfulness of his admission. His elitism and exclusivity discredited, R. Gamliel seeks reconciliation with the sages. He appeals to his dynastic right to leadership, and the rabbis defer. The text thus espouses the democratic ideals of meritocracy while simultaneously deferring to the leadership claims of a privileged class.

10d. b. Berakhot 27b–28a

> Our sages have taught: Once a certain student came before R. Joshua. He asked him, "The evening prayer—is it optional or obligatory?" He said to him, "It is optional." He came before R. Gamliel. He said to him, "The evening prayer—is it optional or obligatory?" He said to him, "It is obligatory." He said to him, "But didn't R. Joshua tell me it is optional?" He [R. Gamliel] said to him, "Wait until the shield-bearers [the sages] enter the academy."
>
> When the shield-bearers entered the questioner stood up and asked, "The evening prayer—is it optional or obligatory?" R. Gamliel said to him, "It is obligatory." R. Gamliel said to the sages, "Is there anyone who disagrees on this matter?" R. Joshua said to him, "No." R. Gamliel said to him, "But didn't they tell me in your name 'It is optional'?" He said to him, "Joshua! Stand on your feet that they may bear witness against you!"

R. Joshua stood on his feet and said, "If I were alive and he [the student] dead—the living could contradict the dead. Now that I am alive and he is alive—how can the living contradict the living?"

R. Gamliel was sitting and expounding while R. Joshua stood on his feet, until all the people murmured and said to Hutspit the *turgeman* [a kind of human "loudspeaker"], "Stop!" and he stopped. They said, "How long will he [R. Gamliel] go on distressing [R. Joshua]? He distressed him last year on Rosh HaShana. He distressed him over the firstling, in the incident involving R. Zadoq. Now he distresses him again. Come, let us depose him. Whom will we raise up [in his stead]?" [After some consideration, they decide upon R. Eleazar b. Azariah] . . .

. . . It was taught: That day they removed the guard at the gate and permitted students to enter, for R. Gamliel had decreed, "Any student whose inside is not like his outside may not enter the academy." That day many benches were added. R. Yohanan said, "Abba Yosef b. Dostenai and the sages disagree. One said four hundred benches were added and one said seven hundred benches were added."

R. Gamliel became distressed. He said, "Perhaps, God forbid, I held back Torah from Israel." They showed him in a dream white casks filled with ashes. But that was not the case; they showed him [the dream] only to put his mind at ease [but he really had held back Torah from Israel].

It was taught: They taught tractate Eduyyot on that day . . . And there was not a single law pending in the academy that they did not resolve.

And even R. Gamliel did not hold himself back from Torah. For it was taught:

On that day Judah the Ammonite, a resident alien, stood before them in the academy. He said to them, "Am I permitted to enter the congregation of Israel [i.e., may I convert]?" R. Gamliel said to him, "You are forbidden." R. Joshua said to him, "You are permitted." R. Gamliel said, "Is it not written, 'No Ammonite or Moabite shall be admitted into the congregation of the Lord' (Deut 23:4)?" R. Joshua said to him, "And are Ammon and Moab in their [original] places? Sennacherib King of Assyria has since come up and mixed up all the nations, as it says, 'I have erased the borders of peoples; I have plundered their treasures and exiled their vast populations' (Isa 10:13). And whatever separates, [we deem it to have] separated from the majority." R. Gamliel said to him, "Has it not already been said, 'I will restore the fortunes of the Ammonites—declares the Lord' (Jer 49:6), and they have already been restored?" R. Joshua said to him, "Has it not already been said, 'I will restore my people Israel' (Amos 9:14), and they have not yet been restored?" Immediately they permitted him to enter the congregation.

R. Gamliel said, "I will go and appease R. Joshua." When he arrived at his house, he saw that the walls of his house were black. He said to him, "From the walls of your house it is evident that you are a blacksmith." He said to him, "Woe to the generation of whom you are the head, for you do not know the distress of the scholars, how they earn a living and how they subsist." He said to him, "I apologize to you. Forgive me." He [R. Joshua] paid no attention to him. [R. Gamliel said], "Do it for the honor of my father's house." He said to him, "You are forgiven."

[This is followed by reconciliation with the sages generally.]

DOCUMENT 11. MIDRASHIC VIRTUOSITY

The following story—at once humorous and tragic—gives voice to the rabbinic author's sense of tremendous distance and difference from the biblical world of Moses and ancient Israel while at the same time affirming a sense of kinship with that world.

b. Menachot 29b

Rav Judah said in the name of Rav: "When Moses ascended to heaven [to receive the Torah] he found the Holy One, blessed be He, engaged in affixing [decorative] crownlets to the letters." Moses said, "Lord of the Universe, why do you bother with this?!" He answered, "There will arise a man at the end of many generations, Akiva b. Joseph by name, who will expound upon each crownlet heaps and heaps of laws." "Lord of the Universe" said Moses, "allow me to see him." He replied, "Turn around." Moses went and sat down behind eight rows [and listened to the discussions]. Not being able to follow their arguments he was depressed, but when they came to a certain topic and the disciples said to the master, "Whence do you know it?" and the latter [R. Akiva] replied, "It is a law given unto Moses at Sinai"—Moses was comforted. Thereupon he returned to the Holy One, blessed be He, and said, "Lord of the Universe, You have such a man and You give your Torah by me!" He replied, "Be silent, for such is My decree." Then Moses said, "Lord of the Universe, you have shown me his Torah, now show me his reward." "Turn around," said He, and Moses turned round and saw them weighing out his flesh at the market-stalls. "Lord of the Universe," cried Moses, "such Torah, and such a reward!" He replied, "Be silent, for such is my decree."

According to the story, Moses ascends to heaven to bring the Torah to Israel, and finds God attaching final calligraphic flourishes to the text. To Moses' astonished query God replies that a man will later derive numerous laws from these seemingly meaningless squiggles. Fascinated, Moses asks to see this man and is immediately transported to the first-century C.E. schoolhouse of R. Akiva where he sits with the least skilled students and is at a complete loss to understand. Moses, the very one to whom God entrusted his Torah and the first to teach Torah to Israel, does not recognize that Torah in the hands of a rabbinic sage, a midrashic virtuoso, some 1,500 years later. Moses' depression is relieved only when R. Akiva declares concerning a particular law that it cannot be derived through midrashic exegesis of Scripture, but has been received independently as a law stretching back to Moses at Sinai.

In the story, Moses never does understand the proceedings of the school-house, the complex exegetical processes by which a vast structure of laws and teachings had come to rest upon seemingly "insignificant" details in the biblical text. Indeed, R. Akiva's midrashic virtuosity makes Moses quite nervous—and in this he surely reflects the rabbis' own anxiety about midrashic exegesis. However, the depiction of God as partner to R. Akiva's midrashic excesses suggests that this anxiety is not absolute. Portraying God as R. Akiva's partner betokens at least a desire on the part of the author(s) to believe that despite the yawning gulf that appears to separate the teachings of the rabbis from the divine Torah of ancient Israel, there is an organic unity between them. Midrashic exegesis may engender an agonizing sense of distance and difference between the Torah and later rabbinic halakhah, but midrash is also the bridge that connects the two, and in Moses' mouth are placed words of praise and approbation for R. Akiva. In this story, the rabbis assert their faith in the power and creative possibilities inherent in the midrashic method despite—or rather because of—their equally explicit anxiety over the (at times) unintuitive nature of its results.

The tragic ending to the story is a reference to the martyrdom of R. Akiva. As a very old man, R. Akiva was flayed alive by the Romans for his support of the Bar Kochba revolt. For such suffering, there can be no explanation or justification—only silence.

DOCUMENT 12. TALMUDIC DIALECTICS: A SAMPLE STUDY TEXT

To this day, traditional Jews view Talmud study as a supreme religious act. Exploring the meaning of God's commandments through dialectical argumentation, exercising the mental faculties in the service of God is a ritual lived out in *yeshivot* and Talmud study circles on a daily basis.

All Talmud study begins with a paragraph of Mishnah that stands at the center of the talmudic discussion. The following example study text centers on Mishnah Avodah Zarah (Idolatry) 3:1 concerning the prohibition of images. The Mishnah's teaching is itself based upon the biblical prohibition of images (see for example, Deut 7:5, 12:3, 13:18). The Bible calls for the utter destruction of idols and images within the land of Israel—nothing of the forbidden thing is to "cleave to one's hand."

At the time of the Mishnah's redaction, however, the land of Israel was under the dominion of Rome, a pagan empire whose cultic practices included the erection and worship of images and statues of all kinds. How, one may ask, in an environment replete with pagan worshippers and symbols, did the rabbis negotiate the biblical zero tolerance policy for idolatrous images within the land of Israel? Following the text is a step-by-step analysis of its argument.

b. Avodah Zarah 40b–41a

Mishnah: All images are prohibited (for any use) because they are worshipped (at least) once a year—the view of R. Meir; but the sages say it is not prohibited unless it holds in its hand a staff, a bird, or a sphere. R. Shimeon ben Gamliel says, also any [image] that holds anything in its hand.

Gemara: If they are worshipped once a year, what is the reason of the sages [for permitting them]?!

R. Isaac b. Joseph said in the name of R. Yohanan: In the place where R. Meir lived, [idolators] used to worship each image once a year; and since R. Meir takes a minority [practice] into consideration, he decreed [against images] in all other places on account of that place. The sages, however, who do not take a minority [practice] into consideration did not decree [against images] in all other places on account of that place.

R. Judah said in the name of Shmuel: The mishnah refers to royal statues.

Rabbah bar bar Hanah said R. Yohanan said: and the mishnah refers to these when they are standing at the entrance of a city.

Rabbah said: There is a difference of opinion in the case of [these statues] in villages, but as for those which are in cities all agree that they are permitted.

What is the reason [they are permitted]? Because they are made for ornamentation.

But is there anyone [who really holds that the images] in villages are made only for ornamentation? Surely those in the villages were made to be worshipped!

Rather, if he [Rabbah] is cited, this is how he is cited: Rabbah said: There is a difference of opinion [with regard to statutes] in cities; but as for those in villages, all agree that they are prohibited.

We see in the opening line that the biblical ban on images is understood as a ban on benefiting from images in any way. Forced to accept the entanglement of Israelite and pagan society the rabbis adopted a strategy of avoiding idolatry as much as possible. Thus, instead of destroying idols, Jews were to avoid either supporting or benefiting from pagan worship whether directly or indirectly. Indeed, most of the prohibitions and regulations contained in tractate Avodah Zarah are motivated by the concern neither to benefit from nor contribute to idolatry.

The Mishnah contains a three-way dispute over the scope of the prohibition of images, with R. Meir asserting that all images are prohibited for any and all uses because all images are worshipped even if only very infrequently. The majority view of the sages, however, is that an image is prohibited only if it holds in its hand certain symbols of authority. R. Shimeon b. Gamliel expands the majority definition of a worshipped image to include images that hold anything in their hands.

The reasons for the three views expressed in the Mishnah are not stated. Thus, the talmudic discussion begins (as it often does) with an exploration of the deeper grounds of the tannaitic dispute. Why does R. Meir hold a different view from the majority? The answer is provided by the amora R. Isaac b. Joseph in the name of an early Palestinian amora, R. Yohanan: R. Meir and the sages have differing legal philosophies. R. Meir allows exceptional and minority cases to govern his legal thinking. Since it was the practice in R. Meir's locale for pagans to occasionally worship their noncultic images, he rules that all images must be prohibited at all times in all localities. The sages, however, do not allow exceptional cases to shape the law for the vast majority of cases. Thus since most images are not actually cultically functional, some criterion is established to determine which are genuinely worshipped and therefore subject to the biblical ban: only those holding certain symbols of authority are subject to the ban.

Perhaps the reference to symbols of authority prompts Shmuel's observation (reported by R. Judah) that the mishnah is referring specifically to royal images or statues. To this may be added the view of R. Yohanan (reported by Rabbah bar bar Hanah) that the mishnah refers to royal images standing at the entrance of the city. This is a significant narrowing of the mishnaic ban on images. A third generation Babylonian amora, Rabbah, then draws a further distinction between images in villages and images in cities. He observes that all agree the images set up in cities do not fall under the ban, but there is a dispute concerning the images set up in villages.

The anonymous editorial voice of the Talmud (the *stam*) explores the reason for this distinction and concludes that images in cities must be permitted because they are purely ornamental and are not worshipped. However, the status of images in villages is a matter of dispute. This suggestion is immediately questioned. Could there really be any dispute about the status of images in a village? Villagers would not spend their limited resources on mere ornamentation—they build images to be worshipped! The record of Rabbah's statement is thus emended to reflect what the *stam* concludes he must have meant: there is in fact no dispute over the images set up at the entrances of villages—they are prohibited because they are surely worshipped; the dispute is over images set up at the entrances of cities. Some hold that they are ornamental and thus exempt from the biblical ban on images while others hold that they are indeed worshipped and thus included in the biblical ban on images.

Notice how the anonymous editorial voice of the Talmud has introduced a critical distinction of great utility to Jews living in an environment that is saturated with idols—the distinction between the purely ornamental and the genuinely cultic. Only the latter must be avoided. Thus, when asked, in m. Avodah Zarah 3:4, how he could bathe in the bath of Aphrodite in light of the biblical ban on idolatry, R. Gamaliel is said to have responded that Aphrodite's statue serves a purely decorative and not a cultic function in the bathhouse. Other rabbinic traditions note that Gentiles use images as decoration on all sorts of items (such as household utensils) and that these images do not qualify as idols that Israelites are biblically commanded to destroy (m. Avodah Zarah 3:1, 3:4). In short, the rabbis maintain that only that which is actually *treated* as an idol (worshipped) falls under the biblical prohibition of idolatry.

Note how well the anonymous editor of this passage has managed to convey sophisticated legal concepts by constructing a lively dialectic among scholars distant from one another in time and place. Principles are not stated outright. Information is delayed, raising questions of meaning and motivation that the student must explore and consider before moving to the next step. There are false moves that encourage the student's own critical thinking (for example, the statement of Rabbah which is emended in the light of logical reflection). This abbreviated example illustrates the degree to which the study of Talmud is not a matter of passive acquisition; it is an exercise in active and critical thinking through carefully orchestrated dialectics.

DOCUMENTS 13a–c. HALAKHIC AND AGGADIC MIDRASH: DIVINE POLYSEMY

Close exegesis of Scripture is the hallmark of rabbinic midrash. Different types of midrash were produced over the course of the rabbinic period. Earlier, tannaitic midrash (to the mid-third century) tended to focus on the legal (halakhic) portions of the Torah. Its discussions are often technical and grammatically focused, showing little interest in an audience outside rabbinic circles. Later amoraic midrash tended to focus on the narrative (aggadic) portions of the Bible and was in many instances rhetorically and literarily crafted to appeal to a wider audience. Document 13a is an example of tannaitic midrash while Document 13b is drawn from amoraic midrash.

Document 13a is taken from the Mekhilta deRabbi Yishmael, a tannaitic midrash to Exodus beginning with the legal prescriptions for Passover in Ex 12. The Mekhilta contains comments on individual biblical verses and phrases. The selection presented here comments on the words "You shall not follow a multitude to do evil" (Ex 23:2). In their biblical context, these words refer to the administration of justice. The verse continues: "when you give testimony in a lawsuit, do not pervert justice by siding with the majority, and do not show favoritism to a poor man in his lawsuit." Through exacting analysis, legal analogy, and logical argumentation the verse yields the teaching that convictions require more than a simple majority. This is not, of course, the plain meaning of the text. The plain meaning of the text is that one should not give testimony for evil purposes, pervert justice, or show favoritism. However, through midrashic exegesis, *additional* teachings beyond the plain meaning of the text could be derived from the text—grounding all of life in the authority of God's revelation.

13a. Mekhilta deRabbi Yishmael, Kaspa 2 on Exodus 23:2

"You shall not follow a multitude to do evil" (Ex 23:2). The sense of this [verse] is that you should not be with them for evil, but you should be with them for good. How?

If twelve are for acquittal and eleven are for conviction, he is acquitted. If thirteen are for conviction and ten are for acquittal he is convicted. Now if eleven are for acquittal and 12 are for conviction, I might think that he should be convicted. But Scripture teaches "neither shall you give testimony [bear witness] in a lawsuit" (Ex 23:2). Torah says you may execute on the basis of witnesses and [it also says] you may execute on the basis of a majority [decision]. Just as there must be two witnesses so also there must be a majority of at least two [judges]. If eleven are for acquittal and eleven are for conviction and one says "I don't know," behold there is a warning to the judge that he not incline the judgment except in the direction of acquittal. Scripture says, "Neither shall you give testimony [bear witness] in a lawsuit to turn aside after a multitude to pervert justice."

The midrash explores the meaning of the phrase "you shall not follow a multitude to do evil" by drawing a logical inference: if a judge is not to follow the majority in doing evil then we may infer that he is certainly to follow the majority in doing good. In concrete terms what might this mean? It means that if the majority wish to acquit, even if it is a majority by one, then the judge may add his voice to that majority to obtain acquittal. However, if a majority by one wishes to convict, the judge may not add his voice to that majority to convict, because Scripture says "Neither shall you bear witness/answer in a lawsuit [to turn aside after a multitude to pervert justice]." Because this verse is written using the second person singular ("you") it is understood to be directed at the individual judge. Conviction requires a majority by two votes. This verse is interpreted as warning the individual judge against creating a majority that can convict, at the same time that it urges him to create a majority that can acquit. The principle is further explored by comparing witnesses to judges. Just as two witnesses are required for a capital conviction so a majority by two judges is required for a capital conviction.

Document 13b is taken from the Pesikta deRav Kahana, a work believed to have been compiled in fifth-century C.E. Palestine. It is a midrashic text based on the Scriptural readings for the Sabbaths and holidays. The following passage is based on the reading for the holiday of Shavuot, which begins with Exodus 19:1 "In the third month after the people of Israel had gone out of the land of Egypt, on this day they came into the wilderness at Sinai." The passage contains numerous creative interpretations of the phrase "in the third month"—many involving puns on the word "third" (whose root letters are *sh.l.sh*). Through puns and multiple meanings the midrashist is able to derive additional meanings from an otherwise lackluster phrase. By linking the phrase to other biblical phrases that contain a similar word, the midrashist builds a web of associations and transferred meanings. To the rabbis, such displays were not only warranted by but proof of the divine origin of the text.

13b. Pesikta deRav Kahana, Piska 12:12–13

"In the third (*shalishi*) month." This verse (Ex 19:1) can be read in the light of [the following verse]: "In [the books of] counsels and knowledge have I not written for you things which are to be trusted (*shalishim*)?" (Prov 22:20). Whenever you seek to find counsel, it is in the Torah you should seek to find it. As David said: When I sought to find counsel, I would look into the Torah and there find counsel: "I will meditate in Your precepts, and look into Your ways" (Ps 119:15), and again "From Your precepts I get understanding" (Ps 119:104).

Even if you wish to erect a building, Ben Huta said, and do not know how to manage its height, look into the Torah and you will learn how. How does Scripture put it? "With lower, second and third (*shalishim*) decks you shall make [the ark]" (Gen 6:16). Hence "in [the books of] counsel and knowledge" (Prov 22:20).

In another comment the verse is read "Did I not write for you excellent things (*shlishim*)?" which Rabbi [=R. Judah haNasi] took to mean: Let the Torah never be for you an antiquated decree, but rather like a decree freshly issued, no more than two or three days old, for the consonants in "Did I not write for you excellent things?" are *sh.l.sh.m*, a word which when read *shilshom*, means "day before yesterday." But Ben Azzai said: Not even as old as a decree issued two or three days ago, but as a decree issued this very day. You can see for yourself that this is the way to regard the Torah. For the verse beginning "In the third month," etc. does not go on, as one might expect, "on *that* day they came," but rather "on *this* day they came into the wilderness at Sinai." Elsewhere Scripture says, "This day the Lord your God commands you to do these statutes and ordinances" (Judg 26:16).

Another interpretation of "in the third month." Torah is likened to three things. The patriarchs are three. The name of the tribe through whom Torah is given is made up of three letters. The month [in which the Torah was given] is the third month. Whence do we know that Torah is likened to three things? R. Abun the Levite beRabbi asked this very question. Why should Torah be likened to three things? It is so likened because in some respects it resembles three things— wine, honey, and peppers. Proof that Torah is like wine? The verse "Come eat of my bread, and drink of the wine which I have mingled" (Prov 9:5). Like honey? The verse "[the ordinances of the Lord] . . . are sweeter than honey" (Ps 19:11). Like peppers? "Every word of God is zestful" (Prov 30:5), which R. Abun the Levite beRabbi took to mean "as zestful as pepper." Now you see why Torah is likened to three things.

The first paragraph features both a pun as well as an intertextual link. The word *shalishim* appears in Proverbs 22:20 where it means "trusted." The midrashist reads Exodus 19:1 in the light of Proverbs 22:20 (an intertextual link), importing the meaning of *shalishim* in the latter text into the former text. Exodus 19:1 can be understood to be saying "In the month of the trusted thing" (i.e., in the month when that which is to be trusted—the

Torah—was given). By the same token, Proverbs 22:20 is then read in the light of Exodus 19:1. If that which is to be trusted is the Torah, then the books of counsel and knowledge referred to in Proverbs 22:20 must also be Torah. This is proven by reference to verses in which David is said to have meditated upon God's precepts (understood to be the Torah) when seeking counsel.

The second paragraph continues the idea of the Torah as the source of all knowledge and counsel, and makes another pun. Here, the word *shelishi* in Exodus 19:1 is linked intertextually to the same adjective in Genesis 6:16 regarding the building of the ark. That the ark was made with decks that were *shalishi* indicates that it was built according to the counsel and information contained in the Torah itself.

The third paragraph continues the discussion of Proverbs 22:20. Punning on the word *shalishim* in that verse, the midrashist notes that the consonants of this word could be read differently—as *shilshom*. This word means "day before yesterday." Now, Proverbs 22:20 seems to be saying "Did I not write for you the day before yesterday?" Rabbi interprets this to mean that the Torah should always seem like a fresh and new document to us—like a decree that is only two or three days old. Ben Azzai takes this idea even further—the Torah should be as fresh and new to us as a decree issued this very day. He bases himself on our verse, Ex 19:1, which says "on *this* day" where we might have expected it to say "on *that* day." Such unexpected locutions are believed by many rabbinic exegetes to signal some additional meaning that would not be conveyed by an alternative locution. In this case, the use of "this day" is to promote the idea that the Torah should be deemed freshly given, at all times.

The fourth paragraph continues to play with the word "*shelishi*" by listing the many things in Israel's history that have occurred in threes or are tripartite in some way. The list includes the Torah because the Torah is likened to three things: wine, honey, and peppers. Three verses are adduced as evidence. The first verse, taken from Proverbs 9:5 is spoken by "wisdom" (commonly understood by the rabbis to be equivalent to Torah) who invites her addressee to partake of her wine. The second and third verses explicitly attribute the sweetness of honey and the zestfulness of peppers to the ordinances or word of God.

With imaginative virtuosity, midrashists employed puns and intertextual links in order to breathe profound meaning into even the most mundane of verses, such as Exodus 19:1's opening phrase: "in the third month."

This midrashic approach to Scripture is predicated on the idea that a divine text can bear many meanings. The insistence on divine polysemy (conveyance of more than one meaning) is thematized in the following text from the Babylonian Talmud.

13c. b. Hagigah 3b

> "The words of the wise are as goads, and as nails well planted are the words of masters of assemblies, which are given by one Shepherd" (Eccl 12:11).
>
> Why are the words of the Torah likened to a goad? To teach you that just as the goad directs the heifer along its furrow in order to bring forth life to the world, so the words of the Torah direct those who study them from the paths of death to the paths of life. But [should you think] that just as the goad is moveable so the words of the Torah are movable; therefore the text says: "nails." But [should you think] that just as the nail diminishes and does not increase, so too the words of the Torah diminish and do not increase; therefore the text says: "well-planted"; just as a plant grows and increases, so the words of the Torah grow and increase. "The masters of assemblies": these are the disciples of the wise, who sit in manifold assemblies and occupy themselves with the Torah, some pronouncing unclean and others pronouncing clean, some prohibiting and others permitting, some disqualifying and others declaring fit.
>
> Should a man say: "How in these circumstances shall I learn Torah?" Therefore the text says, "All of them are given from one Shepherd." One God gave them; one leader uttered them from the mouth of the Lord of all creation, blessed be He; for it is written: "And God spoke all these words" (Ex 20:1). Also make your ear like the hopper and get yourself a perceptive heart to understand the words of those who pronounce unclean and the words of those who pronounce clean, the words of those who prohibit and the words of those who permit, the words of those who disqualify and the words of those who declare fit.

The passage expounds a biblical verse in which the words of the wise who sit in assemblies (understood as rabbinic academies) are likened to goads on the one hand and planted nails on the other. Like goads, the words of the wise direct one along paths of life; like nails, they have a certain fixity; like things that are planted they increase and grow. The text then characterizes the assemblies mentioned in the verse as places where sages occupy themselves with Torah, often with contradictory results. However, the contradictions and controversies should be no occasion for despair, for it is the very nature of divine revelation to contain multiple, even contradictory, meanings and the assiduous student should learn the words of all.

GLOSSARY

Aggadah: The nonlegalistic portions of classical rabbinic literature, as found especially in the Talmuds and the Midrash. The aggadah contains homilies, legends, folklore, anecdotes, ethical teachings, and practical advice.

Amora: Aramaic term for sages immediately following the tannaitic period (ends 220 C.E.) and mentioned in the Palestinian or Babylonian Talmuds. The period of these sages' activity is known as the amoraic period (to 370 C.E. in Palestine and to the fifth century in Babylonia).

Apocalypse (literally, "revealing"): A revelation of hidden things. The literature containing such revelations often depicts the end of historical time and the beginning of a new world order. Apocalyptic writings tend to feature a series of catastrophes, the division of humanity into two groups (a wicked majority and a righteous minority), and a highly symbolic imagery that may include beasts or monsters.

Apocrypha: Writings composed between 200 B.C.E. and 100 C.E. and widely used by Jews of the period, though not included in the Jewish canon of Scripture. These works have become a part of the canon of Catholic Christianity, but were denied equal status with other biblical books by Protestants during the Reformation.

Canon: A collection of writings accepted by a religious community as sacred and authoritative.

Decalogue: The Ten Commandments, known in Jewish tradition as the Ten Words or Statements, are a set of imperatives that introduce the covenant concluded between God and Israel at Sinai. They are listed in Exodus 20:2–17 and repeated with minor variation in Deuteronomy 5:6–21.

Diaspora: Jewish communities outside the Land of Israel.

Documentary Hypothesis: A hypothesis that explains certain literary features of the Bible (contradiction, repetition, etc.) by positing the existence of hypothetical source documents (labeled J, E, P, and D), which are assigned either relative or absolute dates and then analyzed to reveal the different stages of Israel's religious history.

Eschatology: From the Greek "eschaton" meaning "end." An imaginative account of the final events in the history of the world.

Exegesis: Interpretation of a text, especially Scripture. The centrality of Scripture in Judaism spurred the rise of various, often competing, methods of exegesis.

Gemara (literally, "study"): Gemara refers to the commentary on the Mishnah (an early third-century legal text) developed by amoraic (post-220 C.E.) rabbinic sages in Palestine and in Babylonia. Together, the Mishnah and its Palestinian gemara commentary comprise the Palestinian Talmud, while the Mishnah and its Babylonian gemara commentary comprise the Babylonian Talmud.

Halakhah: Jewish law as a collective (the body of halakhah) or a single Jewish law (a halakhah). The term is used primarily with reference to the body of rabbinic laws.

Hebrew: In the patriarchal and Exodus narratives of the Hebrew Bible, the term Hebrew designates the ancestors of the Israelites. The term is not used to designate ordinary Israelites or Jews in the early postexilic period. In Greco-Roman tradition the Greek term Ebraios designates a Jew, and Christian writings adopt this usage, referring to members of the Jewish people as Hebrews. Jews in late antiquity (including rabbinic Jews) do not generally refer to themselves as Hebrews.

Hellenization: The process of acculturation to Greek civic, social, artistic, cultural, material, and economic norms.

Israelite: A member of one of the twelve tribes of Israel, descended from the patriarch Jacob (renamed Israel). This term is the predominant self-designation of biblical Israelites and rabbinic Jews.

Jew: A member of the Jewish people. Originally designating a person from Judah (Yehud), the term took on an expanded and nonterritorial meaning.

Kashrut: The system of dietary laws prescribed in the Hebrew Bible and followed by observant Jews to this day. Food acceptable according to these rules is kosher (or kasher), meaning "fit."

Midrash: The process of interpreting and exploring the biblical text so as to elicit meanings beyond the plain contextual meaning. The term can also refer to the compilation of midrashic teachings in commentaries (the Midrash).

Midrash aggadah: Rabbinic interpretation of nonlegal portions of the Bible. The classic works of midrash aggadah date to the amoraic period or later.

Midrash halakhah: Rabbinic interpretation of legal portions of the Bible. The classic works of midrash halakhah date to the late tannaitic/early amoraic period.

Mishnah: One of the first works of rabbinic Judaism. The Mishnah is a compilation of legal teachings and traditions (halakhah) edited, according to Jewish tradition, by R. Judah ha-Nasi (the Patriarch) in the early third century C.E. The Mishnah and its later commentary, the Gemara, together form the Talmud. An individual paragraph of the Mishnah is known as a mishnah.

Oral Torah: Orally transmitted teachings which, according to rabbinic tradition, were handed down from earliest times and eventually recorded as the main works of rabbinic literature, especially the Mishnah and Talmuds. In contrast to the Written Torah (Scriptures), the Oral Torah is commonly understood to refer to all of rabbinic tradition.

Pseudepigrapha: From the Greek pseudos and epigrapha meaning false inscriptions. The term usually refers to works falsely attributed to an authoritative biblical figure. Some pseudepigraphical works are also apocrypha. The books of the Pseudepigrapha were never part of the Jewish or Catholic canons of Scripture but various ones were accepted among various Eastern Christian groups (e.g., the Coptic, Ethiopic, and Syriac churches).

Rabbi: From *rav*, meaning "great." Literally "my superior [in wisdom, i.e., my teacher]." An honorific for those distinguished in learning; authoritative teachers of the Torah. The related term *rabban* (literally "our superior [in wisdom, i.e., our teacher]" is an honorific term (often used anachronistically) in the Mishnah and Talmuds for the head of the rabbinic assembly or reconstituted Sanhedrin following the destruction of 70 C.E.

Sabbath: From the Hebrew root for "ceasing." A weekly day of cessation from work, modeled (according to the biblical legend) on God's ceasing to labor after the six days of creation. Shabbat begins with sundown on Friday and ends with nightfall on Saturday.

Sanhedrin: From the Greek *synedrion*, meaning "sitting together," hence "assembly." A council of seventy-one Jewish sages who met in the Temple precincts and functioned as a supreme court and law-making body in the Hellenistic period. Later assemblies and courts of rabbis after the destruction of the Temple would also take the name "Sanhedrin."

Septuagint: The Greek translation of the Hebrew Bible produced from the third to first century B.C.E., so named because according to a legend it was produced by seventy-two scholars.

Talmud: See gemara above.

Tanakh: An acronym for the Hebrew Bible, formed from the initial Hebrew letters of the three main sections of the Bible: Torah (Pentateuch or five books of Moses), Nevi'im (prophets), and Khetuvim (Writings).

Tanna: Aramaic term for any sage mentioned in the Mishnah or related rabbinic writings, dating to the period between the destruction and ca. 220 C.E. (the tannaitic period).

Theophany: Manifestation of the divine to humans. Biblical examples include God's speaking to Moses from the burning bush and God's revelation at Mount Sinai.

Tosefta (literally, "supplement"): A compilation of primarily legal teachings and traditions of tannaitic sages that corresponds in structure to the Mishnah. The date of the Tosefta's final redaction is disputed.

Written Torah: The twenty-four books of the canonical Hebrew Bible to which Christian tradition has added other writings in the formation of the Christian canon. Also known as the Tanakh.

Yeshivah (plural yeshivot): Institution of rabbinic study that grew out of the smaller *bet midrash* (school). Fully developed *yeshivot* do not appear until the late Talmudic period in Babylonia.

ANNOTATED
BIBLIOGRAPHY

PRIMARY TEXTS IN ENGLISH TRANSLATION

Hebrew Bible

The Anchor Bible. Garden City, NY: Doubleday, 1964. A multivolume series of book-by-book translations of the Hebrew Bible, New Testament, and Apocrypha, with extensive commentary drawing on archaeology, linguistics, comparative religion, and Ancient Near Eastern sources.

Berlin, Adele, Brettler, Marc and Fishbane, Michael, eds. *The Jewish Study Bible: Featuring the Jewish Publication Society Tanakh Translation.* Oxford: Oxford University Press, 2004. A superb study Bible based on the translation of the Jewish Publication Society. Contains excellent introductions to each section (Torah, Prophets, Writings) and each individual book of the Hebrew Bible, as well as a running sidebar commentary that incorporates both ancient and modern scholarship on the Bible. A collection of scholarly articles on an array of topics (purity and impurity, biblical poetry, textual criticism, archaeology, and biblical religion to name a few) makes this comprehensive volume an essential tool for any study of the Hebrew Bible in its own right or as the foundation of later Jewish tradition.

Sarna, Nahum M. and Potok, Chaim, eds. *The JPS Torah Commentary Set.* 5 vols. Philadelphia, PA: Jewish Publication Society of America, 1996. Hebrew text, English translation, extensive commentary drawing on traditional rabbinic works, medieval exegesis, archaeology, and modern scholarship for each of the five books of the Pentateuch. An excellent resource for the study of the Hebrew Bible and its place in the development of later Jewish tradition.

Postbiblical, Nonrabbinic Writings

Charles, R. H., ed. *The Apocrypha and Pseudepigrapha of the Old Testament in English: With Introductions and Critical and Explanatory Notes to the Several Books.* Oxford: Clarendon Press, 1913. Reprint Oxford: Oxford University Press, 1963. Classic translations with scholarly notes of extra-canonical Jewish writings from the Second Temple and late antique periods.

Charlesworth, J. H., ed. *The Old Testament Pseudepigrapha.* 2 vols. (Anchor Bible Series). Garden City, NY: Doubleday, 1983–1985. Translations of extra-canonical Jewish literature from ca. 200 B.C.E. to 200 C.E., many in the apocalyptic genre. Scholarly introductions precede each translation.

Rabbinic Literature

Bialik, Hayyim Nahman, ed. *The Book of Legends: Legends from the Talmud and Midrash.* Trans. by William G. Braude. New York: Schocken Books, 1992. English translation of a century-old classic anthology of rabbinic legends. This vast collection of Talmudic and midrashic material, topically arranged, is an indispensable resource for students of Jewish folklore and religion.

Blackman, P. *Mishnayoth.* Pointed Hebrew Text, English Translation, Introductions, Notes, Supplement, Appendix, Indexes, Addenda, Corrigenda. 2nd ed. Gateshead: Judaica Press, 1983. A six-volume translation of the six orders of the *Mishnah*, the classic legal work of rabbinic tradition, with helpful introduction and notes.

Danby, Herbert. *The Mishnah.* Translated from the Hebrew, with Introduction and Brief Explanatory Notes. Oxford: Oxford University Press, 1987. One-volume translation of the Mishnah with fewer notes than the preceding.

Epstein, Isadore, ed. *The Babylonian Talmud.* Translated into English with Notes, Glossary, and Indices Under the Editorship of I. Epstein. London: Soncino Press, 1935–1952. Standard English translation of the Babylonian Talmud with helpful notes and full subject and verse citation index.

Freedman, H. and Simon, M., eds. *Midrash Rabbah.* London: Soncino Press, 1983. Definitive English translation of the rabbinic midrash (homiletical, ethical, and creative interpretations) on the Pentatuech and five "scrolls" (Ecclesiastes, Song of Songs, Ruth, Esther, and Lamentations), with notes, glossary, and indices.

Neusner, Jacob, ed. *The Tosefta:* Translated from the Hebrew with a New Introduction. 6 vols. Peabody, MA: Hendrickson Publishers, 2002. Translation of the Tosefta, a work containing legal traditions primarily of tannaitic origin. Especially useful when studied in conjunction with the Mishnah.

————. *The Talmud of the Land of Israel: A Preliminary Translation and Explanation.* Chicago: Chicago University Press, 1982. The only English translation of the Palestinian Talmud, of somewhat uneven quality. Some volumes have extensive helpful commentary.

Steinsaltz, Adin. *The Talmud: The Steinsaltz Edition.* Trans. and ed. by Israel V. Berman. New York: Random House, 1989–1999. Highly accessible, multivolume translation of the Talmud, with step-by-step explanations of the intricate logic, terminology, and necessary background information. Reference Guide volume describes the nature of the Talmud, its history, methodology, legal concepts, language.

Jewish Law

Appel, Gersion. *Concise Code of Jewish Law.* New York: Ktav Publishing House, 1997. Translation of a compilation of Jewish law from traditional sources with introduction and legal annotations based on contemporary legal opinions.

Ganzfried, Solomon. *Code of Jewish Law.* Trans. by Hyman E. Goldin. 2 vols. New York: Moznaim Pub. Co., 1991. Translation of the Kitzur Shulhan Aruch, a condensed compilation of Jewish law. Handy reference.

REFERENCE AND HANDBOOKS

Barnavi, Eli, ed. *A Historical Atlas of the Jewish People.* New York: Knopf (distributed by Random House), 1992. A remarkable work that covers three millennia of Jewish history and culture through texts, maps, photographs, diagrams, and reproductions of paintings. Arranged chronologically, the atlas covers the main themes of Jewish experience.

Encyclopedia Judaica. Jerusalem: Keter, 1974. The classic encyclopedia for Judaica researchers. An updated version is in production.

Freedman, Noel, ed. *The Anchor Bible Dictionary.* New York: Doubleday, 1992. An essential reference for biblical studies, this six-volume state-of-the-art dictionary provides comprehensive accounts of biblical subjects informed by the most up-to-date scholarship.

Holtz, Barry. *Back to the Sources: Reading the Classic Jewish Texts.* New York: Summit Books, 1984. An essential and superb introduction to the classic texts of Jewish tradition: the Hebrew Bible, rabbinic literature, medieval Bible commentaries, medieval philosophical works, Kabbalistic texts, Hasidic writings, and the prayer book. Aimed at the nonexpert with excellent suggestions for future study.

The Jewish Encyclopedia. New York: Funk and Wagnalls, 1901–1906. A classic, but century-old encyclopedia of Jewish history, biography, sociology, literature, theology, and philosophy. Out-of-date but useful for its biographies. Accessible on-line (see below).

Mills, Watson E., ed. *Bibliographies for Biblical Research: Periodical Literature for the Study of the Old Testament.* Lewiston, NY: Edwin Mellen Press, 2002. A mutlivolume work containing detailed bibliographies for each of the books of the Hebrew Bible.

Strack, H. L. and Stemberger, Günther. *Introduction to the Talmud and Midrash.* Trans. by Markus Bockmuehl. Minneapolis, MN: Fortress Press, Reprint 1996. A revision of the classic introduction to the main works of rabbinic literature. A comprehensive work of reference essential for the serious student.

Werblowsky, R. J. and Wigoder, Geoffrey, eds. *The Encyclopedia of the Jewish Religion.* New rev. ed. New York: Adama Books, 1986. Concise and nontechnical information on a range of terms relating to Jewish beliefs, practices, religious movements, and doctrines. Not for in-depth research.

———. *The Oxford Dictionary of the Jewish Religion.* New York: Oxford University Press, 1997. A ready-reference resource with 2,400 entries that emphasize the religious, rather than the historical or political aspects of each topic.

Wigoder, Geoffrey, ed. *The Standard Jewish Encyclopedia.* 7th ed. New York: Facts on File, 1992. A portable one-volume reference work with over 8,000 entries on Jewish history, politics, literature, culture, religion, and historical figures.

ANCIENT NEAR EASTERN CONTEXT

Arnold, Bill T. and Beyers, Bryan, eds. *Readings from the Ancient Near East: Primary Sources for Old Testament Study.* Grand Rapids, MI: Baker Academic, 2002. A convenient, affordable, and well-selected anthology of the most important Ancient Near Eastern primary source texts needed for a full understanding of the Hebrew Bible, including Sumerian creation accounts, Mesopotamian epic literature, Egyptian cultic ritual texts, and Syrian prophetic references.

Benjamin, Don C. and Matthews, Victor H. *Old Testament Parallels: Laws and Stories from the Ancient Near East.* Revised and expanded edition. New York: Paulist Press, 1997. A comprehensive collection of ancient Near East documents that parallel biblical stories and illuminate the broader context of the Hebrew Bible. Comments highlight the points of convergence and divergence.

Coogan, Michael. *Stories from Ancient Canaan.* Philadelphia, PA: Westminster Press, 1978. A slim one-volume translation of four major Ugaritic myths, with introductory essays that underscore the Canaanite background of biblical traditions.

Gordon, Cyrus H. and Rendsburg, Gary A. *The Bible and the Ancient Near East.* 4th ed. New York: W.W. Norton & Co., 1998. Situates the Hebrew Bible in its ancient historical context. Draws on the latest archaeological and linguistic research and points to cultural and literary parallels.

Pritchard, James Bennett, ed. *Ancient Near East in Pictures Relating to the Old Testament with Supplement.* Princeton, NJ: Princeton University Press, 1969. A comprehensive anthology of texts and black and white photographs of artifacts from the Ancient Near East. The texts include, myths, epics, legal materials, historical texts, inscriptions, hymns, wisdom literature, prophecy, proverbs, letters, and provide important context for the study of Biblical Israel. This work is the "parent" anthology of the following smaller, paperback volumes.

————. *The Ancient Near East, Vol. I: An Anthology of Texts and Pictures.* Princeton, NJ: Princeton University Press, 1965.

————. *The Ancient Near East, Vol. II: A New Anthology of Texts and Pictures.* Princeton, NJ: Princeton University Press, 1975.

BIBLICAL ISRAEL

Cross, Frank Moore, Jr. *From Epic to Canon: History and Literature in Ancient Israel.* Baltimore, MD: Johns Hopkins University Press, 1998. An examination of the social structures of ancient Israel, and the institutions of kinship and covenant in particular by a distinguished scholar of biblical and ancient Near Eastern studies.

Finkelstein, Israel and Silberman, Neil Asher. *The Bible Unearthed: Archaeology's New Vision of Ancient Israel and the Origin of Its Sacred Texts.* New York: Free Press, 2001. An important assessment of the incongruity of the biblical text and the archaeological record. Argues that the Hebrew Bible is neither historical truth nor literary fiction but a national saga fashioned from memory (tradition) and hope (vision) during the political crises of the seventh century B.C.E.

Kaufman, Yehezkel. *The Religion of Israel, from Its Beginnings to the Babylonian Exile.* Trans. and abridged by Moshe Greenberg. Chicago: University of Chicago Press, 1960. Reprint New York: Schocken Books, 1972. A highly readable abridgement of a multivolume work in Hebrew by the Israeli scholar Yehezkel Kaufman. Argues for the uniqueness of biblical religion against the backdrop of competing Ancient Near Eastern beliefs and practices.

Matthews, Victor H. *A Brief History of Ancient Israel.* Louisville, KY: Westminster John Knox Press, 2002. Information on the major events in Israelite history, a basic chronology, and a consideration of extra-biblical data.

Mazar, Amihai. *Archaeology of the Land of the Bible, 10,000–586* B.C. New York: Doubleday, 1990. Considered a standard text on biblical archaeology. This award-winning, comprehensive introduction moves from the very beginning of Israel's history to the divided monarchy and the kingdoms of Israel and Judah.

Shanks, Hershel, ed. *Ancient Israel: From Abraham to the Roman Destruction of the Temple.* Upper Saddle River, NJ: Prentice-Hall, 1999. A complete history of ancient Israel that draws on the expertise of many leading scholars. Well illustrated with photos, maps, timelines, and charts.

Stern, Ephraim. *Archaeology of the Land of the Bible. Volume II: The Assyrian, Babylonian, and Persian periods, 732–332* B.C.E. New York: Doubleday, 2001. Sequel to the preceding. Shows the contribution of archaeological research to our understanding of the Biblical texts of the Assyrian, Babylonian, and Persian periods. Contains photographs and illustrations of rare ancient relics.

Vaux, Roland de. *Ancient Israel: Its Life and Institutions.* Trans. by John McHugh. Grand Rapids, MI: W. B. Eerdmans, 1997. Reprint of a classic two-volume work originally published in French. Examines civil, military, religious, and family institutions, setting out the relevant biblical and Ancient Near Eastern material.

Weinfeld, Moshe. *Social Justice in Ancient Israel and in the Ancient Near East.* Minneapolis, MN: Fortress Press, 1995. Considers the relevance of a wide array of Near Eastern material for understanding social practices and ideology in ancient Israel.

THE HEBREW BIBLE

Alter, Robert. *The Art of Biblical Narrative*. New York: Basic Books, 1983. A classic and pathbreaking literary analysis of biblical narratives.

——— *The Art of Biblical Poetry*. New York: Basic Books, 1985. A classic and eminently readable study of the structures and effects of biblical Hebrew poetry.

Alter, Robert and Kermode, Frank, eds. *Literary Guide to the Bible*. Cambridge, MA: Belknap Press of Harvard University Press, 1987. A book-by-book literary analysis of the Hebrew Bible and New Testament written by an international team of leading scholars. The volume also contains several general essays dealing with topics such as the formation of the canon and the characteristics of Hebrew poetry.

Berlin, Adele, Brettler, Marc and Fishbane, Michael, eds. *The Jewish Study Bible Featuring the Jewish Publication Society Tanakh Translation*. Oxford: Oxford University Press, 2004. See above under Primary Texts in English Translation.

Brettler, Marc. *How to Read the Bible*. Philadelphia, PA: Jewish Publication Society, 2005. Examines the Hebrew Bible in its historical setting and employs a critical methodology that traces the interplay of history, myth, and ideology in the composition of the biblical text.

Collins, John J. *Introduction to the Hebrew Bible with CD-Rom*. Minneapolis, MN: Fortress Press, 2004. A critical introduction to the Hebrew Bible that often raises interpretive and ethical issues.

Coogan, Michael. *The Old Testament: A Historical and Literary Introduction to the Hebrew Scriptures*. New York: Oxford University Press, 2006. This introduction is organized historically and includes consideration of archaeological evidence in its discussion of the history of the Old Testament.

Friedman, Richard. *Who Wrote the Bible?* New York: Summit Books, 1987. A lively and engaging study of the problem of the Hebrew Bible's authorship. Considers when the various sources of the Bible were composed and by whom.

Habel, Norman. *Literary Criticism of the Old Testament*. Philadelphia, PA: Fortress Press, 1971. A clear introduction to the method of literary criticism in which considerations of structure, style, and form enable the scholar to identify biblical sources. Concrete examples illustrate the methodology beautifully.

Kugel, James. *The Bible as It Was*. Cambridge, MA: Belknap Press of Harvard University Press, 1997. A popular and engaging book that focuses on early readings (especially midrashic) of the Torah (or Pentateuch) from 100 to 300 C.E. in order to reconstruct the Bible as it was understood at the beginning of the millennium.

————*Traditions of the Bible: A Guide to the Bible as It Was at the Start of the Common Era*. Cambridge, MA: Harvard University Press, 1998. Full scholarly edition of the preceding. Focuses on two dozen central stories in the Pentateuch and shows how early interpreters radically transformed the Bible in the process of reading it.

Levenson, Jon D. *The Hebrew Bible, the Old Testament, and Historical Criticism: Jews and Christians in Biblical Studies*. Louisville, KY: Westminster John Knox Press, 1993. A set of essays that critiques the unacknowledged religious and cultural biases and implicit or explicit anti-Judaism that have shaped much of biblical scholarship.

Reis, Pamela Tamarkin. *Reading the Lines: A Fresh Look at the Hebrew Bible*. Peabody, MA: Hendrickson Publishers, Inc., 2002. Holistic literary analyses of biblical narratives that challenge the assumptions of disunity that inform the historical-critical school.

Sarna, Nahum M. *Understanding Genesis: The Heritage of Biblical Israel*. New York: Schocken Books, 1970. A comprehensive interpretation of the book of Genesis in light of extra-biblical sources.

————*Exploring Exodus: The Origins of Biblical Israel*. New York: Schocken Books, 1986. A comprehensive interpretation of the book of Exodus in light of extra-biblical sources.

Shanks, Hershel, ed. *Abraham and Family: New Insights into the Patriarchal Narratives*. Washington, DC: Biblical Archaeological Society, 2000. A collection of sixteen thought-provoking essays by biblical scholars that examine diverse aspects of the biblical narratives about Abraham and his family.

JEWISH HISTORY

Alon, Gedaliah. *The Jews in Their Land in the Talmudic Age, 70–640 C.E.* Trans. by Gershon Levi. Cambridge, MA: Harvard University Press, 1989. History of the Jews in the Land of Israel until the rise of Islam. Although some of its main claims have been unsettled by more recent scholarship, the book is a classic work by an eminent historian.

Biale, David, ed. *Cultures of the Jews: A New History*. New York: Schocken Books, 2002. A collection of essays by twenty-three internationally renowned scholars, this volume examines the question of Jewish identity and the construction of diverse Jewish cultures throughout history, from earliest times to modernity.

The Cambridge History of Judaism. 4 vols. Cambridge: Cambridge University Press, 1984–1999. A multivolume work for the advanced student, featuring articles on special topics by leading scholars. Volume 1 covers the history of the Jews from the Exile in 587 B.C.E. through the Persian Period. Volume 2 deals with the Hellenistic Age. Volume 3 focuses on the early Roman era. Volume 4 extends from the destruction in 70 C.E. to the rise of Islam in the early seventh century C.E.

Cohen, Shaye J. D. *From the Maccabees to the Mishnah*. Philadelphia, PA: Westminster Press, 1987. An essential and easy-to-read interpretation of ancient Judaism from the Maccabean period to the third century. Documents the shift from Biblical Israel to late antique Judaism identifying major ideas, salient practices, and unifying patterns.

Grabbe, Lester. *Judaism from Cyrus to Hadrian*. 2 vols. Minneapolis, MN: Fortress Press, 1991. An inventory of the primary sources, central problems, and range of scholarly opinions on central issues in the history of the period. An essential research guide.

Levine, Lee I., ed. *The Galilee in Late Antiquity*. New York: Jewish Theological Seminary of America, 1982. Twenty essays by different scholars focusing on the region that was the center of Jewish life in Palestine after the destruction in 70 C.E. Issues include: early Christians, Jewish-Christian conflict, social and economic conditions, Roman rule, the role of the rabbi, the synagogue, Hebrew and Aramaic language, and more.

Neusner, Jacob. *A History of the Jews in Babylonia*. Vols. 1–5. Leiden, The Netherlands: E. J. Brill, 1966–1970. The only comprehensive history of the Jews in Babylonia, based primarily on rabbinic sources.

Safrai, S. and Stern, M. *The Jewish People in the First Century: Historical Geography, Political History, Social, Cultural and Religious Life and Institutions*. Philadelphia, PA: Fortress Press, 1974. A collection of useful and exhaustive introductory essays on the Jewish world of the first century C.E.

Schäfer, Peter. *The History of the Jews in Antiquity: The Jews of Palestine from Alexander the Great to the Arab Conquest*. Luxembourg: Harwood Academic, 1995. A study of the political history of Jews in Palestine in the

Hellenistic age that considers changing social, economic, and religious circumstances.

Scheindlin, Raymond P. *A Short History of the Jewish People: From Legendary Times to Modern Statehood.* New York: Oxford University Press, 2000. An overview of Jewish history that focuses on the major geographical, cultural, and political forces that have shaped Jewish history and emphasizes the interaction of Jews with surrounding nations and cultures.

Schiffman, Lawrence H. *From Text to Tradition: A History of Second Temple and Rabbinic Judaism.* Hoboken, NJ: Ktav Publishing House, 1991. A comprehensive and concise outline of Jewish history that traces the transition from Biblical Israel to rabbinic Judaism. A companion volume of primary sources is listed below.

————*Texts and Traditions: A Source Reader for the Study of Second Temple and Rabbinic Judaism.* Hoboken, NJ: Ktav Publishing House, 1998. A comprehensive source reader intended to complement the historical work listed above. Contains 346 primary sources from the biblical period through the end of the Talmudic period, each briefly introduced and glossed.

Schürer, Emil. *The History of the Jewish People in the Age of Jesus Christ.* Revised by Vermes, Geza, Millar, Fergus, and Goodman, Martin, eds. 3 volumes in 4. Edinburgh: T. and T. Clark, 1973–1987. Translation of a classic text on Jewish History by a nineteenth-century German scholar. This translation has been revised and updated. Although it views Jewish history through the distorting lens of the New Testament, it remains a classic in many ways.

Schwartz, Seth. *Imperialism and Jewish Society, 200 C.E. to 640 C.E.* Princeton, NJ: Princeton University Press, 2001. For advanced students, a groundbreaking and controversial revision of Jewish society from 200 C.E. to the rise of Islam.

Seltzer, Robert. *Jewish People, Jewish Thought: The Jewish Experience in History.* New York: Macmillan, 1980. An excellent and comprehensive review of Jewish civilization, history, and thought. An indispensable guide to every period of Jewish social and political history, culture, and religious and intellectual developments.

Smallwood, E. Mary. *The Jews Under Roman Rule: From Pompey to Diocletian, A Study in Political Relations.* Leiden, The Netherlands: Brill Academic Publishers Inc., 1976. A good readable narrative account of the political relations between the Jews and the Romans from 63 C.E. to 313 C.E. A basic reference work on Jewish-Roman relations.

JEWISH THOUGHT, RELIGION, AND CULTURE IN THE SECOND TEMPLE AND LATE ANTIQUE PERIODS

Baumgarten, Albert. *The Flourishing of Jewish Sects in the Maccabean Era: An Interpretation.* Leiden, The Netherlands: Brill, 1997. A very important study of Second Temple Judaism that offers an insightful explanation for the prominence of sectarian groups (Pharisees, Sadducees, Essenes, the Qumran community) during this period.

Cohen, Shaye J.D. *The Beginnings of Jewishness: Boundaries, Varieties, Uncertainties.* Berkeley: University of California Press, 1999. An excellent set of essays by a leading scholar, that considers the intersection of ethnic, national, and religious elements in Jewish identity in antiquity. Drawing on classical and rabbinic sources, the author discusses intermarriage, matrilineal descent, conversion, and the place of the convert in Jewish society.

Collins, John J. *Between Athens and Jerusalem: Jewish Identity in the Hellenistic Diaspora.* 2nd edition. Grand Rapids, MI: W. B. Eerdmans Publishing Co., 1999. A survey of the literature of Hellenistic Judaism that focuses on the larger question of Jewish identity in the Greco-Roman world.

―――. *Jewish Wisdom in the Hellenistic Age.* Louisville, KY: Westminster John Knox Press, 1977. Study of Jewish Wisdom literature in the Hellenistic period, with special focus on the books of Sirach and the Wisdom of Solomon.

Feldman, Louis. *Jew and Gentile in the Ancient World: Attitudes and Interactions from Alexander to Justinian.* Princeton, NJ: Princeton University Press, 1983. An exhaustive survey of pagan, Jewish, and Christian writings with an eye to the intersection of Jewish and Gentile cultures and Gentile attitudes toward Jews in the Greco-Roman world.

Grabbe, Lester. *Judaic Religion in the Second Temple Period: Belief and Practice from the Exile to Yavneh.* London: Routledge, 2000. An encyclopedic and holistic study of the nature of Jewish religious beliefs and practices from ca. 550 B.C.E. to 100 C.E. covering topics like: views of God, the temple and priesthood, main religious sects, eschatology and messianism.

Gruen, Erich S. *Diaspora: Jews Amidst Greeks and Romans.* Cambridge, MA: Harvard University Press, 2002. A fresh and provocative look at Jewish life in the Diaspora—and Jewish views of the Diaspora—from ca. 330 B.C.E. to 70 C.E.

Levine, Lee. *Judaism and Hellenism in Antiquity.* Seattle: University of Washington Press, 1998. Examines the reciprocal influences of Greek and Near Eastern cultures in Palestine and the diaspora, and the specific question of the Hellenization of Jewish society and culture.

——. *The Ancient Synagogue: The First Thousand Years.* New Haven, CT: Yale University Press, 2000. A study of the evolving role of the synagogue in the Hellenistic and late antique periods.

Nickelsburg, George W.E. *Jewish Literature between the Bible and the Mishnah, with CD-ROM.* 2nd ed. Philadelphia, PA: Fortress Press, 1981. An excellent introduction to extra-biblical, nonrabbinic Jewish writings (e.g. the Apocrypha, Pseudepigrapha, Josephus, Philo, Dead Sea Scrolls) with a CD-ROM containing hyperlinks to the biblical text, Web links, and discussion questions.

Sanders, E. P. *Judaism: Practice and Belief 63 B.C.E.–66 C.E.* Philadelphia, PA: Trinity Press International, 1992. An important presentation of Judaism as a functioning religion in the late Second Temple period that serves as an important corrective to the distortions of earlier scholarship.

——. *Paul and Palestinian Judaism: A Comparison of Patterns of Religion.* Philadelphia, PA: Fortress Press, 1983. A pathbreaking study of Judaism in first-century Palestine that profoundly affected scholarly understandings of the relationship between early Christianity and Judaism.

Schäfer, Peter. *Judeophobia: Attitudes Towards the Jews in the Ancient World.* Cambridge, MA: Harvard University Press, 1997. An excellent study of the emergence of anti-Semitism in antiquity. Concludes that the cradle of anti-Jewish feeling was ancient Egypt, where ethnic resentment based on allegations of impiety, xenophobia, and misanthropy fueled attacks on Jewish communities. Christianity later embedded this hatred and fear in a theological framework.

Segal, Alan. *Rebecca's Children: Judaism and Christianity in the Roman World.* Cambridge, MA: Harvard University Press, 1989. A look at the early histories of Christianity and rabbinic Judaism that views both as a reinterpretation of prior traditions in response to the same social situation.

Shanks, Hershel, and Cole, Dan, eds. *Archaeology and the Bible: The Best of BAR: Archaeology in the World of Herod, Jesus and Paul.* Washington, DC: Biblical Archaeology Society, 1990.

Stone, Michael E., ed. *Jewish Writings of the Second Temple Period. Compendia Rerum Iudaicarum ad Novum Testamentum.* Philadelphia, PA: Fortress Press, 1984. An important collection of essays that introduces students to the major bodies of Jewish literature in the Second Temple Period.

Vanderkam, James. *An Introduction to Early Judaism*. Grand Rapids, MI: William B. Eerdmans, 2001. An accessible survey of Jewish history from the Persian period to the Bar Kokhba revolt. Describes the literature of this period, as well as the most important institutions, sects, and practices.

RABBINIC JUDAISM

Boyarin, Daniel. *Carnal Israel: Reading Sex in Talmudic Culture*. Berkeley: University of California Press, 1993. An important study of ancient rabbinic constructions of the body, gender, and sexuality in the context of competing Hellenistic constructions.

———*Dying for God: Martyrdom and the Making of Christianity and Judaism*. Stanford, CA: Stanford University Press, 1999. Explores and contrasts significant martyr texts from rabbinic Judaism and early Christianity.

———*Border lines: The Partition of Judaeo-Christianity*. Philadelphia, PA: University of Pennsylvania Press, 2004. A pathbreaking study arguing that the distinction between Judaism and Christianity was a late development imposed by heresiologists anxious to create a distinct Christian religion.

Cohen, Abraham. *Everyman's Talmud: The Major Teachings of the Rabbinic Sages*. New York: Schocken, Reprint 1995. A comprehensive and masterly distillation of the substance of the Talmud, topically organized.

Ginzberg, Louis. *The Legends of the Jews*. 2nd ed. New York: Jewish Publication Society, 2003. A classic and comprehensive compilation of Jewish legends concerning the narratives and characters of the Hebrew Bible. An indispensable guide to the contents of rabbinic lore.

Hartman, Geoffrey H. and Budick, Sanford. *Midrash and Literature*. New Haven, CT: Yale University Press, 1986. A series of essays exploring the midrashic approach to interpretation.

Rubenstein, Jeffrey L. *Culture of the Babylonian Talmud*. Baltimore, MD: Johns Hopkins University Press, 2003. A fascinating exploration of the cultural milieu of the late antique rabbinic academies that produced the Babylonian Talmud, through close readings of talmudic texts that reveal rabbinic values and practices.

———*Talmudic Stories: Narrative Art, Composition, Culture*. Baltimore, MD: Johns Hopkins University Press, 1999. A brilliant study of six narratives from the Babylonian Talmud that illuminates fundamental tensions in rabbinic culture and the complex composition and function of talmudic stories.

Safrai, Shmuel, ed. *The Literature of the Sages: First Part: Oral Torah, Halakhah, Mishna, Tosefta, Talmud, External Tractates*. CRINT II.3. Assen/Maastricht: Van Gorcum and Philadelphia: Fortress Press, 1987. Scholarly introductions to each of the major works of rabbinic literature.

Schechter, Solomon. *Aspects of Rabbinic Theology: Major Concepts of the Talmud*. Peabody, MA: Hendrickson Publishers, 1998. A useful if dated presentation of central Jewish principles, concepts, and ideas drawing on the classics of rabbinic literature.

Steinsaltz, Adin. *The Essential Talmud*. New York: Basic Books, Reprint 1984. A summary of the main principles of the Talmud as an expression and development of biblical law.

Stern, David. *Parables in Midrash: Narrative and Exegesis in Rabbinic Literature*. Cambridge, MA: Harvard University Press, 1991. A comparative study of parables as a rabbinic literary form.

Urbach, E. E. *The Sages: Their Concepts and Beliefs*. Trans. by Israel Abrahams. Jerusalem: Magnes Press, 1975. Reprint edition Cambridge, MA: Harvard University Press, 1987. A comprehensive guide to classical rabbinic views on God, humankind, the people of Israel, and a long list of other topics.

WOMEN AND JUDAISM

Baskin, Judith. *Midrashic Women: Formations of the Feminine in Rabbinic Literature*. Hannover: Brandeis University Press, 2002. A study of the portrayal of females and the feminine in aggadic (nonlegal) rabbinic writings.

———, ed. *Jewish Women in Historical Perspective*. 2nd ed. Detroit, MI: Wayne State University Press, 1998. Essays explore Jewish women's history, surveying the experience and activities of Jewish women in various historical periods.

Biale, Rachel. *Women and Jewish Law: The Essential Texts, Their History, and the Relevance for Today*. New York: Schocken Books, Reprint 1995. A historical overview of issues central to the lives of women—marriage, divorce, sexuality, contraception, abortion—as discussed in key texts of the Jewish tradition.

Frymer-Kensky, Tikva. *Reading the Women of the Bible: A New Interpretation of Their Stories*. New York: Schocken Books, 2002. Explores the portrayal of women in the Hebrew Bible and focuses on four groups of women: the victors, the victims, the virgins, and those with voice.

JEWISH LIFE IN THE MIDDLE AGES

Cohen, Mark R. *Under Crescent and Cross: The Jews in the Middle Ages*. Princeton, NJ: Princeton University Press, 1995. An excellent comparative analysis of the legal, economic, social, and religious position of Jews under medieval Islam and medieval Christianity.

Cohn-Sherbok, Dan. *Jewish Mysticism: An Anthology*. Oxford: Oneworld, 1995. A brief introduction to Jewish mysticism that includes a historical overview of major events and figures in Jewish mysticism and excerpts from mystical writings, chronologically arranged on a wide range of topics.

Dan, Joseph. *Jewish Mysticism and Jewish Ethics*. Seattle: University of Washington Press, 1986. Traces the many strands within medieval Jewish thought, leading to the construction of traditional Jewish ethics.

Lewis, Bernard. *The Jews of Islam*. Princeton, NJ: Princeton University Press, 1984. A masterful study of the complex history of Jews and Muslims since the time of Muhammed, by one of the preeminent scholars of the field.

Matt, Daniel C. *The Essential Kabbalah: The Heart of Jewish Mysticism*. San Francisco, CA: HarperSanFrancisco, 1996. An introductory survey of the history and main ideas of the Kabbalah, with topically arranged excerpts from kabbalistic texts with commentary.

Scholem, Gershom. *The Messianic Idea in Judaism and Other Essays on Jewish Spirituality*. New York: Schocken Books, 1971. Details the concept of the messiah, particularly as it developed in esoteric and mystical traditions.

Wasserstrom, Steven M. *Between Muslim and Jew: The Problem of Symbiosis under Early Islam*. Princeton, NJ: Princeton University Press, 1995. A social and intellectual history of Jews and Muslims from the eighth to tenth century, underlining the "creative symbiosis" that characterized early Jewish-Muslim interactions.

CONTEMPORARY JUDAISM

Bloch, Abraham. P. *The Biblical and Historical Background of the Jewish Holy Days*. New York: Ktav Publishing House, 1978. An introduction to the evolution of the Jewish festivals and holidays.

Bokser, Baruch. *The Origins of the Seder: The Passover Rite and Early Rabbinic Judaism*. Berkeley: University of California Press, 1984. Explores the rabbinic reshaping of the Passover night ritual after the destruction in 70 C.E.

Cohn, Gabriel and Fisch, Harold, eds. *Prayer in Judaism: Continuity and Change.* Northvale, NJ.: Jason Aronson, 1996. A series of essays by scholars and Jewish thinkers on various aspects of prayer including the question of emendation.

Cohn-Sherbok, Dan. *Judaism: History, Belief and Practice.* New York: Routledge, 2003. A basic introduction presented in 90 units, with discussion questions and further readings after each unit, as well as links to a free companion Web site that provides further activities, teaching tips, and additional on-line resources.

Donin, Hayim Halevy. *To Pray as a Jew: A Guide to the Prayer Book and the Synagogue Service.* New York: Basic Books, Reissue 1991. An accessible guide to the prayer book and synagogue service.

————. *To Be a Jew: A Guide to Jewish Observance in Contemporary Life.* New York: Basic Books, 1991. A comprehensive practical resource and clear guide to all aspects of Jewish life, law, and thought.

Elbogen, Ismar. *Jewish Liturgy: A Comprehensive History.* Trans. by Raymond Scheindlin. Philadelphia: Jewish Publication Society and New York: Jewish Theological Seminary of America, 1993. A detailed description of each service of the Jewish daily, Sabbath, and festival liturgy. Though dated in places, Elbogen's book is still considered the classic work in the field.

Gaster, Theodor, H. *Festivals of the Jewish Year: A Modern Interpretation and Guide.* New York: W. Sloane, 1952. Not your standard introduction to the festivals. Gaster points to the universal aspect and particular Jewish significance of Jewish festivals through broad comparisons with non-Jewish festivals and rituals worldwide.

Hammer, Reuven. *Entering Jewish Prayer: A Guide to Personal Devotion and the Worship Service.* New York: Schocken Books, 1995. A discussion of the forms, history, and meaning of Jewish prayer and liturgy that is fully informed by scholarly investigation.

Heschel, Abraham Joshua. *The Sabbath: Its Meaning for Modern Man.* New York: Farrar, Straus, and Giroux, 1976. A classic work of American Jewish spirituality, this elegant essay by a leading Jewish religious thinker on the meaning of the Sabbath introduces the idea of holiness in time, not space.

Idelson, A. Z., *Jewish Liturgy and Its Development.* New York: Dover Publications, 1995. A classic study that surveys the development of Jewish worship and liturgy from the ancient period to the nineteenth century.

Jacobs, Louis. *The Book of Jewish Belief.* Springfield, NJ: Behrman House, 1984. An outline of Judaism's basic beliefs by a distinguished scholar.

———. *The Book of Jewish Practice.* Springfield, NJ: Behrman House, 1987. A companion volume to the proceeding, outlining Jewish religious practice.

———. *The Jewish Religion: A Companion.* New York: Oxford University Press, 1995. A compendium of information on nearly every facet of the Jewish heritage, presented in 750 alphabetical entries.

———. *Principles of the Jewish Faith: An Analytical Study.* New York: Basic Books, 1964. A penetrating exploration of major principles of Jewish faith, structured around the thirteen principles of faith set out by the medieval Jewish philosopher Maimonides.

The JPS Holiday Anthologies. A seven-volume series covering the history and celebration of the major Jewish holidays. Each volume is a treasure trove, containing selections from a vast array of Jewish writings—essays, poems, fictional works, theological reflections, liturgy, popular works—that pertain to the history and celebration of the holiday in question.

Lange, Nicholas de and Freud-Kandel, Miri, eds. *Modern Judaism: An Oxford Guide.* Oxford: Oxford University Press, 2005. A collection of thirty-eight essays on social, cultural, historical, and theological issues in contemporary Jewish life and thought.

Petuchowski, Jacob. *Understanding Jewish Prayer.* New York: Ktav Publishing House, 1972. Explores the meaning and function of Jewish prayer.

Raphael, Marc Lee. *Profiles in American Judaism: The Reform, Conservative, Orthodox and Reconstructionist Traditions in Historical Perspective.* San Francisco, CA: Harper Collins, Reprint 1988. Traces the emergence and development of the main branches of contemporary American Judaism from their European roots.

Reif, Stefan. *Judaism and Hebrew Prayer: New Perspectives on Jewish Liturgical History.* New edition. Cambridge: Cambridge University Press, 1995. A valuable historical overview of the origins of Hebrew prayer and the emergence of a Jewish liturgy.

Schauss, Hayyim. *The Jewish Festivals: A Guide to Their History and Observance.* New York: Schocken Books, 1996. An accessible introduction to the Jewish festivals—their origins, development, and symbolism and the many rituals, foods, and prayers involved in their celebration.

Steinsalz, Adin. *A Guide to Jewish Prayer*. New York: Schocken Books, Reprint 2002. A comprehensive and detailed description of daily, Sabbath, and festival prayer services with essays on the nature and meaning of Jewish prayer. A standard resource and the starting point for any study of Jewish prayer.

Unterman, Alan. *Jews: Their Religious Beliefs and Practices*. Portland, OR: Sussex University Press, 1996. A comprehensive introduction to Jewish belief and practice in the modern world.

ELECTRONIC RESOURCES

Davka Corporation CD-Rom Judaic Classic Library. Contains a comprehensive set of classic Jewish Texts in Hebrew and Aramaic and in English translation, including the Soncino Talmud, the Soncino Midrash Rabbah, the new CD-Rom Bible, the Encyclopedia of Judaism and the Dictionary of Jewish Bibliography.

Encyclopedia Judaica on CD-Rom. TES Inc. All twenty-six volumes of the classic encyclopedia with powerful search capabilities and a full multimedia program. 25,000 articles cover the entire gamut of Jewish civilization.

WEB SITES

Academic Guide to Jewish History at the University of Toronto. A database of links to Jewish history resources in libraries and on the Web. http://eir.library.utoronto.ca/jewishhistory.

Ioudaios Review. An on-line journal devoted to the study of ancient Judaism. http://listserv.lehigh.edu/lists/ioudaios-review.

The Jewish Encyclopedia (see above) is available on-line at http://www.jewishencyclopedia.com/index.jsp.

Judaica Libraries and Archives on the Web. A guide to research-level Judaica collections in libraries and archives worldwide. http://www.bibliomaven.com.

The Orion Center for the Study of the Dead Sea Scrolls and Associated Literature at the Hebrew University of Jerusalem's Institute of Jewish Studies. Information on the Dead Sea Scrolls and Judaism of the Second Temple Period. http://orion.mscc.huji.ac.il/.

INDEX

About the Author

CHRISTINE ELIZABETH HAYES is Professor of Religious Studies in Classical Judaica at Yale University. She is the author of *Between the Babylonian and Palestinian Talmuds* (1997) and *Gentile Impurities and Jewish Identities* (2002).